SECONDARY SCHOOL
ADMINISTRATION

EXPLORATION SERIES IN EDUCATION

...

Under the Advisory Editorship of

JOHN GUY FOWLKES

Secondary School
Administration

ROLAND C. FAUNCE

WAYNE UNIVERSITY

HARPER & BROTHERS, PUBLISHERS

NEW YORK

To MAE

Library of Congress catalog number: 55–10941

CONTENTS

....

EDITOR'S INTRODUCTION   ix

PREFACE   xi

1. INTRODUCING THE SECONDARY SCHOOL ADMINIS-
TRATOR   1
The Administrator Is Often Lonely—The Principal
Faces Many Problems—The Secondary School's Role
in a Changing Society—A New Concept of Leadership
Is Emerging—Summary

2. THE BACKGROUND OF THE AMERICAN SECONDARY
SCHOOL   17
The Expanding Secondary School—Some Adjustments
of the Program—The Program of Instruction—New
Subjects Added—A Decade of Studies—Summary

3. CURRICULUM TRENDS IN THE SECONDARY SCHOOL   40
Some General Trends Since 1930—Enriching Individ-
ual Learning—Trends Toward Better Guidance—
Trends Toward the Current Scene—Trends Toward
General Education and the Core Curriculum—Sum-
mary

4. THE PRINCIPAL AS LEADER IN PROGRAM DEVELOP-
MENT   62
What Is the Meaning of "Curriculum"?—A Complex
Task—Setting the Climate—Planning Together—
Summary

5. THE PRINCIPAL AS SUPERVISOR   83
Earlier Concept of Supervision—The Duties of the

Principal—Relationship of Principal to Supervisory
Staff—Achieving the Goals of Supervision

6. THE PRINCIPAL AND THE COMMUNITY   113
    The Schools Belong to the People—Older Concepts of
    Community Relations—The Job of the Superintend-
    ent—Surveying the Community—Advisory Com-
    mittees—The PTA—The Room Parents' Club—Grade-
    Level Planning—Study Committees—Involving Stu-
    dents—The Classroom—The Principal's Task—Sum-
    mary

7. THE GUIDANCE PROGRAM   133
    What Is Guidance?—Guidance and Instruction—Or-
    ganization for Guidance—The Principal as Coun-
    selor—The Principal as Coördinator of Guidance

8. PUPIL RECORDS   161
    Importance of Records—Types of Data Needed—An-
    ecdotal Records—Cumulative Records—Marks—Let-
    ters to Parents—Parent-Teacher Conferences—Marks
    as Records—Need of Coöperation

9. STUDENT ACTIVITIES   201
    Purposes of Activities—Organizing the Activities
    Program—Scheduling Activities—Financing the Pro-
    gram—Credits and Awards—Evaluating Activities—
    Relationship to the Curriculum

10. STUDENT PARTICIPATION IN SCHOOL GOVERNMENT   223
    Background of Student Participation—Steps Toward
    Student Participation in Government—Activities of the
    Council—Role of the Principal

11. THE PRINCIPAL AND THE BUILDING   252
    Importance of the Building—Teachers—Students—
    The Community—Building Better Secondary Schools—
    The Principal

Contents

12. ADMINISTERING FUNDS   276
    Importance of the Budget—The Total School Budget—
    Inventory of Supplies—Administering Activity Funds
    —Summary

13. DEVELOPING THE SCHEDULE   296
    The Secondary School Schedule: A Problem—Faults
    of the Segmented Schedule—Developing the Standard
    Schedule—The Trend Toward A Different Type of
    Schedule—Blocking for Longer Periods—Uses of
    Shorter Periods—Grade-Level Planning

14. PROMOTING AND GROUPING STUDENTS   323
    Secondary Schools for All American Youth?—Should
    More Students "Fail"?—The Value of Success—Fail-
    ing Students Drop Out—Required Courses—Elective
    Courses—Remedial Help—Grouping Students—Sum-
    mary

15. THE BOARD OF EDUCATION, THE SUPERINTENDENT,
    AND THE PRINCIPAL   343
    The Board of Education—The Superintendent—The
    Principal

16. APPRAISING THE PRINCIPAL'S GROWTH   361
    Evaluation Related to Purposes—The Critical-Incident
    Technique—Teacher Judgments — Self-Analysis — A
    Final Word

    INDEX OF NAMES   381
    INDEX OF SUBJECTS   384

The emergence of the secondary schools of the United States as a truly educational institution "for all" marks one of the most important developments sociologically as well as educationally that the nation has enjoyed. The American high school of to-day is a far cry, indeed, from the corresponding agency of even twenty-five years ago, much less that of 1900, at about which date it was decided that all children in our country should have the opportunity of attending a high school.

Similarly, the administration of a secondary school today is a sharply different activity from that involved in the administration of a high school of the past. Because of the expansion and projection of the high school curriculum, the installation and maintenance of a wide variety of student and community services in and by the high school, and increasingly heavy demands on the high school principal for community as well as specialized professional leadership, the role of the high school principal is as complex as it is important to the life of an American community.

The acceptance of the post of professional leader of a high school by an individual imposes an obligation for both previous and continued preparation which cannot be escaped. Broad and intimate understanding of how our high school came to be and what it is trying to do; ways and means of unrelenting appraisal of its effectiveness; how the existing program can be changed by elimination, modification, or addition in terms of our changing society; how the constituents of the school may be best kept conversant with such changes and the reason therefor, how the reactions and recommendations of citizens with respect to the school are some of the major matters which challenge and try the mettle of the high school principal. Sound scholarship and high professional competence in "the detailed know how" of school organization and operation are obviously musts for the distinguished administration of a secondary school.

This volume presents an illuminating backdrop of the American high school, reports a wide variety of distinctive curricular offerings and practices, and presents invaluable material concerning the skills so essential for good high school administration. The author's real scholarship and rich experience have been focused so that the book is philosophical yet practical; challenging rather than arbitrary; exploratory rather than definitive. The volume should prove valuable both for those who are preparing for and those who are experienced in the practice of high school administration.

JOHN GUY FOWLKES

PREFACE

Many books have been written about the important job of the secondary school principal. Perhaps an explanation is due the reader why another volume should be written on this subject.

Historically, the principalship was originally created as a means of enforcing regulations and policies that were drawn up by the board of education. As schools grew larger and more complex, the principal's duties came also to include many clerical and managerial responsibilities. A considerable number of such duties still confront today's principal of a secondary school. They are significantly reflected in textbooks on administration. These volumes give excellent advice about attendance and membership, supplies and equipment, report forms, finance, and schedules.

Meanwhile the important field of curriculum development has come of age. Experience of the past twenty years gives evidence that educational programs for children and youth can be effectively developed only by coöperative planning on the part of teachers, parents, and pupils themselves. It has become increasingly clear that the principal is the crucial agent in this planning process. It is the thesis of this book that the major task of the principal is leadership in program change. This involves administration of people, not things. It is not possible to provide recipes or panaceas for this kind of administration, since human relationships are ever-changing and complex. It is the hope of the author, nevertheless, that this volume will give some direction and offer some practical help in this crucial and difficult role of the secondary school administrator. Other tasks of the principal have been omitted or treated briefly, not because they have no importance, but because they have been discussed so often and so thoroughly in other books on administration.

Sincere appreciation is herewith expressed to Professors Earl C. Kelley, Edgar G. Johnston, and J. Wilmer Menge, of Wayne University, for their inspiration and active help in improving the manuscript. Many fine Michigan principals have been a source of ideas to the author during his long association with them. Thanks are due for their friendly assistance.

ROLAND C. FAUNCE

Detroit, Michigan
July, 1955

CHAPTER 1

....

Introducing the Secondary School Administrator

_____

THE ADMINISTRATOR IS OFTEN LONELY

The principal sits in his office in one of his rare intervals of being alone. He is pondering the schedule for next semester, or the accrediting report which is due Friday, or the request for the band for a parade during school hours. To aid him in thinking about such problems as these he has (1) the traditions and precedents which have been established by past decisions, (2) fragments of vaguely remembered textbooks on administration which he read in a course some years ago, and (3) his own common sense and insight about the people affected by the decisions.

If he were a business or industrial executive he would have the further advantage of the counsel of his peers and associates. Considerable mutual support and many ideas result from discussions at board meetings and luncheon clubs composed of businessmen. The secondary school principal, on the other hand, is often the only one of his kind in town. He represents a specialized kind of administration which people assume is different. The boys at Kiwanis Club even call him professor.

There is help close at hand for the principal. In every room in the building there is a professional worker with a training substantially like his own, and with a personal stake in administrative decisions. The principal may not think of sharing problems with teachers. If he does think of it, he may be deterred from making the necessary first move by (1) his fear of a bad decision, (2) his feeling that his status depends on retaining the power of deciding issues, (3) his ignorance of the techniques through which staff consensus could be achieved, or (4) his personal shyness, which he has been accustomed to conceal behind a bland or abrupt manner.

There are others who could help, too. There are the janitor and the secretary—both human beings with unique backgrounds and with ideas about school operation. There are the citizens of the community, who really own the school whether they have children in it or not. They have ideas about what a good school is and could help develop policies on which a future decision could be based. And there are the students—hundreds of them close at hand. They have ideals and energy and good sense. They have the greatest stake in the school, and would work hard to make it a better school. If only these resources could be tapped! If only the principal had the know-how and the faith to use the help which lies all about him, he would not be so lonely.

There was a time when the school was too small to have a professional administrator. The board of education ran the school then. One teacher was eventually designated the "principal teacher" and charged with reporting attendance and other clerical tasks as an extra assignment. As the school grew in size and complexity the principal teacher became a teaching principal and finally a principal. The role of administration was born in every community when its schools became big business. This same process of growth had a tendency, too, toward isolating the principal from the "mere" teacher. As schools grew larger it became increasingly difficult to communicate directly with the teachers. The barriers which surround many principals were erected initially by these factors of size and numbers. Later, as the principal discovered his condition of professional loneliness, it seemed too late to do anything about it.

A newly appointed principal has usually not been specifically trained for his administrative role. The programs of graduate preparation for administration are still relatively new. In practice, even today, a typical high school principal does not complete such training before his appointment. He usually returns to a professional school and takes courses in administration after his appointment as an assistant principal or as a principal.[1] An overwhelming majority of secondary school principals were teachers —often athletic coaches—before they became principals.[2] They usually entered upon their new career with a minimum of specific preparation for school administration.

The advanced courses which have been deemed appropriate for a graduate degree in school administration have often been aimed at the management of things, not people. There have been courses in school plant maintenance, in finance and budget making, in school law and school district organization and public relations. General courses in school administration have often been aimed at the acquisition of command of rather specialized areas. These courses have sometimes prepared the principal to choose the right brand of floor wax but have not helped him to plan with other people.

In summary, the secondary school principal is often lonely because he lacks the skill to melt away interpersonal barriers and establish effective communication channels between himself and others. Too often, his training has not helped him much in this important task.

Surely the most important thing about any person is his attitude toward other people. Human relations and group dynamics therefore become extremely vital areas for training professional leaders.

[1] Recent studies indicate that from 70 percent to 85 percent of high school principals now hold master's degrees.

[2] But nearly 40 percent of junior high school principals moved into their positions from elementary school principalships.

In recent years much research has been done in the fields of social psychology, sociology, and personnel administration. The contributions which such fields as these can make to the preparation of school administrators are now widely recognized. Many professional schools have been influenced by these disciplines and have moved significantly toward the goal of making group processes effective in school administration.

THE PRINCIPAL FACES MANY PROBLEMS

It is probable that the principal's number one task is that of coöperative planning: with staff, with community, and with students. The day will soon be past when a school administrator could hold the reins tightly in his hands, decide the route of the vehicle, and steer its course by himself. The problems are simply too many and too complex for any one person. Schools have become big business in more ways than in size alone. Increasing urbanization has rendered the task of community relations incredibly more complex. New trends in instruction place a challenging burden upon the leaders, as well as upon the staff. Teachers are becoming more articulate and often less patient with authoritarian administration. Recent attacks upon public education have rendered it imperative that the principal and the staff involve lay persons in curriculum planning. Student activities have come of age, too, and these activities pose perplexing problems of scheduling, financing, and appraisal.

All these and many other developments tend to force the school administrator in the direction of sharing the planning of school policies. But there are serious problems here, too. Barriers to coöperation exist between individuals and groups. The parents are afraid of the teachers, the teachers of the parents. Within the staff there may be cliques which divide people from each other. There are the new teachers and the experienced ones, the young and the old, the various teacher organizations, the resident teachers and the commuters, the pro-administration and the anti-administration teachers. There are curriculum or departmental cliques, based on assumed differences in the status of English and Latin teachers, on the one hand, and shop, physical education, commercial, or vocational teachers, on the other. There are philosophic cliques based on various scales of beliefs ranging from ultra-progressive to rigidly conservative. There are social cliques, too, which form around certain established leaders. In the community the same kinds of barriers exist, but on a vastly more complex scale. These barriers between groups tend to perpetuate themselves in the student body, especially in senior high schools.

The principal is apt to find himself in the middle of these conflicts. If he is untrained in resolving differences, and without special ability for this role, he is usually forced by conflicting pressures into a safe middle course. He becomes a compromiser and mediator. He takes particular care to keep himself free or uncommitted to any point of view. At best he is able to interpret various points of view and prevent open conflict. This is often accomplished, however, by strict avoidance of any discussion of controversies. This is apt to mean avoidance of discussion of all problems that are real to people.

Certain staff members force another kind of role on the principal. Insecure people usually seek a scapegoat outside themselves whom they can blame for any condition that appears objectionable. To some extent, any administrator will discover himself at times in this role of scapegoat. In situations of real conflict the principal may find himself walled off from the faculty by all manner of real and imagined grievances which are really outlets for disturbed feelings. Thus it may become even more difficult for him to help others around him to work together toward the solution of common problems.

The principal, indeed, suffers a special kind of handicap from his very status in a line-and-staff administrative organization. His position is one of responsibility to the superintendent's office for the operation of "his" school. He has power and control over people in the building. He can make their daily lives more pleasant or more difficult by his decisions and assignments. He is an important link in a chain of authority. He may have some difficulty escaping from this power role even if he wishes to do so. It may be hard for him to see how he can share his responsibility for planning when the tradition of his position holds him responsible for the outcomes of such planning.

In the back of his mind lies the uneasy thought that the faculty may make a decision that will cause trouble, a decision to the enforcement of which he may be committed because of his position. He fears that he may lose a measure of his control by sharing it. . . . Even when he shares this power as fully as he knows how, the halo effect of his position still hovers about him with devastating damage to his relationships with his colleagues. There is a barrier between him and the group that sometimes proves surprisingly hard to surmount.[3]

THE SCHOOL'S ROLE HAS CHANGED

The changing social scene has posed many new and perplexing problems for the secondary school. It would be a relatively simple task to administer such a high school program as that which obtained in 1900. In earlier times the school was kept as aloof as possible from the community surrounding it. Both popular traditions and prevalent theories of learning tended to give an academic flavor to the curriculum. Student bodies were relatively homogeneous, at least in respect to educational goals of the students. Few social activities, athletic events, or school clubs existed. A flavor of the ivory tower clung to the old brick high school of 1900.

Today's school leader can no longer live in such academic isolation. The culture in which the secondary school operates and which it reflects is a dynamic culture posing many perplexing problems

[3] Roland C. Faunce and Nelson L. Bossing, *Developing the Core Curriculum*, New York, Prentice-Hall, 1951, pp. 196–197. Reprinted by permission of the publisher.

for the principal. Anyone who hopes to be an effective secondary school administrator must understand the nature of our society.

Perhaps the first aspect of our culture is one of rapid and constant change. Bossard has pointed out the fact that rapid social change is characteristic of our times: "It is the rapidity and scope of social change in recent decades that etch the modern era so sharply against the more stable background of the past. Not simply one, but many aspects of our life have been revolutionized within the past few decades. The present is an era of both rapid and fundamental changes." [4]

Never before in the world's history have so many significant changes occurred in our lives as in the past twenty years. The only thing we can count on about the future is the fact that it will be different from the present. This fact has profound significance for school leaders, and indeed for all persons interested in social adjustment. Kelley has stressed the importance of change to personal adjustment: "The most successful and adjusted people will be those who know that whatever tomorrow may be, it will be different from today or yesterday, and who are ready, know how, and have assurance to meet tomorrow on that basis. They will not be filled with anxiety about tomorrow because they will have confidence and courage with which to meet it." [5]

The school administrator's challenge consists in the development of an educational program which can give youth a measure of this "confidence and courage" in the face of constant change.

Successful adjustment to other people is complicated by the fact that there are so many of them. Our population as a nation has steadily increased until it is nearly 160 million. Today a majority of our people live in urban areas. Approximately two out of every three Americans are now city dwellers. Urban life is carried on in the face of many difficult problems. Cities have sprawled out far

---

[4] James H. S. Bossard, "Social Change in the United States," *The Annals of the American Academy of Political Science,* 265–269, September, 1949.
[5] Earl C. Kelley, *Education For What Is Real,* New York, Harper & Brothers, 1947, p. 61.

beyond their planning. The results are traffic congestion, hazards to health and safety, unsuitable housing, poor zoning, and costly, inadequate schools and recreation areas. Most secondary schools located in cities have no natural community setting. Communication is tremendously difficult. Enrollments are heavy. Teachers are scarce. Many city schools are on staggered schedules with classes running from eight A.M. to five P.M. An increasing number of relatively poor "bed-room" communities have rapidly grown up around every large city. These suburban districts have inadequate tax resources for the support of secondary schools. Attendance areas tend to be large, a fact which results in long commuting trips for many high school students. Teachers in urban areas seldom live near the school in which they teach. This presents serious difficulties to the development of a real community school.

With the rapid change to an industrialized urban economy profound changes have occurred in the American home. The home was once the center, not only of economic production, but of social life. In rural America of a few decades ago, commercial entertainment was almost nonexistent. People derived their security and their fun in the family group. The family exercised considerable influence in forming children's values and in shaping their entire lives.

Today's urban home is no longer an autonomous unit. City dwellers are interdependent to a fantastic degree for both the essentials and the luxuries of life. Over eight million women are actively employed in business and industry. The whole family spends a great deal of time commuting to and from school and jobs. Homes broken by divorce are a common spectacle, with about one divorce for every four marriages. Not only do people leave the home for employment, but also for recreation. The home has tended to become only a place to sleep.

The once powerful influence of the family in educating children has declined. The family has surrendered to social agencies one after another of its responsibilities for the care and education of children. The schools have inherited most of these functions which were once thought the exclusive prerogative of the home. This fact has posed a constant challenge to curriculum planning in many new courses. Such examples as home and family living, sex education, character education, and vocational guidance could be multiplied. It appears probable that this trend will continue and intensify whether we like it or not.

The home was once a place where adolescents had real opportunities to share responsibilities with adults. There were cows to milk, wood to chop, walks to shovel, stock to feed. Today's city boy or girl must leave home to find a task to do. Homes are mechanized to such an extent that the help of the adolescent member of the family is no longer needed. The educational benefits which result from having a task to perform for the common weal are still recognized, but have become the job of the school. This fact has great significance for school leaders who take seriously the "civic competence" purposes of education.

The phenomenon of juvenile crime seems to accompany increasing urbanization. There are many causes for delinquency, among them being the emotional stresses that are produced by city life. Another cause is probably the gap of five years which generally exists between the first legal age for school leavers and the earliest (permanent) employment. The school has a role to play in regard to both of these factors. Its program must provide recreation and constructive channels for emotional release. Its curriculum must also be made functional for the potential school leaver. Youth must have something to do—something recognized by them as worth doing. The modern school leader recognizes the need to adjust the secondary school program to the needs and interests of all youth as the first challenge to administration.

One other kind of cultural change presents a challenge to the schools. This is the vast increase in knowledge. Recent vocabulary studies reveal that high school students know an astonishing number of words. The technological changes of the present century, together with improved communication through mass media, have so increased our total body of knowledge that it is beyond any-one's power to know more than a fraction of it. This fact has certain implications for school administrators. Since selection of subject matter from this vast and growing array of knowledge must be made by someone, it follows that teachers and students have a responsibility for choice. Ways must be found to make these choices possible. For example, the single "basic" textbook for an entire section or class cannot serve the multiple purposes now required. Many school people are unwilling to see all power of choice of subject matter vested in a textbook writer. Flexible classroom libraries, periodicals, and pamphlet materials are being developed to make student and teacher choices possible. Since the sharp increase in knowledge represents a comparable increase in specialization in business and industry, the secondary school must provide many exploratory experiences in new, specialized fields. This will continue to force the expansion of the curriculum into new areas. It will also challenge classroom teachers to enrich learn-ing to keep pace with social change. Both language and concepts become outmoded and must give way to the new.

We have noted that the changing social scene presents a con-stant challenge to the secondary school administrator. The dynamic nature of our culture makes it imperative that education prepare people for change. Urbanization and industrialization have thrust the schools into many new roles once played by the home, and at the same time created perplexing difficulties in the effective per-formance of these new roles. The spectacular growth in knowl-edge forces us to adapt the curriculum to many new specializations, while we simultaneously try to keep general education abreast of the times.

THE SECONDARY SCHOOL'S ROLE IN A CHANGING SOCIETY

In the United States of America, the high school has come to be regarded as the poor man's college. A high school education, once the privilege of a chosen few, has come to be regarded as a "must" for all youth. It is considered a means of realizing our national dream of social mobility, whereby a boy or girl can escape the chains of undesirable social or economic circumstances and move "up the ladder." About four out of every five of the appropriate age group now enroll in high school.[6] It is the highest present level of our common school system, into which we all put our money and to which most of us send our children. It is a vast melting pot in which nearly eight million young citizens rub elbows with others of different social class, color, creed, and national background. It is our chance to teach youth democratic social relationships by association. It is our way of bridging the gap between the elementary school and full-time employment. It is the means of learning independence from home and parents, which all young people must ultimately learn, without revolution or trauma. Above all, the high school is a place for learning to make increasingly wiser choices, a process which is the essence of growing up. It is indeed hard to overestimate the importance of the secondary school in such a culture as ours.

A NEW CONCEPT OF LEADERSHIP IS EMERGING

As titular head of this basic social institution, the secondary school principal is our most important public administrator. Without his leadership and help, no significant improvement can occur in the school. No matter how farsighted or statesmanlike are the superintendent and his staff, nothing good can happen without the active leadership of the building administrator. He will (1) actively lead in efforts at program change, or (2) effectively block such efforts, or (3) have to be by-passed by an energetic superintendent or director of secondary education, who thus in reality becomes the principal. No matter how creative the faculty, no matter how helpful the community, little progress can be expected if the principal blocks the way to program change. The

[6] This point, together with the data on school leaving, will be more fully developed in the next chapter.

administrator sets the tone of a building. His example can set up the contagion of democratic relationships throughout the building, or it can establish the patterns of authoritarianism among all groups in the building. He sets the tone of student morale as well as that of the faculty.

It becomes of the utmost importance, therefore, that the secondary school principal be carefully selected in the first place, and given adequate professional training in the second place. As has been already indicated, these two conditions have not always obtained in the past. There are certain promising symptoms, however, which indicate that the quality of secondary school administration is improving, and will continue to improve. Some of these symptoms arise from the inescapable demands of social changes already mentioned. Others have come about as research in new social disciplines has tended to teach us more about leadership.

The rapidly growing field of personnel work in business and industry has taught us much about administration. Research has been rather carefully conducted in dozens of problem areas connected with the role of leadership. Discoveries made by these researchers for large corporations have influenced labor-management relations and stepped up production by improving plant morale in various ways. Big business organizations are now investing large sums of money in such research. The findings of research in industrial personnel work have also influenced other disciplines, including professional programs in educational administration.

The training of public administrators has also been recently influenced by studies in group dynamics. Social psychologists, following Kurt Lewin, have made detailed investigations into the relationships which exist between groups of people, the techniques of reducing interpersonal barriers, the role of leader and follower, the various techniques of group work, and the methods of evaluating social changes. These investigations have made a significant impact on courses and workshops for school administrators. They have also been reflected in professional conventions and in articles published in professional journals.

Trends in curriculum development have been conditioned by these discoveries in the field of group processes. An analysis of the recently published materials of the Association for Supervision and Curriculum Development,[7] for example, will convince one that this organization has become group-process-centered. The same thing can be said for many other national, state, and local groups concerned with curriculum development. The National Association of Secondary School Principals has reflected this influence in significant ways in its official journal and in its convention programs. On the teacher-education level this trend toward careful study of coöperative curriculum planning has become the dominant note. It has reflected itself in the workshop movement, which has been perhaps the most influential change in method in the past twenty years.[8] The techniques of group work which the workshop popularized have spread to other courses in teacher education. Curriculum courses especially reflect this influence. They often derive course content from participants in the form of actual local school curriculum problems. There has also been a distinct effort to bring principals and teachers together in work groups where actual changes can be planned and carried out.

The techniques of coöperative planning, executing, and evaluating which are now being learned in such workshops and curriculum courses can be of great value to school administrators. They are generally available to interested principals in summer sessions and even in extension courses. They also come to him in professional meetings and in his professional journals and books on administration. The principal who wants to learn how to give

[7] See, for example, *Group Processes in Supervision* (1948), *Leadership at Work* (1943), *Group Planning In Education* (1945), as well as the files of *Educational Leadership* since 1940. Washington, D.C., The National Education Association.

[8] An excellent brief treatment of the workshop movement is Earl Kelley's *The Workshop Way of Learning*, New York, Harper & Brothers, 1950.

leadership in coöperative planning for better schools can now get help.

There is help, too, in the experience of trying out democratic planning with the staff. Many a secondary school principal who had not been back to college for several years has been helped to secure new insights by the gentle prodding of the faculty. There is a growing interest in coöperative planning in faculty groups, in classrooms, and in student activities. Staff planning can develop from an interested group of teachers who have discovered its effectiveness with high school students. The principal is sometimes involved by faculty invitation and by the challenge of programs already under way.

In recent years we have seen a wave of public interest in the schools. In some cases this has stemmed from emotional or irrational attacks, believed to have been fomented by self-interested persons. Even these attacks have had their benefits. Schools which had not got around to involving the community in program planning have found themselves forced to do so for support. They have, in some cases, discovered that only involvement of large groups of lay citizens can save the schools from the worst effects of the attacks.

These developments in school-community relations constitute a further challenge to the principal to learn more about group planning. The incentives for study of group processes are multiplying, and many secondary school principals are responding to these challenges.

SUMMARY

This first chapter has set the stage for this volume on administering the secondary school. We have seen that the secondary school is faced with many new tasks as a result of its focal role in our dynamic urban society. The most important person in this process of program change is the principal. Although he is handicapped by a number of obstacles arising from the traditions of his position, he is also aided by certain recent trends which support and clarify the process of coöperative planning. It is proposed in this volume to examine this challenge to status leaders of secondary schools as it applies to the various tasks of the principal. We shall undertake to study the role of the principal as a leader in democratic planning of all the aspects of the school program. As a beginning it may be appropriate to look at the background of the modern secondary school. The next chapter will review the story of its development as a major social institution in our American democracy.

FOR FURTHER READING

Association for Supervision and Curriculum Development, *Group Processes in Supervision,* Washington, The National Education Association, 1948.

Association for Supervision and Curriculum Development, *Leadership at Work,* Washington, The National Education Association, 1943.

Bossard, James H. S., "Social Change in the United States," *The Annals,* September, 1949.

Bossing, Nelson L., "Wanted: A New Leadership for the Secondary School," *Bulletin of the National Association of Secondary School Principals,* No. 138, 30:92–100, April, 1946.

Briggs, Thomas H., *Improving Instruction,* New York, The Macmillan Company, 1938, chaps. 1 and 5.

Chamberlin, Leo, and Kindred, Leslie, *The Teacher and School Organization,* New York, Prentice-Hall, 1949, chap. 1.

Douglass, Harl R., *Modern Administration of Secondary Schools,* rev. ed., Boston, Ginn & Company, 1954, chap. 3.

Douglass, Harl R., *Organization and Administration of Secondary Schools,* Boston, Ginn & Company, 1945.

Faunce, Roland C., and Bossing, Nelson L., *Developing the Core Curriculum,* New York, Prentice-Hall, 1951, chap. 11.

French, Will; Hull, J. Dan; and Dodds, B. L., *American High School Administration,* New York, Rinehart & Company, 1951, chap. 8.

Jacobson, Paul B., and Reavis, W. C., *Duties of School Principals,* New York, Prentice-Hall, 1941.

Kelley, Earl C., "The Function of the Principal in a Modern School," *American School Board Journal,* June, 1947.

Menge, J. W., and Faunce, R. C., *Working Together for Better Schools,* New York, American Book Company, 1953.

Newlon, Jesse, *Educational Administration as Social Policy,* New York, Charles Scribner's Sons, 1934.

Roethlisberger, Fritz J., *Management and Morale,* Cambridge, Mass., Harvard University Press, 1941.

Spears, Harold, *The High School for Today,* New York, American Book Company, 1950, chap. 15.

Wittenberg, Rudolph, *So You Want to Help People,* New York, YMCA Press, 1947, chap. II.

Yauch, W. A., *Human Relations in School Administration,* New York, Harper & Brothers, 1949.

CHAPTER 2

The Background of the American Secondary School

THE EXPANDING SECONDARY SCHOOL

The phenomenon of rapidly extending public education in the United States is well known to most people. Nowhere in the world has the dream of universal education been more steadily sought. The secondary school, which was once open only to the gifted and propertied, today enrolls over four-fifths of our youth. For over three hundred years the American secondary school has been evolving and extending, always in the direction of more education for more people.

Since 1890, the secondary school has increased its enrollments from 350,000 to eight millions, an increase of nearly 2200 percent! During the same period the number of youth of secondary school age increased 180 percent. In 1900, 11.4 percent of those of appropriate ages were enrolled in high schools. In 1940 the percentage had risen to 73 percent, and in 1950 to 82 percent. The number of high school graduates in 1942 was seventy-seven times as great as in 1870, although the number of 17-year-olds merely trebled. We have made giant strides toward the concept of a high school education for all.

DEMOCRACY DEMANDS AN EDUCATED CITIZENRY

Why has the American secondary school been steadily extended, often in the face of opposition? One reason lies in the unique need of our democratic system of government. Democracy demands an educated citizenry. As early as 1787 Thomas Jefferson wrote in a letter to James Madison: "Above all things, I hope that education of the common people will be attended to; convinced that on this good sense we may rely with the most security for the preservation of a due degree of liberty." [1]

In 1816 Jefferson wrote to Colonel Yancy: "If a nation expects to be ignorant and free in a state of civilization, it expects what never was and never will be. There is no safe deposit for the functions of government but with the people themselves; nor can they be safe with them without information." [2]

When James Madison was President he gave voice to a widely quoted judgment about the need for popular education: "A popular government without popular information, or the means of acquiring it, is but a prologue to a farce or a tragedy, or perhaps both. Knowledge will forever govern ignorance; and a people who mean to be their own governors must arm themselves with the power which knowledge gives." [3]

Not all our early statesmen, of course, held views as strong as those of Jefferson and Madison in regard to the importance of universal education in a democracy. Indeed, some of the founding fathers, and many of our statesmen since, have opposed popular education. Yet the views expressed by some of our great leaders eventually prevailed because they made sense to most of our people. It came to be the common view that people who are illiterate are likely to be poor citizens. They are judged to be more likely to become the dupes of propagandists than critical thinkers who can successfully pass on the noble heritage of self-government.

The world has grown vastly more complex since Jefferson's day.

[1] Quoted in E. H. Wilds, *The Foundations of Modern Education*, New York, Farrar & Rinehart, 1942, p. 418.
[2] *Ibid.*, p. 418.
[3] *Ibid.*, p. 419.

The processes of democracy have accordingly become much more difficult to achieve. Communication has become a major difficulty. The problems of our fast-moving, complex industrial society place a terrific burden on us to maintain our mental health. If we are to make wise choices among a welter of conflicting values, and do our share in helping achieve a good life for all, a major challenge confronts education.

In this connection, a recent volume on curriculum development has pointed out that

The insights, the skills, and the knowledge that might have enabled citizens to live successfully in 1900 are quite inadequate today. Our world has become a complex, technological maelstrom of rapid mobility, constant change, and interdependence in which the citizen must acquire certain critical abilities in order to survive. To live as an integrated, secure individual, he must understand what is going on about him and within him. With the relative dissolution of home and family life in our urban communities, the burden of providing these necessary insights and abilities has fallen upon the schools. Thus the high school of today serves a vastly increased enrollment of widely differing mental and cultural backgrounds, and confronts a radically new challenge stemming from the personal and social needs of youth who live in a world like ours.[4]

In our day an elementary education no longer suffices for vocational preparation or for civic understanding. The understanding of this basic fact has done much to maintain popular support for more education.

YOUTH EMPLOYMENT IS NOT NEEDED

A second reason for the rapid extension of the American secondary school lies in the astonishing increase in technological invention which has released our youth for more schooling. In the rural culture which prevailed for the first one and one-half centuries of our history as a nation, the economy depended heavily on

---

[4] R. C. Faunce and N. L. Bossing, *Developing the Core Curriculum*, New York, Prentice Hall, 1951, p. 40. Reprinted by permission of the publisher.

manpower. Young people could not be spared for extended schooling. Consider the following figures on the net output per man-hour. In 1850 the net output was 17.3 cents, based on 1940 prices. In 1890 it had risen to 29.6 cents. From 1900 on, the output increased dramatically.[5]

1900	35.7
1910	40.1
1920	43.1
1930	52.3
1940	74.0
1950	87.5

On the basis of the 1947 price levels, production in the United States rose from 54 cents per hour in 1900 to 80 cents in 1930, $1.13 in 1940 and $1.20 in 1950.

Since about 1850 we have steadily replaced man power with steam and electrical energy. During the ninety years from 1850 to 1940 our national income increased more than sixteen times, while total man-hours increased less than four times.[6]

Thus we have emancipated our adolescents from farm and industrial production by the development of labor-saving devices. Boys and girls can go to school for more years because their labor is not needed any longer. The beginning of permanent employment has been steadily deferred. Many of our own fathers assumed their permanent vocations at the age of 16 or 17. Today this vocational launching occurs, on the average, at age 21. Even with the possibility of universal military service for men, it is reasonable to expect most youth to continue their education at least to age 18. Thus the extension of public education upward, which has resulted in our increasing secondary school enrollment, has been in harmony alike with our political creed and our economic development.

[5] J. Frederic Dewhurst and Associates, *America's Needs and Resources,* New York, The Twentieth Century Fund, 1947, p. 23, Table 3.

[6] *Ibid.,* pp. 680–682.

THE LATIN GRAMMAR SCHOOL

The secondary school did not spring into being full blown. It was developed gradually (and often painfully) from humble beginnings. The grandfather of the American high school was the Latin grammar school, the first of which was established in Boston in the year 1635. The Latin grammar schools were set up by colonial towns and supported largely by fees paid by the parents of the boys enrolled. Most of the pupils were college-bound, and they spent their school days chiefly in the study of Latin and Greek. At most there were only about forty of these schools, all with small enrollments. Thus the Latin grammar school was limited both in the number served and in the curriculum offered. It was significant in that it set a precedent for legal and public recognition of a community's responsibility for education beyond the elementary level. The period of the grammar school was roughly 1650–1750.

THE ACADEMY

The academy (1750–1850) further strengthened the trend toward youth education at the local level. Benjamin Franklin founded the first academy in 1751. It emphasized the practical in education and prepared boys for some professions other than law or the ministry. Both boys' and girls' academies were developed, although without coeducation. Many of the academies were financed and controlled by church groups, but all students paid tuition. By 1850, toward the end of the dominant period of the academy, there were over 6000 such institutions serving about a quarter of a million youth. Some academies have persisted to our own time. In a sense, the academy was the father not only of the public high school but of our present normal schools and liberal arts colleges.

THE HIGH SCHOOL

The failure of both the grammar school and the academy to serve the needs of the vast majority of adolescents gave rise to the public high school. The first high school was opened in Boston in 1821 under the title English Classical School. It was renamed English High School in 1824. As its name implied, this first high school stressed the teaching of English as opposed to the previous intensive training in Latin and Greek. Its broader curriculum reflected the effort to prepare students for many vocations. Girls were later admitted to the high schools. Massachusetts passed a state act in 1827 requiring larger communities to establish high schools, but the act was not strictly enforced for many years. There was even doubt in the minds of many citizens whether a local community had a constitutional right to tax all its citizens for the support of education beyond the elementary level. This issue was resolved by the Michigan Supreme Court in the Kalamazoo Case (1874). The court ruled, in effect, that a community could establish a tax-supported high school. Many authorities in school law hold that this Kalamazoo decision played a significant role in the rapid extension of the "free" public high school. At any rate, the growth of the high school from 1870 on was most phenomenal. The number of high school graduates from 1870 to 1946 is shown in the accompanying table from a recent bulletin of the Federal Office of Education:[7]

Year	Number Graduated
1869–1870	16,000
1879–1880	23,634
1889–1890	43,731
1899–1900	94,883
1909–1910	156,429
1919–1920	311,266
1929–1930	666,904
1939–1940	1,221,475
1941–1942	1,242,375
1943–1944	1,019,233
1945–1946	1,080,033

[7] *Bienniel Survey of Education in the United States, 1944–46*, Chap. 1, Statistical Summary of Education, 1945–46, p. 14.

SOME ADJUSTMENTS OF THE PROGRAM

It seems pertinent to note developments in the program of the secondary school which occurred as a result of the dramatic increase in its enrollments. With a 2200 percent increase in secondary school students since 1890, it is clear that the pupil population is considerably less homogeneous today than it was sixty years ago. The program which then may have seemed appropriate to the needs of the adolescent has become less and less serviceable as more youth of varying abilities, interests, and needs remained in school beyond the elementary level. Nearly any study of individual differences will today reveal a wide range, in each high school grade, in reading power and rate, command of numbers, vocabulary, spelling, written usage, and so-called intelligence. These differences are natural and inevitable. They are not something to be ashamed of, or to blame pupils for. On the contrary, the very differences between pupils can become a source of strength in a dynamic instructional program. Many constructive changes in the secondary school have come about through the need to adapt the program to the different needs of the millions of added pupils who have stormed our high school doors since 1890.

THE ACTIVITIES PROGRAM

Among the changes which this century has witnessed should be listed the programs of athletics, clubs, music, speech, journalism, and social activities which the secondary school has finally acknowledged to be legitimate members of its family. Nearly all these activities originated in the out-of-school lives of boys and girls, entered the school through the back door, were merely tolerated for several decades, and have finally achieved a status of acceptance. Further discussion of the rapid extension of these student activities will be included in subsequent chapters.[8]

[8] See Chapters 9 and 10.

GUIDANCE

The guidance movement began (in a formal sense) with the development of the home room in the early 1920's. It spread rapidly as a means of providing a "home-in-the-school" for boys and girls. Great results were expected from this movement, and a few schools have persisted in making the home room function. In most schools, however, the original enthusiasm ebbed and the home-room period shrank in length until it served no purpose other than that of announcements and clerical routines.

Meanwhile, to supplement the guidance work of the home room, the position of counselor was developed during the late 1930's and 1940's. The counselor movement has been, and still is, basically an urban school phenomenon. The counselors have been full-time, part-time, and extra-duty persons. They have been sub-assistant principals, attendance officers, home visitors, clerks, and disciplinarians; some of them have done some fine guidance work, in spite of their impossible pupil loads. Most counselors are not satisfied with the effectiveness of their guidance efforts. Further evidence on this point will be included in the chapter on guidance.[9] In general the guidance movement represents an attempt to supplement the curriculum, or to humanize its effects in meeting the needs of individual pupils.

THE JUNIOR HIGH SCHOOL

The organization of the secondary school has changed and is still changing in an effort to adapt to the needs of millions of new students. The junior high school was developed beginning about 1910 in an effort to broaden the program and enrich the experiences of early adolescents. Since it has generally been justified as an exploratory experience, the junior high school has added specialized laboratories, shops, and other facilities. It has also tended to specialize the teaching personnel in comparison with the

[9] See Chapter 7.

typical elementary school. In 1945–46 there were 2654 of the three-year junior high schools, enrolling about one and one-quarter millions of pupils. This represented an average enrollment of 481. In addition there were 6366 six-year high schools which included the junior high school grades with the senior high school.[10] By 1952 the trend toward the junior high school had accelerated, particularly in urban areas. In that year it was found that 57.2 percent of the high schools in the United States had reorganized, either into the 6–3–3 or the 6–6 pattern. Of the 42.8 percent of schools retaining the 8–4 pattern of organization, only about 6 percent were in cities of 10,000 or over.[11] Gaumnitz and Hull present a comparison of the arguments for the junior high school and the traditional 8–4 high school:

I. *Some advantages of the junior high school:*

1. The junior high school gives young adolescents some status and deals effectively with their unique problems.
2. Junior high schools emphasize student activities and give pupils some responsibility.
3. The junior high school provides a gradual shift from the self-contained elementary room to the departmentalized senior high school.
4. Junior high schools provide guidance personnel and better pupil records.
5. Better provision for individual differences is possible in junior high schools.
6. Junior high school positions attract better teachers than elementary schools.
7. Junior high schools can better gear school building programs to needs of children at various grade levels.
8. Junior high schools can make possible greater flexibility in building space management.

---

[10] *Biennial Survey of Education, 1944–1946,* pp. 8–9.
[11] Walter H. Gaumnitz and J. Dan Hull, *Junior High Schools Vs. the Traditional (8–4) High School Organization,* U.S. Office of Education Circular No. 373, Washington, U.S. Department of Health, Education, and Welfare, May, 1953.

9. The junior high school can enable school systems to make desired program changes at reasonable cost.

II. *Some advantages of the 8–4 system:*

1. Retention of grades 7 and 8 in the elementary school tends to extend upward such practices as accepting every pupil and grading him in relation to his capacity.
2. The 6–3–3 plan creates two gaps instead of bridging the original one.
3. Provision of junior high schools with expanded facilities tends to rob elementary schools of auditoriums, gymnasiums, libraries, etc.
4. Through better planning of the elementary school, all the flexibility desired can be attained.
5. The elementary school achieves better instruction by emphasizing continuous relationship of a teacher and a room group.
6. The elementary school permits children to mature naturally instead of bombarding them with adult-world stimuli.
7. The elementary school achieves better guidance because of its natural, familylike relationship of teacher and pupils.[12]

Whatever the arguments pro and con, the junior high school seems to have become established, at least in urban areas, as a means of cushioning the transition from elementary to senior high schools. If it is to become effective in this cushioning role it appears that the junior high school must develop a program that will help pupils to adjust to the additional school shift which it entails. Its chief error may be that it has introduced specialization too early in an era when permanent employment or admission to college is still relatively remote for the junior high school pupil. It is no longer necessary for the junior high school to ape the elective program of the senior high school, if indeed it ever was necessary.

THE COMMUNITY COLLEGE

In addition to extending downward, the high school is also beginning to extend upward to include (free) thirteenth and four-

[12] Adapted from *ibid.*

teenth grades. Legislation empowering districts to provide such a "community college" is already in effect in many states. California and New York appear to have gone farther than other states in providing for such an extension of the secondary school. Koos and others have proposed that the secondary school should include two sections. The junior secondary school would include grades 7–10 and the senior school grades 11–14.[13] Whatever the organization, it seems in harmony with trends discussed in this chapter to include the thirteenth and fourteenth grades in the secondary school rather than to build up another separate unit of only two years.

THE PROGRAM OF INSTRUCTION

Thus far we have examined the trends which have emerged in the secondary school since 1900 as it has attempted to adjust to the needs of its rapidly growing student body. We have seen that a program of student activities has grown up and been officially adopted, that various efforts have been made to provide for guidance of students, and that the secondary school has extended both downward and upward as a means of integrating the total program of education. No mention has been made of curriculum changes or of adaptations in teaching methods which the changing character of the pupil population demands.

THE COMMITTEE OF TEN

We have noted that the early high school was still, like the academy before it, mainly a college preparatory institution. The increasing number of students who were not interested in preparing for college gradually compelled educators to broaden the curriculum of the high school. The Committee of Ten of the National Education Association began its report (1892) with the statement that the high school was not and should not be a college preparatory institution for all its students. The committee went on

[13] Leonard V. Koos, *Integrating High School and College,* New York, Harper & Brothers, 1946.

to make recommendations which were intended to liberalize the curriculum, though they sound to our modern ears to be in strange conflict with the liberal opening statement of the report.

COMMISSION ON REORGANIZATION OF SECONDARY EDUCATION

In 1912 another committee of the National Education Association was appointed to study the total function of the high school curriculum in relation to its generally accepted goal of preparing students for college. This group, the Commission on the Reorganization of Secondary Education, published in 1918 a now famous report called *Cardinal Principles of Secondary Education*. An introductory paragraph of the report voiced this warning to secondary school educators:

Secondary education should be determined by the needs of the society to be served, the character of the individuals to be educated, and the knowledge of educational theory and practice available. These factors are by no means static. Society is always in process of development; the character of the secondary school population undergoes modification; and the sciences upon which educational theory and practices depend constantly furnish new information. Secondary education, however, like any other established agency of society, is conservative and tends to resist modification. . . . The evidence is strong that . . . a comprehensive reorganization is imperative at the present time.[14]

In this widely discussed statement we have the first official recognition that curriculum adjustments were demanded by the changing responsibility of the secondary school. The report went on to list and discuss the now famous seven objectives which the commission considered basic for all subjects in the secondary school:

1. Health
2. Command of the fundamental processes

[14] Commission on the Reorganization of Secondary Education, *Cardinal Principles of Secondary Education*, Bulletin No. 35, Washington, Bureau of Education, 1918, p. 7.

3. Worthy home membership
4. Vocation
5. Civic education
6. Worthy use of leisure
7. Ethical character

NEW SUBJECTS ADDED

Some changes were made in the secondary school curriculum during the 1920's in an attempt to respond to the changing responsibility of the school. Agriculture, homemaking, industrial arts, and commercial subjects were added in most high schools. Art and music courses increased in number. Physical education was strongly emphasized. Such courses as citizenship, civics, and economics were added in an effort to meet civic and consumer needs.

By 1930 the secondary school had generally made such adaptations as these to the changed and still changing needs of their growing student population. Yet there was evidence during the 1930's that the high schools still needed to make even more basic adjustments in their programs. Although enrollments in early high school years increased by about 50 percent between 1930 and 1940, dropouts continued to be high also. About half of our young people were rejecting the high school, usually after a brief trial. Since jobs were scarce during this period of the depression, there was no constructive role for these millions of adolescents to play in our society. The whole nation became alarmed by the problem. Young people roamed the country, unemployed and often homeless. The federal government took steps to correct the situation through the NYA and the CCC, in the face of considerable opposition from professional school people.

The entry of our national government into the realm of education convinced many educators that the local secondary school had thus far failed to get itself into gear with the real needs and interests of youth. This realization is highlighted in the following satirical passage, written in 1938:

Here is a scene for the pen of a satirist. . . . Place: An American high school. Setting: A democracy struggling against strangulation in an era marked by confused loyalties in the political realm, by unrest and deprivation, by much unnecessary ill health, by high pressure propaganda, by war, by many broken or ill-adjusted homes, by foolish spending, by high crime rates, by bad housing, and by a myriad of other urgent, real human problems. And what are the children in this school, in this age, in this culture learning? They are learning that the square of the sum of two numbers equals the sum of their squares plus twice their product; that Millard Fillmore was the thirteenth President of the United States and held office from January 10, 1850 to March 4, 1853; that the capital of Honduras is Tegucigalpa; that there were two Peloponnesian wars and three Punic wars; that Latin verbs meaning to command, obey, please, displease, serve, resist, and the like take the dative; and that a gerund is a neuter verbal noun used in the oblique cases of the singular and governing the same case as its verb.[15]

A DECADE OF STUDIES

The 1930's have been called the decade of secondary school studies. Never before had there been so many formal and informal studies of the secondary school curriculum. The interest which prompted these state, regional, and national studies was due to a general realization of the ineffectiveness of the high school program. It stemmed also from certain developments in the curriculum of the elementary school. In 1930 the better elementary schools had already been experimenting for three decades with basic changes in method. Generally free from such extrinsic pressure as domination by colleges, some elementary schools had been busy with studies since the early 1900's. The early experiments were chiefly in laboratory schools of education, but discoveries of educational psychologists and curriculum specialists were soon tried in various city school systems. The project method had significantly

---

[15] Educational Policies Commission, *Purposes of Education in American Democracy*, Washington, The National Education Association. 1938, p. 147.

influenced elementary schools in the direction of learning by doing. There was considerable interest in problem solving as an educational method. Many elementary schools had experimented with the activity movement, which emphasized children's activities as a means of learning the fundamental knowledge and skills. Some schools had developed the "experience curriculum," which added certain criteria for evaluating the educational contribution of children's activities. Such activities, the experience advocates held, are educative when

1. They stem from real purposes in the learner
2. They are geared to his present problems and interests
3. They derive their sequence from the learner's normal growth and development
4. They are interpreted, analyzed, or intellectualized as an aid to redirection of the learner's purposes [16]

The evolving concept of the experience curriculum led many elementary schools to help children base their activities on units of study, which "correlated" the various learnings around one topic or problem.

These developments were far from universal in the elementary schools of 1930; indeed, some of them are still not found in all elementary schools today. Some schools at the lower level, however, were attempting to involve pupils in planning activities, striving to involve the group in study of problems that were real to pupils, and organizing the learning experiences around a series of life centered units. These developments in the elementary schools provided a further challenge to secondary education of the 1930's. There was some concern over the sharp cleavage which had developed between the methods and philosophy of the elementary and secondary schools. Under these conditions it was perhaps natural that numerous studies of secondary education should be undertaken during the 1930's.

[16] Faunce and Bossing, *op cit.*, p. 43.

THE EIGHT-YEAR STUDY

The first of these, and in some ways the most important, was launched in 1932 by the Commission on the Relation of School and College of the Progressive Education Association. The thirty member schools were given a guarantee from the start that the colleges would not ban their graduates on the basis of their lack of conventional patterns of preparation. A staff was organized to assist the schools in studying their current programs and the needs of their students. The faculties were encouraged to consider and try out various ways of reorganizing course offerings and teaching methods. As the study drew to a close in 1940, an influential series of five reports was published.[17] These books described the curriculum innovations and student activities developed in the thirty schools, and presented the evaluative data regarding the study.

These five volumes have had a far-reaching influence on our thinking with regard to the secondary school curriculum. One of them, *Did They Succeed in College?*, deserves special mention at this point. The member schools of the study had been protected from the beginning by an agreement with the three hundred colleges and universities which their graduates usually entered. This agreement permitted graduates of the thirty schools to enter college without presenting the usual high school subjects required, provided they were recommended from among the more able students. This agreement was designed to prevent the subject requirements of the colleges from establishing a rigid pattern for the high schools. In small schools the conventional college preparatory curriculum was likely to be the only available program for all students. Teachers in the high schools were so used to the as-

[17] Wilford M. Aikin, *The Story of the Eight-Year Study*, New York, Harper & Brothers, 1942; H. H. Giles, S. P. McCutchen, and A. N. Zechiel, *Exploring the Curriculum*, New York, Harper & Brothers, 1942; E. R. Smith *et al.*, *Appraising and Recording Student Progress*, New York, Harper & Brothers, 1942; Progressive Education Association, *Thirty Schools Tell Their Story*, New York, the Association, 1942; Dean Chamberlin *et al.*, *Did They Succeed in College?* New York, Harper & Brothers, 1942.

sumption that requirements were fixed for them by the colleges that it was often difficult for them to think boldly and objectively about the needs of youth—both of the college-bound and of the vast majority who would never enter college. Since it was possible under the old plan to blame the college admission requirements for whatever seemed wrong, these requirements constituted a convenient scapegoat which blocked their thinking. The new agreement provided a significant stimulus toward evaluation, planning, and actual change.

The volume *Did They Succeed in College?* is a report of a carefully conducted evaluative study of the comparative success in college of graduates of the thirty schools. A total of 1475 matched pairs were carefully selected, one of each pair of students from an experimental and one from a conventional high school. Analysis of the data showed that the graduates of the experimental schools were more successful than the control group of graduates when judged by the standards of the college, the judgments of fellow students, and the student's own self-appraisals. A further study was made of the graduates of the six most experimental high school programs. These graduates were significantly superior to their matched pairs in college marks, achievement ratings, academic honors, intellectual curiosity, scientific thinking, and citizenship qualities. The investigators concluded that "the more experimental the school, the greater degree of success in college." [18]

In summary, this important major investigation clearly demonstrated that no single pattern of subjects has been found to be sacred for the preparation of students for college. It disproved the commonly held belief that success in college depends on the students having taken in high school a specific set of courses labeled as "college preparatory." The reassurance which this finding has given high school principals and teachers has been an important factor in curriculum development since 1942.

[18] Chamberlin, *op. cit.*, p. 209.

OTHER NATIONAL AND REGIONAL STUDIES

In 1933 the Cooperative Study of Secondary School Standards was initiated. This study began with the efforts of the regional accrediting associations to find some more effective method of appraising high schools for accreditation. One result was the development of the *Evaluative Criteria,* which has been applied in high schools throughout the country since 1940. It provides a method, and an instrument, for the self-study of a school by the local faculty, followed by an appraisal by a visiting team of school administrators.

An inquiry into the "character and cost" of secondary schools in New York state was launched in 1935 by the State Board of Regents. The Regents' inquiry was reported in several volumes.[19] The Regents' report was one of the first examples of widespread follow-up studies of former high school students. In addition, it recommended some ways in which the State Department of Education might improve the secondary schools of New York.

In the same year (1935) the American Council on Education created an American Youth Commission to study for five years the education and care of American youth. The report, *Youth Tell Their Story,*[20] has been widely read by those interested in secondary education. Basing the study on evaluations made by graduates and dropouts, the report accents the problems and needs of adolescents more effectively than had ever been done before.

Some other regional and national studies were launched during the 1930's. These included the United States Office of Education Committee on Youth Problems (1934), the Southern Association Commission on Curriculum Studies and Research (1935), the National Association of Secondary School Principals' Study of the Adjustment of Secondary Youth to Post-School Occupational Life

[19] Prominent among these was Francis T. Spaulding, *High School and Life,* New York, McGraw-Hill Book Company, 1938.
[20] Howard M. Bell, *Youth Tell Their Story,* Washington, American Council on Education, 1938.

(1939), and the various reports of the Educational Policies Commission, which was set up by the National Education Association in 1935. The various reports of the Policies Commission have had an important influence on secondary education.[21]

STATE STUDIES

The decade of studies was also a period of state studies. These included a five-year study of ten California high schools (1935), the Ohio plan for Curriculum Reorganization in Secondary Schools (1938), the Florida Program for the Improvement of Schools (1938), and the Michigan Study of the Secondary School Curriculum (1938). A number of other states made less ambitious surveys, involving the development of new curriculum programs for secondary schools during the 1930's.

The Michigan Study. An example of the state programs which followed the Eight-Year Study was the Michigan Study of the Secondary School Curriculum. Initiated in 1938 after a year of preliminary planning, the Michigan program enrolled fifty-five member schools for a period of twelve years. Again, following the example of the Eight-Year Study, an agreement was reached with all Michigan colleges and universities to admit recommended graduates of the member schools without specific regard to the pattern of their high school subjects. A staff worked with the schools for the first six years, after which the study was lodged in and served by the State Department of Public Instruction. As a result of the communication techniques which were developed, a number of curriculum innovations were tried out in these high schools. Many of these experiments became an integral part of the curriculum after a period of successful trial. A follow-up study of the success of the graduates in Michigan colleges revealed that they did as well as college students generally.

[21] Especially *Purposes of Education in American Democracy* (1938), *Learning the Ways of Democracy* (1940), and *Education for All American Youth* (1944). Washington, The Educational Policies Commission.

In 1946 a revision of the college agreement was developed and offered to all high schools in the state whose staff and leaders would agree to (1) conduct studies of their curriculum, (2) make follow-up studies of graduates and dropouts, (3) improve guidance records, (4) intensify guidance in vocational and college selection. A state committee was established in 1947 to administer this new Michigan Secondary School-College Agreement, which presently was endorsed by all Michigan colleges and universities. Two hundred and eighteen high schools had joined the program by 1954. They were organized into five regions for purposes of study and sharing of ideas. Both secondary school and college personnel have profited from the ten to twelve camp conferences held annually, the action research carried on by subcommittees, and the publication of developments in regional newsletters.

The Illinois Program. A somewhat similar curriculum program is actively under way in Illinois. The State Superintendent of Public Instruction and the University of Illinois have joined forces to provide leadership for a very extensive program of local "consensus" studies. A number of valuable reports have emerged from the Illinois program, ranging from studies of "hidden tuition costs" and participation in extra-class activities to holding power and human relations.[22]

THE LIFE ADJUSTMENT PROGRAM

In 1945 the United States Office of Education launched a national program aimed at improving instruction and guidance of "neglected" groups of youth, who often drop out of high school before graduation. This program went forward under the label "Life Adjustment" education and depended primarily on the various states for implementation. It was defined in the following language from a U.S. Office of Education bulletin:

[22] A number of the early Illinois studies are reported in the monograph by H. C. Hand, *Principal Findings of the Illinois Secondary School Curriculum Program,* Bulletin No. 2, Springfield, Ill., State Superintendent of Public Instruction, 1949.

Life adjustment education is designed to equip all American youth to live democratically with satisfaction to themselves and profit to society as home members, workers, and citizens. It is concerned especially with a sizable proportion of youth of high school age (both in school and out) whose objectives are less well served by our schools than the objectives of preparation for either a skilled occupation or higher education. Some leaders have for years been at work in secondary schools developing a guiding philosophy and bringing about program reorganization in the direction of life adjustment education for every youth. Under such leadership many high schools have made considerable progress in building programs of study and providing educational services basically useful to each participating pupil.

Many high schools, however, continue to be dominated by traditional curriculum patterns which emphasize verbal and abstract learning or place undue emphasis on specialized courses useful to a relatively small number of pupils. As a result many pupils unable to benefit from either of these types of instruction are left to flounder or to leave the schools as soon as the compulsory education laws will permit.[23]

The emphasis of the original Life Adjustment program has now been broadened to include the improvement of secondary education for all youth. It represents an effort on the national level to stimulate the more general adaptation of instruction to the real needs, problems, and interests of adolescents.

SUMMARY

We have noted in this chapter that the secondary school in the United States has emerged from its limited origins and advanced in enrollments by leaps and bounds. Some program changes were made to adapt to the new types of students who filled the high schools in the early decades of this century. Since 1930, however, an intensive series of national, regional, and state studies have

[23] *Developing Life Adjustment Education in a Local School,* Circular No. 253, Washington, Office of Education, February, 1941, p. 3.

been aimed at reducing the high dropout rate by gearing the program of instruction and activities to all youth, whatever their economic status or verbal ability.

Much progress has been made in the direction of a more functional curriculum. Better guidance programs have been developed. Some efforts have been made to increase student participation in school activities. Teaching methods have tended to improve, and instructional materials have become much better.

Most students of secondary education, however, are not yet satisfied with our progress. When about 50 percent of our youth still reject the high school before graduation, it seems evident that there is still room for improvement. If we are to realize the American dream of universal public education up to at least the age of marriage or permanent employment, there is still work to be done.

FOR FURTHER READING

Aikin, Wilford M., *The Story of the Eight-Year Study*, New York, Harper & Brothers, 1942.

Biennial Survey of Education in the United States, 1944–46, chap. 1, Statistical Summary of Education, 1945–46, Washington, U.S. Office of Education, 1946.

Chamberlin, Dean, *et al.*, *Did They Succeed in College?*, New York, Harper & Brothers, 1942.

Cubberley, Ellwood P., and Eells, Walter Crosby, *An Introduction to the Study of Education*, Boston, Houghton Mifflin Company, 1933, chaps. I, II.

Dewhurst, J. Frederic, and Associates, *America's Needs and Resources*, New York, The Twentieth Century Fund, 1947.

Educational Policies Commission, *Education for All American Youth*, Washington, The National Education Association, 1944.

Educational Policies Commission, *Purposes of Education in American Democracy*, Washington, The National Education Association, 1938.

Faunce, Roland C., and Bossing, Nelson L., *Developing the Core Curriculum*, New York, Prentice-Hall, 1951, chap. 3.

Gaumnitz, Walter H., and Hull, J. Dan, *Junior High Schools Vs. the Traditional (8–4) High School Organization,* U.S. Office of Education Circular No. 373, Washington, U.S. Department of Health, Education, and Welfare, May, 1953.

Giles, H. H., McCutchen, S. P., and Zechiel, A. N., *Exploring the Curriculum,* New York, Harper & Brothers, 1942.

Hand, Harold C., *Principal Findings of the Illinois Secondary School Curriculum Program,* Bulletin No. 2, Springfield, Ill., State Superintendent of Public Instruction, 1949.

Koos, Leonard V., *Integrating High School and College,* New York, Harper & Brothers, 1946.

Leonard, J. Paul, *Developing the Secondary School Curriculum,* New York, Rinehart & Company, 1946, Part One.

Progressive Education Association, *Thirty Schools Tell Their Story,* New York, the Association, 1942.

Smith, E. R., *et al., Appraising and Recording Student Progress,* New York, Harper & Brothers, 1942.

Spaulding, Francis T., *High School and Life,* New York, McGraw-Hill Book Company, 1938, chaps. II, XIV.

Wilds, Elmer H., *The Foundations of Modern Education,* New York, Farrar & Rinehart, 1942.

....

CHAPTER 3

Curriculum Trends in the Secondary School

SOME GENERAL TRENDS SINCE 1930

In the previous chapter the efforts to adapt the secondary school to its changing student population have been noted. Beginning about 1930 there has been a continuous procession of studies of secondary education. Since most of these studies have dealt with the basic functions of the secondary school and its program of general education, it is not surprising to find that some important changes have resulted. In the present chapter an overview of those changes will be presented as an aid to understanding the task of the principal as a leader in curriculum revision. It is not proposed to make at this point a complete analysis of all the trends since 1930 in the secondary school.[1] Within the scope of this chapter an effort will be made to highlight the most important trends that have appeared as secondary schools have become involved in studies of their communities, the nature of adolescence, and the learning process.

The program of the secondary school of the 1950's is not like

---

[1] Among several excellent books which present such an analysis, see especially Harold Alberty, *Reorganizing the High School Curriculum*, New York, The Macmillan Company, 1947; J. Paul Leonard, *Developing the Secondary School Curriculum*, New York, Rinehart & Company, 1946; and William Alexander and J. Galen Saylor, *Secondary Education*, New York, Rinehart & Company, 1950.

that of the 1920's. The activity movement has become well established as a legitimate companion program to classroom instruction, and has also entered the classroom in certain significant ways. The concept of the community school, as earlier defined by Hanna, Olsen, and others,[2] has tended to effect bridges from the secondary school to the community and from the community to the school. Efforts have been made to correlate certain courses and units within courses. Unified studies and core courses have emerged as a part of the trend toward reducing the departmentalized nature of both junior and senior high schools. The schools have intensified and enriched vocational offerings in an effort to give exploratory experiences in earning a living. Work experience programs have lent reality to such efforts. Art and music courses have become more versatile in their adaptation to individual interests and special abilities. The impact of two wars and the prospect of permanent mobilization have had an influence in the direction of preinduction training [3] and physical education. Secondary schools have generally discovered the present tense in their curriculum programs. Such emphases as home and family living, consumer economics, local community government, personal and public health, conservation of natural resources, driver training, and the air age have appeared either as courses or as major units within courses in most secondary schools.

Not all these trends have appeared in any large number of schools. Some schools still present little evidence of any of these trends. In general, however, such developments as these may be found in most junior and senior high schools in the United States today. This is not to say that the secondary school has achieved a new curriculum. In many schools modern trends appear only here

---

[2] Paul R. Hanna *et al.*, *Youth Serves the Community*, New York, Appleton-Century-Crofts, 1936; E. G. Olsen, *et al.*, *School and Community*, New York, Prentice-Hall, 1945; E. G. Olsen, *School and Community Programs*, New York, Prentice-Hall, 1949.

[3] Presently reduced in scope since the period of full educational mobilization of the early 1940's, but still evident in guidance programs.

and there as individual teachers gain security in changed procedures. School-wide change develops slowly—some wit has said "with geologic speed." It is often difficult to note the changes which have gradually emerged until one compares an institution with its prototype of two or three decades ago. The gradualness of change is emphasized also by the realization that the task still before us is so vast and so urgent. It may therefore be profitable to devote some thought to certain curriculum trends, which, in combination, appear to be slowly changing the nature of the secondary school's program.

ENRICHING INDIVIDUAL LEARNING

It has been said that the major challenge to teaching method is that of individual differences and their acceptance by teachers. This problem is especially real in the modern secondary school, with its wide range of pupil abilities and interests. As has been pointed out in Chapter 2, the secondary school enrollment includes pupils representing a wide range of differences. Instead of bemoaning these differences, or fruitlessly seeking ways to restore homogeneity to the high school pupil enrollment, the staff must come to accept the fact of differences, and to accept fully the youth who do not measure up to the academic standards of another day.

There has been some progress made in this important task of learning to accept all youth. Teachers are gradually escaping from the old stereotypes which attached greatest social value to the skills of academic readiness. The curriculum, too, has been modified to provide for individual enrichment.

In small schools most of this individual enrichment must be done in required courses because there is a limited offering of electives. Such curricula as agriculture, industrial arts, and homemaking, for example, have made significant progress in recognizing that individuals differ and that a wide range of learning experiences must be provided. These particular curricula have been largely developed in modern times, and perhaps they have benefited from research in child development to a greater extent than have the older, traditionally required curricula. In any case, the so-called practical arts courses have pioneered the trend toward (1) accepting all boys and girls as worthy citizens of the class, (2) providing a wide variety of learning experiences, (3) recognizing the value of successful achievement in other lines of effort than reading and writing, and (4) evaluating individual achievements without regard to the (mythical) class norm. In agriculture classes boys have discovered that they can be successful in raising hogs or in keeping an accurate record of soil improvement. Girls in homemaking classes have changed the whole pattern of social life in their homes by their new knowledge of interior decorating or of healthful menus. The student in shop has learned that *his* interests, *his* abilities, and *his* needs can determine the project he chooses. To some degree, too, these students in the practical arts courses have discovered that their progress is being evaluated in terms of their own abilities rather than in terms of some abstract grade level standard.

The curriculum has also been enriched for the individual whose interests and abilities are in the area of the graphic arts. Urban high schools have well-equipped art laboratories with facilities for silver and copper design, reed weaving, ceramics, leather work, and a dozen other fine-arts activities. Crayon, pencil, and oil and water coloring are also provided for the boy or girl who is interested in creative activity in the graphic arts. Some city high schools have art laboratories which are so well equipped that they bear comparison with commercial or university studios. Rural high schools are not usually as well equipped with facilities for the fine arts. Yet these art programs, too, are often characterized by great freedom from the usual subject limitations and are thus free to adapt the standards of art achievement to the drives and interests of the individual learner.

School music programs have vastly expanded since 1920. School bands, orchestras, and choirs have become a part of the "regular" curriculum, meeting every day for credit. Within the rather flexible requirements of these large group activities, there is a place for the student of great or little talent. If he cannot master one instrument, he is encouraged to study a different one. Seldom is he discouraged or barred from pursuing a sincere interest in music because of group standards or national norms.

The talented student finds an outlet in solo or ensemble work, even in small secondary schools. This is a part of the astonishing expansion of the public school music program. Even the typical rural consolidated high school provides opportunities, either in the regular school day or closely allied to it, for the talented musician who wishes to secure special help to go beyond the artistic challenge of the band or choir.

The speech activities of the high school were once highly stereotyped and standardized. Changing cultural standards have had an effect on these activities also. Many of them are offered as a part of the regular program of class offerings. Within these speech or dramatics classes are offered many opportunities for the flowering of the individual talent. The so-called extracurricular realm, too, is rich in activities in which the talented speaker can engage and thus learn greater competence in creative communication. The program today goes far beyond the old oratorical activities. Dramatics now has its place, as well as humorous readings, extempore speaking, debate, and discussion.

Although there is an increasing tendency for high schools to employ a speech teacher and to schedule speech courses as such, the majority of schools still provide the training in oral expression as a part of instruction in English classes. Written work also reflects to some degree the trend toward individual enrichment. In many schools creative writing has replaced the older stereotyped theme. The student often chooses a topic to write about, sometimes after he has had a challenging experience to provide stimulation for writing. This may be a moving picture or some mood music; it may be a trip to some place of special interest in the community;

or his inspiration for written expression may come from a lively discussion of problems which are of real concern to him and his classmates. Whatever the occasion for writing, he is often given a choice, not only of topic, but of the form, length, and style of his writing. The themes suggested for writing include autobiographies and such topics as "If I had three wishes" or "I would like to be . . ." These can furnish valuable data for individual guidance. Some written work may not be collected and appraised daily, but kept in a file accessible to the student and submitted to his teacher at such times as he wishes to get some specific help. Evaluation of his work in English may be in terms of his own growth since he entered the course instead of comparison with other students' work. English teachers who use such methods as these are providing individual enrichment through creative writing. They are also discovering that better writing skills can result from intensive individual effort.

The reading activities in English classes also tend to reflect the trend toward individual enrichment. Many English teachers are discovering the individual through "free reading" programs. Instead of attempting to make all students read the same story, essay, or poem and react to it exactly as their fellows, they are making available to students a rich classroom collection of all kinds of good literature, written at many different vocabulary levels. Through exhibits, films, and discussions the reading interests of boys and girls can be stimulated to the point where they will return to their earlier interest in books. Appreciation and understanding are tested not by examinations or formal book reports, but by round table discussions, by informal story or poetry sessions, or by individual conversations with the teacher. A reading log may be kept as a means of recording the student's impressions and criticisms of the books he has read. Periodical literature also has its place in a lively program of free reading. Much stimulation comes from the theater and the moving pictures. Standards of critical analysis are formed gradually through class discussions and individual counseling. A collection of interesting books is maintained in the classroom to facilitate introduction to new reading vistas. The school library is used as a major resource, as are also the community library and book collections in the home.

Other experiences enrich individual growth in a modern secondary school. The science laboratories are a source of keen enjoyment and expanding intelligence to students interested in plants, animals, electricity, atomic energy, and many other facets of natural and physical science. A creative program in science is not a series of workbook exercises seeking answers already recorded in the text. It is rather a wonderful adventure of exploration and discovery with a sympathetic teacher and a well-equipped laboratory. The individual with special interests in science is encouraged to go as far and as fast as he can in his experimental search for new truth. The Science Talent Search [4] is an example of a number of current efforts to identify and encourage these young scientists in their careers.

Similar encouragement of individuals with special interests goes on in other departments of the secondary school. There are programs of reward—scholarships, cash, or simply recognition—for boys and girls interested in invention, in poster design, in architecture, engineering, automobile and other kinds of industrial design, garment styling, radio and television acting, plastics, and a number of other fields. Only a few students, however, can qualify for these awards or scholarships. The schools must operate in such fashion that every boy and girl will get a chance to pursue an individual interest and achieve success in some line of activity. This is largely a matter of teaching method. Indeed, it is difficult to separate curriculum from teaching method, since both combine to govern the experiences which the learner has. In addition to the way in which the teacher operates, there can be overall planning to insure that the curriculum includes enrichment for every learner. This trend appears to be established in secondary schools.

[4] Conducted annually by the Science Clubs of America, 1719 N Street N. W., Washington 6, D.C.

TRENDS TOWARD BETTER GUIDANCE

The guidance movement is well known to observers of the secondary school since about 1920. Many guidance activities go on in apparent disregard for, or independence of the curriculum. In some schools guidance means an adaptation or adjustment of the student to the current curriculum, rather than an adjustment of the curriculum to the learner's needs. A dynamic curriculum must be accompanied by an equally dynamic guidance program designed to (1) help discover the learner's needs, abilities, and interests; (2) help the learner to discover school experiences which will capitalize upon those needs, interests, and abilities; and (3) help the learner plan for future experiences in the light of his growth, including successes and failures. Thus the functions of guidance, curriculum, and teaching method are inextricably intertwined in the modern secondary school.[5]

The guidance movement has affected the curriculum in many significant ways. The trend toward core or general education, which will be discussed later in this chapter, has owed its growth to the need for better guidance programs. The block program which retains one teacher with the same section for two or three class periods represents basically an effort to know pupils better and to aid their adjustment. That is one reason why such programs have developed so rapidly at the junior high school level.

Occupational information was once the job of the home-room teacher or counselor or librarian. Today many secondary schools have required courses in occupations or vocational choice and thousands of other schools include units in occupations in other required courses. Such instructional efforts are usually concentrated in the ninth and twelfth grades.

Another guidance area which has graduated from the extra-curricular is orientation to the new school. In seventh, ninth, and tenth grades in many schools the opening unit in some required course is one on orientation. Here the new student learns about his

[5] A more detailed analysis of the guidance program will appear in Chapter 7.

school—its curriculum, its activities, building plan, traditions, rules, and teaching staff.

Many high schools provide help in selecting a college or a vocation as a part of some twelfth-grade class, such as "problems of democracy." The resources of the community are frequently brought to bear on this selection process, through "Business-Industry-Education" conferences. Leaders in various vocational fields represented in the community are brought together for discussion of the opportunities in their respective fields with the high school seniors. Often college representatives are also present at these BIE days, for the purpose of supplying information about their respective admission requirements and training opportunities. In some schools, the college representatives are invited to a separate "College Day" conference to confer with interested students. The curriculum is often geared to these conferences, as students in some required course plan the conference and their particular part in it, followed by evaluation of it and study and discussion of materials distributed at the conference. College days held on a particular college campus for several neighboring high schools are also made the topic of study in senior classes.

VOCATIONAL EDUCATION

The guidance trend has affected the so-called vocational offerings, too. There was a time when vocational educators claimed for their field the task of preparing students for specific operations needed in a particular job. The difficulty was that there was no assurance that the students would follow the particular job trained for, or use the particular skill acquired in high school. In jobs where processes or machines have become generally standardized, a close relation may appear between training and operation on the job. This is somewhat true of typing and shorthand. It is less true of bookkeeping, due to the variety of accounting methods prevalent in business. It is even less true of industrial machine operations, where the machines used in production are far too expensive, too specialized, and too rapidly changing to be practicable for a high school shop.

It is furthermore true that young people change jobs frequently before assuming a (more or less) permanent vocation. Any survey of jobs held by graduates five years after high school would reveal that most of them are no longer doing what they trained for in high school. The outstanding exceptions to this rule are home-making (which is so universally a "second" vocation for women that it might rather be considered a part of general education) and agriculture, which is usually a part of the curriculum in rural areas.

The realization of these facts has gradually brought about certain trends in secondary schools. We no longer think of the commercial and shop courses as strictly vocational, nor try to justify them on a basis of specific job training. We consider them exploratory, in the sense that through these courses we give students an opportunity to try themselves in tasks comparable to those on a particular job, and discover their aptitude or lack of it for a particular kind of job. We also justify these courses by their contribution to the goals of general education—good citizenship, social relationships, and individual growth. Finally, such courses as industrial arts and bookkeeping can help a student to understand the economic world about him and thus become better prepared as a consumer as well as a producer or seller of goods. With such goals as these, the various "vocational-exploration" courses are directly a part of the guidance trend in secondary education.

A more direct training in specific vocational skills occurs in such part-time programs as the coöperative apprentice training courses in trade or industry. Here the student spends part of his day on the job, learning a particular operation by actually performing it, and comes to school for the background and auxiliary education related to the job. Many kinds of work-experience programs are in operation in high schools across the land. They range from the casual recognition of the need to dismiss students from some of their school day to take a job to the formal apprentice-training programs, which involve a formidable series of operations to be learned by experience over a two-year period. All these programs make some kind of a contribution to better guidance. Not all of them equally affect the curriculum. There is a trend, however, toward planning school experiences which will relate to the student's work experience and capitalize on his interest in it for more functional learning.

TRENDS TOWARD THE CURRENT SCENE

It is obvious by now that modern curriculum trends cannot be neatly divided into separate categories. The heading immediately above would be quite suitable for the occupational-exploration courses just discussed. Throughout secondary education we have discovered the present tense. The older "current events" period (for ten minutes each Friday!) has grown to lifelike proportions and become the heart of the curriculum in many schools. The spread of such courses as "problems of democracy," usually combining the traditional civics and economics courses in the senior year, is evidence of our concern that students go out of our schools with some understanding of the current world scene.

Units in such courses may include political and economic concepts as a means of understanding "the home," "marriage and divorce," "crime and its correction," "public education," "religion," "city planning," "money and banking," and many other similar problems to be found in every community.

The study of current economic and civic problems extends into other kinds of secondary school courses. It is a common procedure in core classes. It has affected the chapter organization in many recent textbooks in history, civics, and sociology. Some English anthologies have appeared in which readings are selected and arranged around current problems.

The trend toward home- and family-life courses has become rather general in high schools. These courses often differ from the older homemaking field in that they include both girls and boys, and stress insights and understandings rather than the skills of home management. They are a vital phase of the guidance program in many schools. The contents of a typical textbook [6] include the following chapters:

> What You Are
> How We Meet Our Problems
> Getting Along With Others
> Dating
> Use of Alcohol
> Family Understanding
> Mate Selection
> Engagement
> Marriage
> Is It Love
> What About Quarreling
> You and Your In-Laws
> Learning to Manage the Family Income
> Consumer Economics
> Divorce
> Size of Families
> Approaching Parenthood
> Parents and Children
> Childless Homes
> The Successful Home

Such courses are now required in many schools, elective in a host of others. They do not all use a textbook. They vary also in the extent to which they deal with sex problems and give information about sex. It is clear that some approach to the problems of marriage and family living is increasing as a part of the secondary school curriculum.

Other current problems are studied in junior and senior high schools. Many schools make a frontal attack on racial and religious

[6] Judson T. Landis and Mary G. Landis, *Personal Adjustment, Marriage and Family Living,* New York, Prentice-Hall, 1950.

prejudice through units in various courses on the Negro in American life, the nature of prejudice,[7] facts about various religious beliefs, and facts about the nature of man. The problems related to achieving world peace are studied in thousands of secondary schools, either in history or core classes or in "international relations" courses. Units on United Nations, UNESCO, and other agencies related to UN appear in many required courses in both junior and senior high schools. The air age has penetrated the modern curriculum through its influence on science, geography, and history materials, and through special units in various courses. Even arithmetic texts use problems in air distance. Special projects in various classes give students experiences in model airplane construction as an aid to recognition of planes, as well as to the understanding of aerodynamics and the theory of flight.

Conservation has joined the curriculum. This is only partly because of its importance to adult citizens. It has become a vital concern to youth, too, in thousands of communities. The school camping program in some states has drawn secondary school students into service projects of various kinds pointed at the conservation of our resources. Through soil erosion control, tree planting, contour plowing, fish and game management, road, dam, and bridge construction, and a hundred other activities in conservation, youth in such programs are learning to know and appreciate the interdependence between man and his environment.

Personal and public health is another current problem that has become a part of the curriculum. Both in health classes, as such, and in science and social studies classes students are learning practices and understandings which will prolong and enrich life. This is another area of learning that cannot be acquired exclusively from books. The materials and subjects for study are likely to be people and their interaction with their environment.

Economic understanding was once the province of a one-

---

[7] An example of text material on this theme is Hortense Powdermaker's *Probing Our Prejudices*, New York, Harper & Brothers, 1944.

semester course toward the end of the senior high school. Analysis of older textbooks in economics indicates that authors and teachers alike depended on the historical-legal approach for teaching economic principles. Today economics is taught in more classes than bear the name, and in a hundred direct applications of economic life. Students are learning through direct experience how to earn, spend, save, and borrow money; how to budget; how to judge products and test the validity of advertising claims; and how to buy wisely. They are learning about loans and insurance and taxes. They are gaining some insight into inflation control and the province of government in economic matters. The very pervasiveness of economic concepts in our culture has brought such experiences as these into thousands of classrooms.

The community school perhaps exemplifies this trend toward the present in its curriculum and methods. One state curriculum committee has defined the community school in terms of its functions in the local community:

1. The community school serves community needs and resources.
2. The community school gives initial leadership to constructive community improvement projects.
3. The community school helps to develop a sense of community, both in children and adults.
4. The community school expands and diffuses leadership throughout the community.
5. The community school practices and promotes democratic procedures.
6. The community school coordinates all constructive efforts to improve community living.
7. The community school uses human and material resources in the instructional program.
8. The community school builds the curriculum around major human problems.
9. The community school involves all persons concerned in planning and appraising the school program.

10. The community school is genuinely life-centered as a social institution.[8]

A school which exemplified all of these activities would, it has been submitted, be a true community school. Not all of the criteria are met by many secondary schools,[9] but most can be found in some schools. In summary, these criteria appear to represent a trend toward meeting the challenge of our present social order and its problems in the curriculum of the secondary school.

It should perhaps be emphasized that an accent on the present does not preclude an understanding of the past and its contributions. Indeed, it may help students to appreciate and understand past cultures if they begin to study the current scene. Most secondary schools still have courses in world history and American history. An effort is made, however, to motivate the study of history by first arousing interest in the world of today. Every modern problem has its roots in events of the past, in which students can become interested when the problem approach is used in the classroom.

TRENDS TOWARD GENERAL EDUCATION AND THE CORE CURRICULUM

Both "general education" and "core" are terms which have come to mean all things to all people. Perhaps the trend can best be defined by stating the conditions it seeks to correct, as a recent volume on the core curriculum begins by doing:

1. There is too much emphasis [in the high school of today] on subject matter, without much relationship to the pupil's real needs, interests, or abilities. . . .
2. The traditional school program is too departmentalized. . . .

[8] Report of the Department of Public Instruction, Lansing, Michigan, State Committee on Instructional Program of the Community School, April, 1953.

[9] Perhaps the most striking approach was made in the Holtville School in Alabama. See Southern Association Study, *The Story of Holtville*, George Peabody College, Nashville, Tenn., 1944.

3. The conventional curriculum takes too little account of real life. . . .
4. The classroom experiences are planned and conducted without sufficient regard for what we now know about the learning process. . . .
5. The pupils themselves receive little or no experience in assuming responsibilities or in making choices. . . .
6. The class periods are often too short for extended activities that vitalize learning. . . .
7. The traditional school offers little real opportunity for guidance: teachers and pupils do not become well enough acquainted.[10]

The trend toward core thus arises from an excessive emphasis on subject matter and from the departmentalized character of the secondary school. In brief, the core class is designed to correct these conditions through its four distinctive aspects:

1. Freedom from subject matter patterns and . . . emphasis upon vital life problem situations;
2. . . . emphasis upon group problem-solving;
3. . . . use of a long block of time; and
4. . . . emphasis on guidance by the classroom teacher.[11]

Programs embodying these four characteristics had emerged in 833 high schools by 1950, according to a survey report published by the United States Office of Education.[12] Although this number constituted only about 3 percent of the high schools in the United States, the author indicated that various factors may combine to make the total number of programs aimed at the core concept much larger. It appears from other surveys that, in the junior high school particularly, the block of time in which one teacher employs teacher-pupil planning procedures, free from the restrictions of subject-matter frames of reference, is a fairly typical modern trend.

[10] Roland C. Faunce and Nelson L. Bossing, *Developing the Core Curriculum,* New York, Prentice-Hall, 1951, pp. 1–3. Reprinted by permission of the publisher.
[11] *Ibid.,* p. 8.
[12] Grace Wright, *Core Curriculum in Public High Schools, an Inquiry into Practices,* 1949, Bulletin 1950, No. 5, Washington, Federal Security Agency, Office of Education, 1950.

The core curriculum is known by many different titles. In some schools it is called "general education." In others it may be titled "common learnings" or "basic living" or "basic communication." Some schools call it "unified studies," which was historically a forerunner of the core curriculum.

The core curriculum emerged from efforts in the early 1930's to extend into the secondary school the experience curriculum of the elementary schools. It was recognized that one of the chief obstacles to a truly functional curriculum at the secondary level was the separation of learning into subject compartments, and the further fortification of these separate dominions by excessively departmental organization of the school staff and curriculum. The elementary school, where one teacher lived all day with the same section of pupils, provided maximum flexibility for such new trends as project construction, the school trip, the activity movement, and the unit method. These developments tended to stop at the doorstep of the departmentalized secondary school because they required time, freedom from subject restrictions, and continuity of relationships between a teacher and a learning group.

The first assault on these limiting factors appeared in the secondary school as "broad fields" courses in which certain separate but related subjects became one broad course. In this category fell general mathematics, general science, and social studies. (English itself had generally become a broad-fields course linking the formerly separate language-arts subjects.) This broad-fields trend led to the combination of ancient, medieval, and European history into "world history" and the combination of geography, history, and citizenship into courses called "social studies" at certain grade levels. The broad fields or survey courses constituted an effort to relate an entire area of human experience for study purposes. Thus they were in at least this one respect forerunners of the core curriculum, which aims at linking all pertinent areas of human experience for problem solving by the learner.

A little later, unified-studies courses were devised with two or more subjects linked together in a double or triple period, and with either a single teacher or a team of subject specialists working in coöperation. English and some social science classes were the most frequently used combinations, although experiments were also conducted in the unification of science and mathematics, homemaking and shop, science and geography, science and hygiene, and many others. In many schools the unified-studies plan has been undertaken as an initial step toward the core curriculum. There are many schools which have not gone beyond the unified-studies level. They have still retained the subject-matter-to-be-learned point of view, and the separate textbooks which exemplify these separate contents. They have developed units in which, for example, American history and American literature have been fused for a six weeks 'period of studying the westward movement in our national history. Such units usually appear as eddies where two separate streams merge briefly before continuing their respective courses. It is true that the unified-studies plan does provide some advantage in reduction of the number of different pupils for whom a single teacher is responsible as a guidance functionary.

During the Eight-Year Study described in Chapter 2 some high school staffs were dissatisfied with the unified-studies organization and sought other ways to organize learning in general education. Among the other forerunners of the core curriculum thus developed was the fusion of learning around units determined by the "cultural epochs" of man. A plan embodying the cultural-epochs approach was used in the Horace Mann School in New York City. Another version was the "social demands" approach in which the curriculum of general education was organized around the major demands of our societal system upon its citizens. A number of state curriculum programs of the 1930's employed this social-demands type of organization. The Ohio State University School set up its early core program on an "adolescent needs" basis, which meant that the curriculum was organized loosely around major

units selected in turn because of their contribution to the needs
which research reveals adolescents confront and recognize.[13]

Certain aspects of the core curriculum deserve clarification because of the frequent misinterpretation of its nature and purpose.

1. *The core curriculum is not proposed as the total curriculum
of the senior high school.*   Even though some advocate that the
entire curriculum of the seventh and eighth grades be organized
as core, few authorities propose that it be the sole program of
learning in senior high school grades. The Educational Policies
Commission proposed such a division as the accompanying chart
shows for grades 10–14.[14]

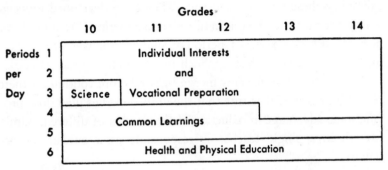

2. *The core curriculum is not a combination of subjects.*   Even
though periods devoted to separate subjects are initially combined
to provide a scheduled time for core classes, the true core class
derives its content from many different subject fields. Any subject
matter is acceptable as a means to the solution of a problem. No
subject matter is regarded as sacred or indispensable in its own
right.

3. *Other subjects should not be thought of as independent, un-*

13 These and other related types of organizing early core classes are described in
detail in two of the volumes reporting the Eight-Year Study: Progressive Education
Association, *Thirty Schools Tell Their Story*, New York, the Association, 1942; and
H. H. Giles, S. P. McCutchen, and A. N. Zechiel, *Exploring the Curriculum*, New
York, Harper & Brothers, 1942. Also see Ohio State University High School, Class of
1938, *Were We Guinea Pigs?*, New York, Henry Holt & Co., 1938.

14 Educational Policies Commission, *Education for All American Youth*, Washington, The National Education Association, 1944, p. 244.

related, or in conflict with core classes. As its name implies, the core class seeks to establish an integration of learnings in the student which will make some sense out of his total school day. All his subjects will contribute to his attack on problems in the core class. To facilitate such integration it has been proposed that every teacher in the secondary school have at least one section of core, as was the goal of the earlier home-room program.

4. *The core teacher does plan.* Through the construction of resource units around large, general areas the core teacher prepares herself to help students plan a learning experience on some aspect of the general area concerned. The core teacher also makes careful, specific analysis of the students themselves, their home situations, the community, and the available resources for learning.

SUMMARY

This chapter has presented some of the trends which appear currently in the secondary school curriculum. The available evidence seems to indicate that these trends will continue. If they do, the secondary school of the future will be characterized by some or all of the following curriculum practices:

1. There will be less dependence on the single basic text. Multiple learning aids will be used.

2. Students will be grouped with one teacher for most of the day in grades 7 and 8, a half day in grades 9 and 10, and two hours in grades 11 and 12.

3. There will be continued emphasis on teacher-pupil planning or coöperative problem solving.

4. Evaluation will tend to be based on *individual* growth toward *individual*, not group, standards.

5. The Carnegie unit will not represent the sole means of determining course length.

6. A large number of short courses will be tried, especially in the last year of the senior high school.

7. The work-experience trend will continue and intensify.

8. The specific subject requirements for college admission will disappear.

9. Bridges from school to community and from community to school will strengthen. The school will become increasingly community-centered.

10. The guidance movement will continue to be built basically around the core teacher as its most important agent.

Some or all of these developments seem likely to characterize the curriculum and the classroom methods of the future secondary school. How these conditions may be brought about is the question in the minds of many school leaders. Whatever kind of secondary school we are to have in the future, the principal will have a crucial role in its evolution. In the next chapter we turn to the ways in which the principal can aid in program development.

FOR FURTHER READING

Alberty, Harold, *Reorganizing the High School Curriculum,* New York, The Macmillan Company, 1947, chap. VI.

Alexander, William, and Saylor, J. Galen, *Secondary Education,* New York, Rinehart & Company, 1950.

Bossing, Nelson L., *Principles of Secondary Education,* New York, Prentice-Hall, 1949, chap. I.

Douglass, Harl R., *Modern Administration of Secondary Schools,* rev. ed., Boston, Ginn & Company, 1954, chap. I.

Educational Policies Commission, *Education for All American Youth,* Washington, The National Education Association, 1944.

Faunce, Roland C., and Bossing, Nelson L., *Developing the Core Curriculum,* New York, Prentice-Hall, 1951, chap 1.

Hanna, Paul R., *et al., Youth Serves the Community,* New York, Appleton-Century-Crofts, 1936.

Kelley, Earl C., "What Dare We Leave Out?", *Educational Leadership, XI:* 4, January, 1954, pp. 209–213.

Leonard, J. Paul, *Developing the Secondary School Curriculum,* New York, Rinehart & Company, 1946, pp. 151–186.

Loving, Alvin D., "Crystallizing and Making Concrete the Community School Concept in Michigan," unpublished doctoral dissertation, Detroit, Wayne University, 1954.

National Society for the Study of Education, *General Education,* Fifty-first Yearbook, Chicago, University of Chicago Press, 1952, chaps. I, III, IV.

Noar, Gertrude, *Freedom to Live and Learn,* Philadelphia, Franklin Publishing and Supply Company, 1948.

Ohio State University High School, Class of 1938, *Were We Guinea Pigs?,* New York, Henry Holt and Company, 1938, chaps. II, XII.

Olsen, E. G. (ed.), *School and Community,* New York, Prentice-Hall, 1945.

Olsen, E. G. (ed.), *School and Community Programs,* New York, Prentice-Hall, 1949.

Planning for American Youth, National Association of Secondary School Principals, Washington, 1944 (rev. 1951).

Southern Association Study, *The Story of Holtville,* George Peabody College, Nashville, Tenn., 1944.

Spears, Harold, *The High School for Today,* New York, American Book Company, 1950, chaps. 5, 6, 7.

Wright, Grace, *Core Curriculum in Public High Schools, an Inquiry into Practices,* 1949, Bulletin 1950, No. 5, Washington, Federal Security Agency, Office of Education, 1950.

....

The Principal as Leader in Program Development

WHAT IS THE MEANING OF "CURRICULUM"?

In earlier usage the school's curriculum was thought of as the content of courses taught. In this sense it was usually manifested by the various courses of study, or (more often) by the tables of contents of the textbooks used in required and elective courses. Today few educators would accept such a limited concept of the curriculum. With the growing belief that learning proceeds out of actual experience, more and more school people have come to accept the thesis that the school's curriculum consists of all the experiences the child has under the school's guidance. These experiences may be planned or spontaneous; they may be direct or indirect, intentional or incidental; they may occur within the classroom itself or in the school program as a whole, including student activities; they may, indeed, take place outside the school building and beyond the school day. If they are actual experiences that are built into the pupil's learning, they together comprise the total curriculum.

This concept of the curriculum places a marked accent on the actual, as opposed to the merely planned for, experiences of the individual pupil. To an enormous degree, the direction and impact of a pupil's experience are influenced by the behavior of his teachers. Their attitudes and their relationships tend significantly to influence the attitudes and relationships of pupils. This fact acquires greater importance when one considers that attitudes and relationships condition all human experience. As Sharp has pointed out: "The teacher is the key figure in the process of guiding children in their experiences, for it is he who has direct and prolonged contact with them. The quality of these experiences rests largely on the kind of person the teacher is. His background, his insights, his sensitivity, and his effectiveness determine to a great extent the caliber of the work accomplished in the school." [1]

The older concept of the curriculum as a body of content to be mastered placed no such responsibility on the teacher. Since the focus was on subject matter, both teacher and pupils were of secondary significance. With the shift to real experiences as the means of learning, the relationships and attitudes existing among the learners, and between them and their teachers, assume a new and crucial importance.

A COMPLEX TASK

The process of curriculum development is thus immensely more complicated than it was once thought to be. It seems simple enough to draw up a new course of study for required or elective classes. But the new course of study is likely to remain in the teacher's desk drawer unless she fully accepts it as a desirable departure from the older arrangement of content. Even if she thus accepts it, the pupils are likely to detect no difference, and behave no differently as a result of the new course of study. (This is especially probable if the teaching method and the classroom climate remain substantially the same as they were before.) And even if some significant changes occur in the classroom procedure and in pupil attitudes, these changes are not likely to be built into the pupils' behavior unless they are supported by the rest of the learners' experiences

[1] George Sharp, *Curriculum Development as Re-education of the Teacher*, New York, Bureau of Publications, Teachers College, Columbia University, 1951, p. 2.

in the school, at home, and in the community. The fact is that real learning is conditioned more significantly by attitudes and relationships in school and out than by any particular content or arrangement of content. That is why the real task of the teacher is to structure the learning situation in such a way that constructive attitudes and relationships are developed and strengthened. Dewey has stated the task thus: "The only true education comes through the stimulation of the child's powers by the demands of the social situation in which he finds himself." [2]

Thus the teacher is the architect of the social learning situation. It is his task to arrange the total learning environment in such ways that relationships will be friendly and strong, that attitudes will be constructive, and that the individual learner will be strengthened, supported, and challenged. For this task the teacher's own attitudes, and his own relationships with others, are of immense significance.

The principal who sets out to improve the school program must begin with an awareness that he is really dealing, not with content or concepts, but with people. He must accept the fact that changing programs really amounts to changing people—specifically and most centrally, the teachers who structure the pupils' experiences and thus (daily) compose the curriculum of the school. Now it is not an easy matter to change people. For one thing, they usually do not want to change. It is natural to resist any change because change usually implies present inferiority or blame. For another thing, no one (including the principal) has anyone's sanction to change him. For that matter, it is probably impossible to change another person's set of values and attitudes without his support of the idea. The changes must occur in people by their own responsibility and by their own acts. Their volition must actually be involved. It is highly probable that changes can only come about through experiences that are satisfying and successful. Since the

---

[2] John Dewey, *My Pedagogic Creed*, New York & Chicago, E. L. Kellogg & Co., 1897.

teachers' consent and even volition are needed, they must be involved in a real sense in the choice and planning of these experiences. This is the real reason for democratic staff planning. Any other kind simply does not furnish the human involvement through which attitudes and relationships can be changed.

SETTING THE CLIMATE

One of the important tasks of the leader as the group sets out to improve the school's program is that of establishing a social climate in which group interaction is possible. Since changes in attitudes and relationships can come about only through actual involvement in satisfying experiences, the climate of the school must be such that teachers enjoy working and living together in it. This climate involves more than the school building, although that can contribute or limit interaction, too. It involves also opportunities for teachers to get better acquainted, to melt away barriers that separate them, to discover that they need and can reinforce each other. Social interaction is thus important because of its possible contribution to effective group planning and execution of group plans. This social orientation is important at all stages of the planning process. It is especially crucial at the beginning, or at any stage where new teachers join the staff. This is true because new barriers to communication are created by the introduction of each new person into the planning process.

Problems on which people are willing to work must be real ones. They must "make sense" to the participants if they are to spend themselves working on them. Most people are unwilling to confess their most urgent needs or problems to strangers. This fear is partly the reason for barriers that we build about ourselves. We are often unwilling to articulate real problems even to ourselves, much less to strangers. One of the first steps in arriving at a group problem, therefore, is to get better acquainted. If this step is omitted or poorly achieved, the group may define an area for work that is essentially a "phony" one for many of the participants. When the problem is not real, people will not remain with it in a psychological sense. They will give lip service to the problem, sometimes in order to escape the hard process of continued discussion and definition, but they will not stick to a problem in which they have no genuine interest. If circumstances permit they may drop out of the group. If they are forced to be on hand they will give evidence of apathy by remaining aloof from the discussion, by carrying on side conversations, or by correcting papers in a committee meeting. Sometimes they will express their indifference to the group's problem by wisecracking, by attacking others, or by introducing irrelevant points into the discussion. There is a real need to reach agreement about what problems are worth attacking together. The achieving of consensus about the problem must await acceptance of each other and a feeling of mutual trust. This is a part of the climate of interaction.

The need for such a social climate, as well as the difficulties in creating it, have been well stated by Earl Kelley:

Each has his own ego to enhance and defend. Each seeks ways by which he can strengthen his ego, but an obvious part of this enhancement is also its defense. We are not all that we would like to be, and consequently not all that we hope others will think we are. We therefore try to cover up our weaknesses by preventing others from seeing too deeply into our real personalities. The more deeply we feel our own inadequacies, the more we try to hide them by building an outer person which we show to the world, and which no one is permitted to get behind. The inner guarded person is forever lonely because no one can join him. The wall gives a certain sense of security, but it prevents the acquisition from the outside of those knowings, attitudes, and concepts which would enhance the individual. The defense, built up, then becomes the nemesis of enhancement. Social intercourse is reduced to a trickle, and since social relations are the essence of life, life itself, in its significant aspects, is reduced.[3]

[3] Earl C. Kelley, *The Workshop Way of Learning,* New York, Harper & Brothers, 1951, pp. 75–76.

REDUCING SOCIAL BARRIERS

The first need, then, is to provide a social situation in which barriers between people are reduced to a minimum. The situation should provide a kind of fluidity, in which people have a chance to move about and mix freely with others. A degree of physical activity seems useful in reducing interpersonal barriers. Games and dancing and group singing have an important role to play in building a climate in which people accept and trust each other. Such activities may be especially essential in any faculty group where old barriers still remain or new ones have developed. A cup of coffee can contribute to social readiness. Meals together are even better. A year of work together might well begin with a faculty party, a week end in a camp setting, or a preschool conference that includes in its program a series of well-planned social events.

In this establishing of an appropriate social climate the principal plays an important role. He can prevent or inhibit social intercourse if he operates the faculty meetings on a tightly planned, all-business agenda, or he can encourage and set the stage for lively social interaction among the teachers. He can help break down social barriers by the example he sets, too. If he accepts others in an open, friendly manner and treats them with informality and warmth, they will usually respond in a similar manner and follow the principal's example in their treatment of each other.

The nature of social activities will vary with the needs of the group. It is not always a simple matter to plan a social program for a group of teachers. Activities that are successful in one group may not be well received by another. Menge and Faunce have pointed out the need for intelligent planning of social activities:

The social activities should be planned intelligently, in keeping with the cultural backgrounds and social readiness of the participants. Some activities will be highly successful with certain groups and will fail with others. Leaders should be sensitive to the feelings of the participants and avoid forcing them into social activities they resent. Most people can be induced to enter into such activities by gradual steps and will eventually reach the stage where they welcome it. The more they resent the social role, the more they are likely to need it. The more they need it, the more skillful and sensitive must be the approach to social activities.[4]

In spite of the difficulties that sometimes attend the launching of social activities, however, groups usually come to accept and welcome these experiences because of the reinforcement they receive from them. They enjoy the lift of the spirit that results from successful social experiences. They treasure the friendships that develop and they usually recognize the value of such activities in freeing communication and in building morale. In most schools the principal will soon discover that there are faculty leaders who can initiate and carry on social activities more effectively than he. His role at that point may shift to participant. He should continue to encourage and facilitate such experiences as much as possible. He may be in the best position to secure funds or building facilities for social events. Above all, his own example, in his dealing with individuals and groups on the faculty, will be important in setting the climate of interaction.

The quality of leadership is the most important single factor about any group. Lewin has pointed out: ". . . it will be easily understood why a change in methods of leadership is probably the quickest way to bring about a change in the cultural atmosphere of a group. For the status and power of the leader or of the leading section of a group make them the key to the ideology and organization of the life of that group."[5]

Wiles has called attention to the importance of respect for personality:

[4] J. W. Menge and R. C. Faunce, *Working Together for Better Schools*, New York, American Book Company, 1953, p. 36.

[5] Kurt Lewin, *Resolving Social Conflicts*, New York, Harper & Brothers, 1948, p. 49.

The basic way for a supervisor to help create a satisfying emotional tone is by respecting the personality of all individuals with whom he comes in contact. . . . [This] involves being concerned about them and their problems, being willing to place their desires ahead of his own, giving full consideration to their ideas and suggestions, creating the type of staff meetings in which each teacher has an opportunity to make his opinions known, encouraging socializing activities that build friendly relationships among the staff, providing working conditions that are comfortable and attractive, and such commonplace things as maintaining an even disposition and showing courtesy.[6]

The administrator sets the tone of relationships within a building. He acts toward other people every day as though he had faith in them. He exhibits skill in his relationships with others. He recognizes that his own behavior is likely to serve as an example and a model for others to emulate. He knows that "real progress toward a better curriculum will not be made until all persons concerned with curriculum improvement are treated with respect, until it is demonstrated in countless ways that their opinions are valued."[7] He treats teachers with respect. He keeps channels of communication open, even when he disagrees with views that are expressed. He deals fairly with people. He works constantly to keep the way open for continued discussion and appraisal. He seeks always to release the power that is in other people, by reducing the barriers to group unity and group action.

PLANNING TOGETHER

Program development is, then, a coöperative enterprise involving, first of all, the entire staff. At other levels the process must also involve lay citizens [8] and the pupils themselves. Since a beginning must be made with the school's faculty, we have noted that

[6] Kimball Wiles, *Supervision for Better Schools,* New York, Prentice-Hall, 1950, p. 13. Reprinted by permission of the publisher.
[7] Alice Miel, *Changing the Curriculum,* New York, Appleton-Century-Crofts, 1946, p. 170.
[8] Analysis of the problems and techniques of bringing parents and other lay citizens into the planning of school programs will be presented in Chapter 6.

it is essential to develop social unity and a climate of interaction within that group.

It is probable that coöperative planning will seldom succeed when the problems under study are not real to all participants. At this point some administrators have made a costly mistake. Many school principals have entered upon their new positions with a considerable number of ideas and goals. They have studied the existing curriculum and have made a list of the outstanding problems that seem to them to need some attention. They may be quite right in their selection of the problems that are most urgent. Yet these particular problems may have no significance for the faculty group. Because of the prestige of the leader, teachers may go along with a program of study; sometimes they may even give the appearance of accepting the leader's proposals for study. If their interest and concern are not rooted more deeply than that, however, the study has little chance of success. The problems on which teachers spend themselves must be real to them.

The principal should be concerned, therefore, to discover first of all what the matters are that are so urgent from the teachers' point of view that they will be likely to devote themselves to a solution of them. To the principal, these teachers may not appear to be aware of the really urgent needs for program change. They may be at the stage where their primary concern is how to control behavior of pupils in the halls, or how to eliminate gum chewing, or how to get extra pay for coaching activities. If the real problems of teachers are on the level indicated by these examples, some administrators may feel that they are scarcely worth the attention of professional people.

This attitude is likely to prove mistaken. However trivial the problems of teachers may appear, they can furnish a beginning for faculty discussion and study which can develop broader lines of inquiry and finally eventuate in significant program changes. Even more important is the realization that groups cannot begin work at any other point than their present level of insights and values.

They cannot adopt the leader's purposes and program, even if they want to do so. They must begin where they are.

Even when this fact is recognized by the leader, it is not easy to arrive at problems that appear worthy of study to all members of the group. Some small segment of the faculty may be successful in imposing a problem on the entire group when there is not general interest in it. The result will usually be as futile as though the principal had imposed the problems. The techniques of reaching consensus on a problem are not easy, nor are they quickly mastered. Yet the productive quality of the group depends so directly on its dedication to the problem that it behooves the leader to seek patiently to attain a reasonable consensus on what problems the group should study. This may, in some situations, even require anonymous surveys of what individuals want before there can be open discussion of the problems. It will be most successful in situations where there is a good morale—a good "social climate." The process will, of course, be helped immensely if there has been previous successful experience in group planning. At the very least there must be a feeling of freedom to express any views, however unpopular they may be to the majority.

There are other barriers to good group planning. Sometimes it is attempted without any time provision. Effective planning requires plenty of time, and some of it should be "school time" in fairness to busy classroom teachers.

The room situation can help or hinder group planning. It is more effective in rooms with flexible, comfortable furniture. It is probable that real consensus demands a group of twelve persons or less. This means that a room should be selected that permits the faculty to break up into small groups for part of the time. For example, the problem census may be preceded by a listing of problems for study in small groups of six or eight persons. The lists can then be brought together in the large group, combined, classified, and discussed, and selections made for study.

Group planning is premised on a belief in people. Some principals avoid its use because they think no worth-while result can come from the faculty:

"They only want to gripe about the rug they want in the teachers' room."

"They argue and argue—they never reach any agreement."

"They only sit and listen, for the most part, while a few hotheads or screwballs shoot off their mouths."

"They only want to be left alone—they want me to decide these matters."

These comments, and others like them, betray a basic lack of faith in the capacity of the average teacher to

1. Develop values and goals
2. Recognize problems that prevent attainment of goals
3. Share problems and answers with others
4. Find resources
5. Arrive at consensus about what should be done
6. Try solutions
7. Appraise results

If teachers appear to be slow and clumsy at carrying out these steps in group planning, it may be owing to their inexperience with such skills. Perhaps no one has ever given them an opportunity to plan together a solution of their own problems. Perhaps no leader has ever helped them discover the skills needed in that process. Such inexperience with group process is still widespread among teachers. Yet those who have had the good fortune to experience successful planning have demonstrated great capacity for it. People derive an astonishing degree of reinforcement and courage from even small successes in planning. As their courage mounts, their skills increase. They are ready in a surprisingly short period of time to tackle any problem, as a group.

Such experienced groups have usually had intelligent leadership. They have learned to be patient with one another, to understand one another's motives, and to share one another's resources. They control even the "screwballs" who want to talk all the time and prevent agreement. They have acquired the techniques of group self-appraisal and have discovered how to make group discussions constantly more successful.

ROLE OF THE PRINCIPAL

The principal, as leader of the faculty, plays a significant role in this coöperative planning effort. It is highly probable that no faculty planning can be successful without his coöperation and leadership. He sets the stage for the planning by arranging a situation in which teachers can have time and opportunity to work together on real problems. He helps them to become better acquainted through social activities. He opens the way for individuals to suggest problems, and for the group to consider them. He avoids imposing his own ideas but keeps channels of communication open for all to participate. He helps to increase the resources of the group by encouraging the contributions of the less verbal members.

A bulletin on supervision has summed up the role of the status leader in group planning as follows:

Status leadership helps groups and group members to:

1. Discover group goals sufficiently vital so that they will call forth a maximum of cooperative effort.
2. Set up a system of values enabling the group to define, select, or choose the needs and interests of first priority.
3. Instill in others a desire to "belong" and take active part in group action.
4. Discover their skills, competencies, interests, and abilities so that each, while taking part in group processes, may gain the maximum security which results from each having a part to play and a contribution to make.
5. Develop good human relationships and satisfactory personal interactions, so that a cooperative, permissive atmosphere characterizes group functioning.[9]

[9] Association for Supervision and Curriculum Development, *Group Processes in Supervision*, Washington, The National Education Association, 1948, p. 59.

The process of democratic planning carries in it the seeds of emerging leadership. A leadership of function, as opposed to a leadership of status, tends to emerge from the successful operation of a planning group. The principal sets the stage, helps to launch the process, and then steps into the group and becomes a participant. Other leaders arise as the planning makes their help appropriate. One of the important skills of the successful principal is the ability to "move over" and become a follower when leaders emerge from the faculty group.

This ability is perhaps especially difficult to master because the principal plays many roles in succession. He is a group leader and a group participant. He must stand ready, however, to become a status leader again for such purposes as these:

1. To administer or execute policies or plans agreed upon by the group.
2. To interpret the group's activitiy and progress to the central office, the board of education, and the lay public.
3. To facilitate group plans by securing funds or other resources.
4. To evaluate the effectiveness of group planning and of group structure.
5. To prepare for next steps in the development of the group's program.

Other faculty members may share these roles, it is true. Yet the principal is likely to be challenged most often to shift roles with ease and skill from the various tasks demanded of him as a line-and-staff administrator to the tasks intrinsic in coöperative planning. If he cannot shift his role with facility he may actually block or defeat his own goals for program improvement. What are the characteristics of a successful coöperative group? The following list is adapted from criteria developed by a workshop group at Wayne University. It appears to represent the goals of the principal as he works with the faculty group.

CHARACTERISTICS OF A GROUP SUCCESSFULLY
WORKING TOWARD THE SOLUTION OF A PROBLEM

1. *A completely accepted goal*
   a. Do all group members understand the group's goals?
   b. Is the purpose or goal genuine to all members of the group?
   c. Do group members feel that they are solving the group problem?
   d. Do they try the solutions experimentally?

2. *Ability to keep and use a written plan as a definitive record of progress*
   a. Does the group operate within a group adopted, written plan?
   b. Does the group use written records effectively?

3. *Enthusiastic participation of each member*
   a. Do group members voluntarily arrive promptly and use the available time?
   b. Do all members take part in discussions?
   c. Do members make a special effort to be present?

4. *Concern by all for growth of each individual*
   a. Do they listen with respect to each other?
   b. Do they encourage contributions from each other?

5. *Leadership disseminated throughout the group*
   a. Does the real leadership reside in the group, not in the principal?
   b. Can the group achieve order and progress without domination?
   c. Are leadership roles assumed by group members generally instead of being constantly assumed by some one member?

6. *Sense of responsibility to the group*
   a. Do group members assume responsibilities on behalf of the group project between meetings?

7. *Habit and skill of critical self-evaluation*
   a. Can the group accept and engage successfully in critical self-evaluation?

b. Can the group accept evaluation by an observer?

c. Can members evaluate each other's growth as a group member?

8. *Understanding of group process and awareness of its values; Skill in achieving them*

a. Does the group succeed in reaching a consensus?

b. Can the group endure and survive its confusion?

c. Do group members understand the various roles people play in a group?

d. Do group members avoid negative roles and adopt positive roles?

e. Do group members identify their own roles and shift them in accordance with the needs of the group? [10]

Wiles has suggested that the faculty group itself can select one of its members as a process observer, who will evaluate the group's effectiveness in terms of such criteria as the following:

General

Was the meeting slow in getting started?

Was the atmosphere easy, relaxed, and comfortable?

Was the tempo slow, hurried, or satisfactory?

Was the interest level high?

Was the purpose clear to all?

Were members cooperative?

Was information shared?

Were members sensitive to each other?

Were tensions brought out into the open?

Was there evidence of feelings of superiority?

Were ideas forced on the group?

Was the group able to accept differences?

Was the group able to discipline itself?

Was any decision reached?

Was there resistance to group decisions?

[10] Unpublished report, Education Workshop, Wayne University, Detroit, Mich., 1950.

Participation

Was participation spread throughout the group?

Was discussion centered for a long period in one portion of the group?

Was the discussion initiated by group members?

Were there difficulties in communication?

Was there a feeling of give and take?

Were members eager to speak?

Were certain members taking more than their share of the time?

Were members showing aggression?

Was the discussion limited to the topic?

Were members assuming responsibility for the success of the meeting?

Were members attempting to draw out each other?

Leadership

Did the leader help the group to establish a direction?

Did the leader give encouragement ?

Did the leader attempt to bring in non-participating members?

Did the leader volunteer more help than was needed?

Did the leader recognize those who wished to speak?

Did the leader dominate the meeting?

Did the leader manifest feelings of superiority?

Did the leader keep things going?

Did the leader bring the specialized skills of members to bear on the problem?

Did the leader summarize as necessary?

Did the leader try to give answers for the group?

Did the leader get a consensus? [11]

Further discussion of the techniques for improving staff meetings will appear in the next chapter, in connection with the principal's relationship to instructional supervision.

IS CÖOPERATIVE PLANNING EFFICIENT?

There are some secondary school principals who regard demo-

[11] Wiles, *op. cit.*, pp. 264–266.

cratic planning as an inefficient procedure. Their motto is, "If you want a thing well done, do it yourself." They point out the amount of time that is consumed ("wasted") in group discussion and groping for consensus. They quote the remarks of teachers, too, who would prefer to leave policy making to the administration and be "let alone" to teach their classes.

It is certainly true that coöperative planning is a slow, difficult business. There are always some persons who tend to reject it, who are uncomfortable and impatient in the planning process, and who would prefer that some leader accept the responsibility. "That's what he's paid to do," they say.

It is also true that there are areas of activity for which coöperative planning is wasteful and inappropriate. The faculty need not be called together, for example, every time the furnace needs some coal; but the janitor and administrator might be well advised to have faculty consensus on policies regarding heating and ventilating. In brief, the function of group planning is to establish policies on which administrative decisions can be based.

Democracy is more efficient in the long run in achieving purposes that are consistent with democracy itself. The goals of free public education in the United States are closely bound to democracy. The schools represent our means of achieving the American dream of political and social democracy. The operation of any social institution in a democratic culture can be most efficient when it is steered and evaluated by the voice of all persons concerned.

The Educational Policies Commission suggested some years ago the reasons for the superiority of democratic policy making:

There are three main reasons . . . why inefficiency of procedure is bound to occur in an autocracy. All three of these reasons are inseparably related to the problem of purpose, because every efficient procedure is derived from the purpose to be served.

In the first place, no agency, mechanical or human, remains efficient very long unless it is subjected to continuous evaluation. When only the man at the top dares to criticize the administration, the quality of the criticism necessarily remains low. . . .

In the second place an autocracy is inefficient because it throttles inventiveness. Every improved procedure is likely to affect policies. In an organization where the policy-making function is a prerogative of the leader, it is therefore dangerous for a member of the group to invent new procedures.

A third source of inefficiency in autocratic procedure is the fatal degeneracy of management represented by the glorification of procedure for its own sake—commonly known as "red tape." The man who is appointed to carry out procedures of any kind in an autocracy is condemned to work with fixed formulas. The procedure constitutes his job. The leader rates him on the basis of loyalty to that job and regards coldly any tendency on his part to question the purposes the job serves. Thus, to be safe, the worker under an autocratic regime must love the procedure for its own sake and leave consideration of its goals to the boss.[12]

Thus the democratic way of operating a school, for example, is likely to be the most efficient way in the long run to serve the social and human purposes for which schools were established in our culture. These goals include respect for individual personality, enhancement of each person to his maximum growth, enabling each individual to contribute to the common good, developing and extending leadership and responsibility. Schools exist for such purposes as these, which cannot efficiently be achieved without maximum involvement of all persons concerned in an enterprise.

It is sometimes assumed that the efficient administrators are those who know all the answers and run "their" schools themselves. Social agencies that operate that way are condemned to continuous inefficiency because they have no channel by which honest evaluation can be secured. The only source of truly efficient operation is the people—their ideas, their resources, their leadership in making good schools better.

[12] Educational Policies Commission, *Learning the Ways of Democracy*, Washington, The National Education Association, 1940, pp. 22–23.

In practice, however, the administrator will not be furnished with a complete set of policies that the faculty has prepared to cover every contingency. Teachers, it has been pointed out, must begin planning together on matters that are real to them—and that seem to them urgently to justify their efforts at planning. These problems that are real to teachers will not include all administrative problems. Teachers cannot be expected to adopt all the principal's problems as their own. He will have to go on dealing with some matters—making policy himself, if necessary—until others on the staff are ready to work on them too. Thus the principal will often be proceeding partly on policies established by the group and partly on his own. If he is interested in efficient administration, he will constantly seek to widen the scope of policies that have been planned (and supported) by the faculty and to diminish the area of one-man policy making.

Only in this manner can genuine support be built for a program. As long as it is "his" program, based on "his" policies, the support of the staff cannot be assured nor firmly secured. Unfortunately, every policy that really matters must have widely-based support throughout the school in order to affect practice in any positive manner. In short, "his" program is likely to remain confined to the principal's office. As we shall see in a later chapter, this same principle extends also to the people who own the schools—the parents and other citizens of the community.

SUMMARY

In this chapter we have looked at curriculum development from the broad view. We have noted that the program consists of experiences that pupils have, and thus is most affected by the attitudes and relationships of people. The principal who sets out to change programs must change these attitudes and relationships, particularly among the staff members of the school who are so influential in establishing the climate for learning. Such changes can come about by involvement of people in work on a common project, which in turn demands a constructive setting, intelligent leadership, and adequate resources. The principal plays a crucial role—indeed many related roles—as he undertakes this business of coöperative program planning. The difficulties are numerous, but the rewards of success are highly satisfying. Success paves the way for subsequent planning efforts, which are continuously crowned by the achievement of a better life for boys and girls. The good administrator of today's school can visualize no greater goal.

For Further Reading

Association for Supervision and Curriculum Development, *Group Processes in Supervision,* Washington, The National Education Association, 1948.

Caswell, H. L., and Associates, *Curriculum Improvement in Public School Systems,* New York, Bureau of Publications, Teachers College, Columbia University, 1950.

Douglass, Harl R. (ed.), *The High School Curriculum,* New York, The Ronald Press Company, 1947, chap. 16.

Educational Policies Commission, *Learning the Ways of Democracy,* Washington, The National Education Association, 1940.

Faunce, Roland C., and Bossing, Nelson L., *Developing the Core Curriculum,* New York, Prentice-Hall, 1951, chap. 5.

French, Will, Hull, J. Dan, and Dodds, B. L., *American High School Administration,* New York, Rinehart & Company, 1951, chaps. 9, 11.

Hagman, Harlan L. and Schwartz, Alfred, *Administration in Profile for School Executives,* New York, Harper & Brothers, 1955, chap. VI.

Kelley, Earl C., *The Workshop Way of Learning,* New York, Harper & Brothers, 1951.

Koopman, G. R., Miel, Alice, and Misner, P. J., *Democracy in School Administration,* New York, Appleton-Century-Crofts, 1943, chaps. 5, 6.

Krug, Edward, *Curriculum Planning,* New York, Harper & Brothers, 1951.

Lewin, Kurt, *Resolving Social Conflicts,* New York, Harper & Brothers, 1948.

Menge, J. W., and Faunce, R. C., *Working Together for Better Schools,* New York, American Book Company, 1953, chaps. 3, 4.

Miel, Alice, *Changing the Curriculum,* New York, Appleton-Century-Crofts, 1946, chap. VI.

Sharp, George, *Curriculum Development as Re-education of the Teacher,* New York, Bureau of Publications, Teachers College, Columbia University, 1951, chap. 1.

Spears, Harold, *The Teacher and Curriculum Planning,* New York, Prentice-Hall, Inc., 1951.

Wiles, Kimball, *Supervision for Better Schools,* New York, Prentice-Hall, 1950, chap. 1.

Wittenberg, Rudolph, *So You Want to Help People,* New York, YMCA Press, 1947.

Yauch, Wilbur, *Human Relations in School Administration,* New York, Harper & Brothers, 1949, Parts 4, 5.

CHAPTER 5

··

The Principal as Supervisor

EARLIER CONCEPT OF SUPERVISION

"Supervisor" seems to have become a naughty word. Teachers tend to take a dim view of the title and the process it implies. Professional literature increasingly reflects this attitude and newer terms have been invented, in many school systems, to designate the supervisory staff. Perhaps the most popular substitute is the title "consultant," which seems to carry a different connotation from that of "supervisor."

Supervision (or overseeing) may have brought opprobrium upon itself by the authoritarian methods which have been carried over from the past. In earlier usage the supervisory function was essentially an inspectorial one, as the word itself implies. Inspection, in turn, implies the process of checking up on teachers by someone who is presumed to know more than the person inspected about the purposes sought by instruction and the most effective means of achieving these purposes.

Supervision, or inspection, was once thought of as a regulatory or disciplinary function. As such, it was supposed to be needed by (1) the poor or ineffective teachers, or (2) the new or young teacher. Since it was a function assigned to one's superior, it followed that the supervisor had considerable power over the teacher. He could prevent promotion, bring about demotion or transfer, or even get the teacher discharged from his position. The punitive or disciplinary functions were closely linked with supervision. It is not surprising that the word has acquired ill repute with many teachers.

The rating of teachers has often been a part of the supervisor's duties. Rating schemes still persist in many school systems. When they are connected with promotion or tenure, rating plans are always a threat rather than an inspiration to teachers. Such devices are more likely to arouse and confirm fears and self-doubts than to develop courage or self-confidence. When rating is done on a basis of criteria which the teacher has had no part in developing, it is basically an authoritarian process. Even when rating plans are administered by kindly, sincere persons, they are unlikely to strengthen or improve teachers. It is probable that the use of teacher rating has contributed to the unpopularity of the supervisory function.

Not only poor teachers but skillful ones, too, object to "snoopervision." They reject rating plans that are undemocratic; they object to being judged on a basis of a few brief visits to a class. They do not like secret reports that find their way into their personnel file without their knowledge or consent. They dislike "surprise" visits and efforts by superiors to impose their ideas, and interruptions of their classes to take care of obtrusive and awesome visitors. It goes without saying that they object to being corrected or criticized in front of their pupils.

In all these matters teachers are on excellent ground. They are quite right in objecting to the kinds of interference and authoritarianism that have too often characterized the supervisory process. These procedures are wrong because they induce fear instead of self-confidence in teachers. They completely violate the kind of coöperative planning described in the preceding chapters. Schools can no longer afford this negative, authoritarian type of supervision.

Fortunately, today's trend in supervision is leading us increasingly in a different direction. Though there are many arbitrary, inspectorial types of supervisors still to be found in public school systems, there are evidences that the overseer is on the way out. Professional literature, the leadership of the universities, and the practices in outstanding school systems today support the concept of the consultant or helper, who works with teachers on a request basis and whose very strength lies in his lack of power or control over individual teachers. There is still much perplexity, however, as to how these permissive roles can be assumed by the principal of a school. The position of the administrator places him in a power role within the building. Certain responsibilities are assigned to him as a result of the line of authority, and these responsibilities, along with delegated authority, cannot be disregarded. It may be helpful to examine the role of the principal as supervisor and try to discover how he can escape the handicaps of his power position in order to become more effective as a leader in instructional improvement.

THE DUTIES OF THE PRINCIPAL

The time-honored concept of the principal has been that of efficiency expert. Not too long ago the graduate courses in school administration dealt exclusively with budgets, time schedules, and building maintenance. It was considered that the efficient principal was he who maintained good order in "his" school, assigned tasks, enforced their performance, and reported neatly and punctually on routine matters to his superior.

The instructions to school principals in 1891 in the city of St. Paul have been quoted by Spears as typical of the characteristics of the principalship at the turn of the century. No item on the list of duties dealt directly with the evaluation or improvement of instruction. The list mentioned enforcement of punctuality and good order, ventilation, and records. There was considerable emphasis on attendance reports and inventories. Some sample items quoted by Spears were as follows:

The principal in each school building shall see that teachers are prompt in opening and closing schools. It shall be his duty to see that all clocks belonging to the building are properly regulated each morning, and that all teachers conform to this standard in making their records of attendance both for themselves and . . . pupils. He shall be at his school thirty minutes before the time of opening the morning session. He shall within two weeks after the commencement of each term furnish the superintendent with the program of the daily exercises of the different rooms of the school.

The principals shall have fire-alarm drills once each fortnight in all the buildings.[1]

It appears that the improvement of instruction was but a minor phase of the principal's duties in 1891, if indeed it was included in them. In more recent years the principal has come to be considered as the leader in program development, but he still retains most of his former administrative routines. Consider the following list of tasks for which the principal is responsible, as given by Edmonson, Roemer, and Bacon:

1. Select, rate, and promote the teaching staff.
2. Make daily schedule of classes after gathering all information necessary for use as a basis for the schedule.
3. Help determine and execute the policy of the school.
4. Make plans for the opening and closing of the school year.
5. Plan public relations activities.
6. Supervise the making of students' programs.
7. Interview and hold conferences with superintendent, board members, and other school officials in regard to business matters.
8. Confer with local, county, and state supervisors in regard to changes and improvements in instruction.
9. Participate in curriculum studies and supervise curriculum planning activities.
10. Supervise classroom work of teachers.

---

[1] *Thirty-third Annual Report of the Superintendent of Schools,* St. Paul, Minn., 1891. Quoted in Harold Spears, *The Emerging High School Curriculum and Its Direction,* New York, American Book Company, 1948, pp. 350–351.

11. Supervise athletics, contests, home-room programs, assemblies, and other school activities.
12. Receive parents and other visitors to discuss problems of the school.
13. Confer with teachers and students.
14. Direct innovations, experiments, and research.
15. Plan and supervise testing programs, summarize results, and adjust the program of the school in accordance with the facts brought to light by tests.
16. Help coordinate social, health, recreational, and other services of the community.
17. Attend court and confer with officials when pupils get in trouble.
18. Find ways and means of helping handicapped children.
19. Write recommendations for students who are going to college or applying for employment.
20. Study causes of failure and help students overcome their obstacles.
21. Keep check on absences and tardiness.
22. Answer questionnaires and handle correspondence.
23. Cooperate with and participate in civic organizations.
24. Fill out or check inventories.
25. Make reports to local, county, or state school officials.
26. Requisition equipment and supplies.
27. Confer with agents, visitors, and inspectors.
28. Make budget for the school and keep or check records of all financial accounts of school activities.
29. Sign checks, pay bills, and prepare payroll of school, or see that such activities are performed.
30. Help with administration of cafeteria.
31. See that economical and efficient use is made of equipment, light, heat, and water.
32. Attend professional meetings, conventions, and discussion groups.
33. Keep in touch with recent educational literature and new movements in secondary education.
34. Arrange and attend faculty meetings.

35. Help select textbooks, library books, auditory aids, maps, pictures, and other visual aids.
36. Enforce school laws.
37. Speak before school assemblies, clubs, home rooms, and community groups.
38. Hire and supervise janitors, bus drivers, and engineers.
39. Represent the school before accreditation associations.
40. Help student council, senior class, and other groups with special problems.
41. Plan for special events such as American Education Week, Book Week, Health Day, World Goodwill Day, and Commencement.
42. Direct counseling and guidance work.
43. Supervise fire drills and safety activities.
44. Serve as chief disciplinary officer of the school.[2]

This rather staggering list of administrative duties assigns little priority to the major task of the principal, which is surely the improvement of instruction. If one performed all these forty-four duties, even occasionally, he would have little time left to plan or to carry out coöperative programs of school improvement. The usual effect of assuming so many and so varied responsibilities is that routines become established and eventually bury the principal under their sheer weight. He becomes too busy doing the things he "has to do" to have any time for the things that are his major responsibility. Some things must be attended to on schedule every day. These get done. Other tasks are creative or reflective in nature, or are ongoing and dynamic. They are the kinds of jobs we think we can always return to because they pose no deadlines. These tasks the busy principal may never get around to assume. Some of the most urgent challenges to administration are in this category of deferrable (and never-completed) tasks.

The principal who has decided to put first things first will have to do something about those forty-four items. Fortunately, there are ways of dealing with most of these tasks without directly as-

---

[2] J. B. Edmonson, Joseph Roemer, and Francis L. Bacon, *The Administration of the Modern Secondary School,* rev. ed., New York, The Macmillan Company, 1953, pp. 86–89. Reprinted by permission of the publisher.

suming them oneself. Such responsibilities as the schedule of classes, school policies, plans for opening and closing the year, public relations activities, curriculum studies, research, arranging of faculty meetings, selecting textbooks, and planning for special days should not be the principal's unique responsibility. All these, and any other operations that stem from total school policy, are the business of the whole staff and should be shared with them. As pointed out in the preceding chapter, leadership of the staff will shift from one person to another in terms of the functions or processes undertaken. Others will emerge as leaders besides the principal. He need not, nor should he, assume sole responsibility for tasks that ought to be group responsibilities.

Other items on the list can be more efficiently delegated to other responsible individuals on the staff. These items include supervision of student program making, athletics, the home-room program, the student council, school assemblies, and testing programs; court visits; coördination of the use of community resources; the student activities budget and financial accounting; the school payroll and cafeteria; and the representation of the school at conferences.

In summary, the principal can create time for his basic job of program improvement if he does not try to do everything himself. He must remember that a better program will emerge from coöperative planning and execution by all persons concerned. He must bend every effort to cause faculty leadership to emerge. He must be ready to delegate the leadership role to others who may be as competent and responsible as he.

DO PRINCIPALS SUPERVISE?

There is some evidence that secondary school principals have not yet freed themselves from the routines of administration and become free to devote adequate time to supervision. In 1921 Davis reported that the typical principal spent his day as follows: [3]

[3] Adapted from C. O. Davis, "Duties of High School Principals," Part I, *20th Yearbook,* North Central Association, 1921, pp. 49–69.

	Percent
Inspecting the building	9.5
Teaching	21
Supervising	9-14
Conferring with teachers	7
Interviewing pupils	7
Talking with callers	7
Attending to student collateral activities	7
In charge of session rooms	9.5
Routine office work	14
Attending to civic and out-of-school professional matters	7

Billett's study of the principal's day in 1932 gave the following time allotment to various duties: [4]

	Percent
Administrative duties	22.9
Clerical duties	11.1
Public relations	7.3
Research	3.8
Supervision	15.2
Teaching	36.5
Guidance	6.3
Other activities	.3

Twenty-five Michigan secondary school principals reported in 1954 that their average distribution of time was as follows:

	Percent
Office administration	21
Teaching classes	7
Supervision	11.7
Conferring with teachers	9
Conferring with pupils	6.5
Conferring with parents	3.7

[4] National Survey of Secondary Education, Bulletin No. 17, Monograph 11, Washington, U.S. Office of Education, 1932, p. 117.

Teachers meetings and committees	5.9
Parent meetings	2.5
Attending community affairs	6.5
Records	6.1
Supervising building maintenance	3.5
Planning schedules, etc.	6.4
Miscellaneous activities	3
Student activities	7.2

These twenty-five principals reported that they spent an average of 55.2 hours per week on their job, as compared to the 35 hours weekly for the principals in Davis's study in 1921. In spite of this dramatic increase in the number of hours per week, they spent about the same percentage of their time on supervisory duties. When the items of indirect supervision, classroom visiting, and faculty meetings and committees are combined in the 1954 study, the percentage of time spent on supervision totals 16.6 percent as compared with 9 to 14 percent in the Davis study and 15.2 percent in the Billett study of 1932.

Routine office administration consumed 14 percent of the principals' time in 1921 (Davis) and 34 percent in 1932 (Billett), as compared with 27.1 percent reported in 1954 by the Michigan principals. The Michigan group reported an average of 7.2 percent of their time as devoted to student activities as compared with 7 percent in the Davis study.

With respect to teaching responsibilities it is difficult to make any valid generalizations, since the amount of teaching by the principal varies inversely with school enrollments. The principals of large schools enrolling 800 or more students seldom teach at all. In schools of 500 to 800 the practice seems to be for the principal to teach only one class, if at all. In schools of 200 to 500 it is fairly common for the principals to have two or even three classes, while in schools enrolling less than 200 they may have full teaching loads.

Detailed comparison of the results of these studies is not fully justified for several reasons. Yet it appears probable that the percentage of time devoted to supervision, direct or indirect, has not markedly increased since 1921. This condition does not accord with the way the principals themselves say they would like to spend their time. The Michigan principals referred to were asked to complete the sentence "If I could change things, I'd try to spend more time than I do now on . . ." Thirteen of the twenty-five completed the sentence with the word "supervision." Eight more wished they could spend more time on "classroom visiting." Five mentioned student conferences, four conferring with teachers, and four planning. Thus the goal of supervision is an unrealized dream for some secondary school principals. These were principals of schools enrolling from 500 to 1800 students. The principal of the really small high school does not usually regard himself as a supervisor. He teaches a full load of classes and leaves administrative and supervisory responsibilities to the superintendent of schools. There is some evidence that the superintendent does not get around to do much supervising, either.

RELATIONSHIP OF PRINCIPAL TO SUPERVISORY STAFF

In the school of medium size, enrolling 400 to 1000 students, the principal is likely to have some time (theoretically!) for supervision. In such schools he is also quite often the only supervisor available. Principals of large urban high schools are free of other conflicting assignments, but often work in buildings served by members of the supervisory or consultant staff for the city school system. Faced with a division of responsibility, urban principals may leave all supervisory work to the staff members assigned to it and titled as supervisors.

This dual responsibility for instructional improvement, involving the principal responsible for the program of a secondary school and the city supervisory staff, represents a persistent problem in urban school systems. Open conflict has arisen in some instances between the principal and the supervisor who entertain different philosophies of education. Since the supervisory staff is often not responsible to the building principal, but rather to an assistant superintendent or a director of instruction, there can be conflicting goals and confusion of responsibility. These situations will be resolved only as the supervisory staff redefines its roles of responsibility and authority, and becomes truly a coöperative resource staff that operates on call. No organization can be tenable that does not recognize and support a large measure of authority of a school staff and principal over the program of the school. Division of this responsibility between two separate agencies of a school system cannot produce a better program.

Thus the principal and the staff of a given school must be responsible for its program. The administrative leader in the task of improving a school's program must be the principal. Supervisors can work effectively in a building only as they recognize a large measure of autonomy of the staff and principal and regard themselves as resources to be drawn upon in the process of improvement. The principal is the responsible leader, whether he directly supervises instruction or works through others on the staff.

DEPARTMENT HEADS

The large school presents a further complication in that there are often department heads who may also be engaged, at least part time, in supervision. There is much disagreement regarding the desirability of the position of department head. Superintendents and authorities in supervision seem to be generally agreed that the position constitutes a hazard to staff unity.[5] Teachers often give a low rating to the help they receive from the department head.[6] The department head is usually given little authority and little time for supervision. There is considerable perplexity among department heads over just what they are supposed to

[5] See, for example, Harl R. Douglass and Charles W. Boardman, *Supervision in Secondary Schools*, Boston, Houghton Mifflin Company, 1934, p. 87.

[6] A. S. Barr and Nels O. Reppen, "The Attitudes of Teachers Toward Supervision," *Journal of Experimental Education*, 4:237–301, June, 1936.

accomplish. There is a belief among curriculum leaders that the chief effect of supervision by the department head is likely to be increased emphasis upon separate subjects as opposed to totality of pupil experience.

In spite of these doubts regarding the usefulness of the department leadership, this position still remains in most urban senior high schools. In some schools it is rotated among various members of each department. In others there is little or no extra salary attached to the chairmanship. Its tendency to emphasize divisiveness between departments can be lessened if the total faculty can be engaged in coöperative planning of the instructional program. It is important that a central problem or area of focus be found on which planning can develop between departments. Grade-level planning by a group representing all departments may supply this need. It is probable that grade-level organization should ultimately supplant departmentalization entirely, as has occurred in most elementary schools.

PURPOSE CÖORDINATORS

One plan of organization which might stimulate the move toward grade-level planning has been proposed by French, Hull, and Dodds in their book, *American High School Administration*.[7] They suggest an organization based on purposes of the secondary school, with four or five instructional coördinators, each providing leadership for a major purpose that the school intended to stress. Such purposes as health, vocational exploration, citizenship, and leisure and recreation would be organized on a total school basis with the coördinators representing each area serving, in effect, as assistant principals. The authors urge this proposal as a means of overcoming excessive departmentalization:

. . . the necessity for teachers from different departments to work together should be facilitated by the leadership of four or five pur-

---

[7] Will French, J. Dan Hull, and B. L. Dodds, *American High School Administration*, New York, Rinehart & Company, 1951, pp. 167–171.

pose coordinators. Where schools are highly organized along subject (process) lines and where such departmentalization cannot be abandoned, the need for the coordination that can be secured through purpose coordinators is even more acute if a school is seriously interested in a better achievement of its purposes.[8]

Whatever plan is used in organizing for supervision, the principal should be the person responsible for the program. This does not mean, of course, that he must make all the decisions or control the making of policies. Johnston pointed out some years ago that responsibility can be efficiently shared:

The principal has no monopoly on sound professional technique or educational philosophy. In the long run that administrator will accomplish most who frankly recognizes this fact and encourages members of his staff to help in shaping educational policies and to take responsibility for them. . . . His task is that of coordinating the activities of the various members of the staff so that they may lead toward a common goal and not result in a number of divergent and unrelated activities. . . . The principal must draw together the various strands which compose the pattern of democratic administration and weave them into one continuous fabric, a task requiring a maximum of patience and tact.[9]

CONTROL OF PROGRAM MUST REST WITH LOCAL SCHOOL

School programs will be effectively improved only through teamwork on the part of all persons concerned. Such teamwork calls for shared responsibility and an accepted goal on the part of all persons concerned with the program of a building. The team must have autonomy for the program. It cannot be controlled from some outside source if real responsibility is to be assumed by teachers, parents, or youth in a given secondary school. Such influences as the following are in basic conflict with this principle and should be sturdily resisted:

[8] *Ibid.*, p. 171.
[9] Edgar G. Johnston, "The Principal as Coordinator," *The School of Education Bulletin,* University of Michigan, January, 1931, pp. 52–54.

Enactment of state laws that define or control curriculum

Enforcement of state or county courses of study

Financial or administrative controls of instruction by state or federal governments

Control by divisions of instruction with staff responsible to someone other than the building principal

Efforts to develop identical (lock-step) programs in all schools within a system

Efforts by colleges or universities to control the secondary school's program

Efforts by accrediting agencies to control the instructional program

Most of the above efforts at control of a program from sources outside the building are launched in the name of uniformity. Research has shown that it is vain to hope for uniform programs throughout a county or city, even when written courses of study are standard for all schools. Worse yet, the very effort to secure uniformity will operate to stultify creativity in the building staff. The trouble with such efforts lies in the fact that they constitute a removal of responsibility from those who must assume it if they are to help build good programs. Any move that reduces the feeling of responsibility or ownership of a program from the staff, parents, and students of a given school and locates it elsewhere is a move toward mediocrity. It removes a degree of creativity and experimentalism without which a program cannot be improved.

PURPOSES OF SUPERVISION

All supervision must be aimed at producing better experiences for youth. There is no other justification for the supervisory function. This purpose will be served only as teachers are helped to operate more effectively, for teachers are the key persons in the effort to develop better programs.

This central purpose can be defined in terms of a number of functions which the principal and other supervisory leaders serve. At least the following functions should guide the process of supervision:

Building staff morale
Helping unify purposes
Disseminating and developing leadership
Developing effective machinery for group action
Developing creativity
Meeting needs, giving help
Helping staff and others to evaluate the program

BUILDING STAFF MORALE

Morale is hard to define but easy to recognize. It consists of the feelings that each staff member has about his relationships with others. Some teachers come to school each day with high hopes and a good feeling about what will probably happen that day. They may find it embarrassing to admit, but they like the kids, they like their colleagues, and they enjoy the life in their school. They often refuse attractive offers to work in other schools because they find life so rewarding right where they are.

Other teachers are really depressed and fearful about their work. They dread Monday mornings and are members in regular standing of the FTG (Friday Thank God) Club. Kelley has pointed out that these teachers may be products of an unpromising work environment.

It is too often true that after a teacher has taught a long time she becomes less effective. She becomes a "type." She often becomes unsympathetic to youth, and difficult for all who cross her path. Indeed, in some cases she may become so queer as to be considered psychopathic. Why should this be so? The teacher does not start out that way. She starts out full of hope and enthusiasm. We cannot escape the conviction that the change in her personality is due to the kind of life she has led. Her life has been so routinized, she has so long worked in an enterprise in which she has had no sharing of objectives, she has for so long been required to indulge in repressive and coercive activities, that sterile routine and coercion have become a way of life.[10]

---

[10] Earl C. Kelley, "The Function of the Principal in a Modern School," *American School Board Journal*, June, 1947.

Whatever the cause of low morale, the principal should make its improvement one of his major concerns. He should seek to identify those teachers who will need special help and encouragement, and he should supply these aids. He should be concerned about helping teachers to get better salaries, an adequate retirement plan, a credit coöperative, and other provisions for financial security. He should be concerned about parking problems and about classroom heating, lighting, and cleaning, which make a daily impact for good or bad morale. A pleasant teachers' room where smoking is permitted can be a decided asset in building morale. There should be another room where teachers can simply rest for a while without noise or interruption.

The principal's own example is a vital factor in building morale. If he is courteous, considerate, and fair, he will aid morale. If he is all these things, and in addition can listen attentively to the complaints that even normal people must occasionally dispense, he will help staff morale further. If, finally, he has all these desirable attributes and in addition is a warm, friendly person whom people just like to be with, he will be likely to be blessed with a staff which reflects these same happy characteristics.

Kelley has indicated the importance of real sharing as a means of developing morale:

The principal can do much to make the teachers feel that the school is a common enterprise by always sharing common lot with them in the privileges of the school. This can be done by simple acts such as taking chances with the rest on a parking place, or seeing to it that the principal is not the only one who ever needs to go to a convention or a conference. He should see himself in the role of a service person, subject to the needs inherent in a good program. He should avoid, in every way, the inference that his time is more valuable than that of a teacher or that he is somehow superior to those who are to share the enterprise of the school. Superiority and sharing do not mix.[11]

[11] *Ibid.*

The principal can build morale in other ways, too. He should be depended on to back the teacher to the limit when the facts warrant that kind of support. When the teacher is wrong the skillful administrator will help him to see that he is wrong, but without creating a new set of fears in him. He will help him to share responsibility for the outcomes desired in a good program, and to play his part in creating it.

HELPING TO UNIFY PURPOSES

Discussion in a previous chapter has dealt with the staff's effort to reach consensus on the school's purposes. It has been suggested that this consensus can come about more readily from successful group attack on mutual or common problems than from preliminary verbalization of the "philosophy of the school" as such.

It is possible—sometimes deceptively easy—to develop a staff philosophy. The trouble is that the words in it may be only words. They may not really reflect the thinking of the staff, but instead may be the product of a few verbal and aggressive leaders. The staff may accept it in a mood of wishing to have done with further discussion and get back to teaching school. They may even sincerely believe that the statement represents their own views, until a test case arises that reveals how far from their thinking their "philosophy statement" is.

Beliefs about education are dynamic and complex. They are influenced by all the experiences people have had, by the adequacy of their own self-image, by the faiths they have developed in others. Faith is developed by successful experiences. It is highly probable that the principal's first concern in developing unified staff purposes should be to help the staff members to define some current problem that all consider demands a solution and then to help them solve it successfully. In the process, separate elements of the common purpose may be verbalized as a statement of what "we believe" about the particular problem under study. This is most apt to occur during an evaluation session in which the faculty members are appraising the effect of their group effort on the problem.

A series of such (successful) problem-solving experiences will ultimately provide an accumulation of beliefs that all members share. These will be reinforced by the strength and courage that gain momentum from successful group efforts.

DEVELOPING LEADERSHIP

The older conception of leadership as an inherent trait has been generally discredited in recent years. It is now agreed that leadership traits are produced by the experiences one has, and that leadership may shift from one person to another as the particular function or process demands. The good administrator realizes the leadership potential in the faculty group and tries to operate in such a way as to release it. He thus evokes leadership in others by structuring the group efforts in such a way as to bring one member or another to the fore. Since the improvement of instruction is a group operation, it becomes a major goal of supervision to develop and disseminate the leadership role throughout the professional staff. Only the insecure or fearful administrator will regard faculty leaders as a threat to his own status. He will realize instead that the staff group has an enormous collective power that should be released. He will see the process of supervision as basically concerned with the release of that power. Only thus can the experiences of boys and girls be improved.

DEVELOPING MACHINERY FOR GROUP ACTION

In some schools the teachers work as individuals. They seldom or never see each other in action. It is unfortunately common enough for teachers to occupy classrooms across the hall from each other for ten years and yet never work together on any common task, or even see each other in operation. In such schools the faculty meetings are few and far between. When they are held it is for the purpose of listening to announcements or instructions or hearing someone speak.

The principal of such a school may justify the lack of faculty meetings by citing evidence that teachers do not want to attend them. This attitude is likely to prevail when (1) the meetings do not contribute to the solution of problems, (2) the teachers have no hand in setting up the agenda for the meetings, (3) they play no active role in carrying on the meeting, and (4) the whole business is held after school hours. Such meetings make no contribution to group action. Indeed, in such schools there is likely to be no machinery at all for group action. Without some such machinery there can be no effective efforts by all concerned to improve the program of the school. The provision of a machinery for group action is a basic function of supervision.

DEVELOPING CREATIVITY

Another important supervisory function is the task of encouraging and releasing creative ideas in teachers. The greatest need in every school is for a climate of experimentalism. Teachers need to feel that they can try any idea and that they are actually encouraged to think of better ways. Any condition, any regulation, any administrative act that tends to discourage experimentalism will contribute to the stultification of teaching—to reducing all staff members to a mediocre level of imitative routines. It is a major goal of supervision to give every teacher the feeling that he is an important professional "seeker" for exciting truth—for new and better ways to accomplish the most significant and influential task in the world today. The creative teacher will not want to move to another situation too soon; he will want to see the outcome of an important professional venture in which he plays a leading role. He will realize that not only will the experiences of youth in his own school profit by his skill and ingenuity; he will hope also to do some good on the larger educational scene of the state and nation by his discovery and publication of better methods. This is the essence of the creative professional person. It is also the only basis on which general improvement in education can be achieved.

The creativity of teachers is a direct product of democratic administration. The chief objection to authoritarian or regulatory administration is that it prevents the development of the experimental climate without which a building program cannot be improved. Corey has pointed out this objection to the use of directives by supervisors:

. . . the chief difficulty when teachers are told what to do is that the directions cannot ever be sufficiently explicit because teaching by its very nature requires much individual initiative and resourcefulness. A second difficulty is that the followers of directions are chronically unable to accept personal responsibility for the success of the activity. A third difficulty is that people who are constantly following administrative directives lose something as persons. They tend to act like cogs in a machine or automatons on assembly line—to become things rather than people.[12]

MEETING NEEDS AND GIVING HELP

Good supervisors seek to be helpful. The modern concept of supervision has moved away from the role of inspection toward that of a helper and resource for the teacher. It is the goal of the modern supervisor to earn the respect and support of every teacher by becoming recognized as a source of real help. This assistance can extend beyond the classroom into the personal life of the teacher. The good supervisor is always welcome. As some wit has said, a good supervisor is one about whom teachers say, "Oh good! Here she comes," instead of "Oh God, here she is." The effective supervisor is helpful to teachers with whose philosophy he disagrees as well as to those with whom he is generally in accord. His help is available on the teacher's own terms, not on those of the helper. It is never forced on the teacher, but it is always available and earns its own reception.

[12] Stephen M. Corey, "The Importance of People—Teachers ARE People," *Educational Leadership*, May, 1944, pp. 491–493.

HELPING TO EVALUATE THE PROGRAM

Closely linked to the unification of purposes is the continuous evaluation of their achievement. This is another total staff job that the supervisory staff can help teachers to perform. It is unlikely that any help will be derived from such externally based evaluations as ratings by the supervisor or comparisons of test scores made by various sections of pupils. The chief difficulty with external appraisal is that the teacher has no part in establishing the criteria for evaluation. The only really effective standards for improvement are those which teachers set for themselves, as a result of critical thinking about the effectiveness of their work. They can be individually established or coöperatively developed by the group under certain conditions. The important point is that the teachers must share in the process of developing the criteria and applying them to their own work. This process should be a continuous one in a faculty group which is on the way toward a better program. It is not an easy task. Indeed, it is often a perplexing and frustrating experience. Self-analysis is seldom a comfortable business. It is probable that effective evaluation can occur only after the faculty has achieved a degree of rapport and mutual respect through successful group planning. The evaluative process is a challenge to supervisory leadership because it is a test of the security feelings of teachers. The first task is to develop a feeling of security in those who are to engage in self-evaluation.

ACHIEVING THE GOALS OF SUPERVISION

CLASSROOM VISITING

In concluding this chapter on supervision it may be helpful to discuss briefly some of the methods used by supervisors in working to improve instruction. One important method is classroom visiting. Principals generally spend much less time than they feel desirable in visiting classes. It is a time-consuming task which busy administrators often fail to include in their daily schedule. It is easy to rationalize this failure if teachers have not invited one to visit their classes. Sometimes the problem of getting oneself invited appears insoluble. It is easy to forget the whole matter and tell oneself that the teachers do better if they are left to their own devices.

Yet most principals rate classroom visiting high in importance as a means of improving instruction. It appears generally recognized that no other device can give the principal as real a picture of what goes on in the daily life of the school.

The problem of getting time to visit classes can be solved if first things are put first. This fact is evident from the experiences of those administrators who regularly visit classes. The invitation to visit is chiefly a product of the climate of interaction between teachers and principals. If there are frequent and interested discussions about teaching methods and pupil achievement it is a natural development for the teacher to ask the principal to come and see for himself. After the first visit, there will be other invitations if the principal and the teacher have *both enjoyed the experience and derived some help or support from it.* Under normal circumstances the time will soon arrive when the invitation is a standing one.

Some principals have elicited the first invitation by frankly admitting to a teacher that he needs the experience. If he enters upon a series of visits in this humble spirit, and maintains the attitude of one who is an interested learner throughout the visit, he is likely to build a good base for continued interaction and repeated visits. It need not be added that he will not help his own cause or the teacher's by any of the following practices: interrupting the class, criticizing the teacher's method, looking for mistakes, assuming a negative attitude.

Wiles suggests that the visitor may ask himself such questions as the following during visits to classes:

Is the classroom one in which children feel secure in their relationships with each other and with the teacher?

Do the children see purpose in what they are doing?

Are the children seekings ways of carrying out their purposes or are they seeking to discover what the teacher wants done?

Is there opportunity for creative thinking and activity in the classroom?

Is cooperation encouraged?

Are children stimulated to evaluate their ways of working and to plan revision of procedures that will make their work more effective?

Are the classroom equipment and materials organized to increase the efficiency with which the group achieves its purposes? [13]

The object of classroom visiting is to be helpful to the teacher. The administrator whose visits and subsequent conferences with a teacher are a source of help will be asked to visit again. Incidentally, teachers can provide much help to each other through visits. One goal of a good supervisory program should be to make it possible and worth while for teachers to visit each other's classes and discuss what happened there.

INTERVIEWS

Much good would be done for faculty morale if the principal merely visited classes and left with a bit of justified praise for something he saw. In a long-range program, however, teachers will not be satisfied to stop there. They want (and deserve) a follow-up interview, however informal, in which discussion can point up the strong points of the methods and suggest even better techniques. These suggestions need not all come from the visitor. They may be voiced by the teacher as a goal to be later achieved. Better yet, they may emerge from a nondirective discussion as the creative product of both teacher and principal. The teacher's own classroom is a better setting for this discussion than the office where the principal is enthroned and fortified. A still better site would be a neutral one such as the teachers' room or cafeteria.

[13] Wiles, *op. cit.*, p. 260.

Wiles has suggested some questions for opening the discussion if an opening is needed:

How do you analyze the experience we've just had?

What were the things about the class period that pleased you most?

What things do you think worked out to make the situation a good learning experience? . . .

How do you feel the experience could have been made more meaningful to the group?

What changes would you make if you were planning the experience again?

What materials did you feel you needed that were not available?

How can I be of assistance to you in continuing the work this class has undertaken? [14]

The interview should be on a friendly, informal basis if it is expected to achieve a more creative job of teaching. Any aspect of it that threatens the teacher's security will nullify its effect as a supervisory technique—and probably interrupt further invitations to visit the teacher. Some principals are expected to submit written reports of classroom visits to the office of the superintendent or personnel director. Such reports can do damage to the process under discussion here, unless they are skillfully and openly developed with the teacher. It is safer to avoid any procedure that smacks of rating if rapport and creativity are the goals.

FACULTY MEETINGS

There has been some discussion of faculty meetings in an earlier section of this chapter. The common trouble with them is that they are not teachers' meetings but the principal's meetings. Unless teachers help to set up the agenda, participate actively in the meeting, and help evaluate it as a guide to improving subsequent meetings, it is unlikely that the faculty meeting will be very useful in supervision. It is unnecessary and shortsighted to bring teachers together after school is over to read announcements to them from

[14] *Ibid.*, p. 261.

a bulletin that could just as well be mailed. As a matter of fact, some principals do place the bulletin in the teachers' boxes and then use the faculty meeting to read them aloud! It is small wonder that such meetings are resented.

If teachers have a hand in setting up the agenda, they might better run the meeting themselves. An elected chairman can perform this function. The principal will then be released to participate more functionally in the meeting as a colleague instead of a status leader.

Some faculty meetings should be held on school time, in fairness to teachers. This is especially necessary when meetings are frequent as is the case in a lively program of curriculum revision. Most teachers will respond well to this gesture by contributing their share of time to the task. Coffee and cookies may help the meeting to get off to the promising start. There is no reason why faculty meetings should be as dull and as solemn as they often are. They can, on the contrary, be informal gatherings of good friends who have common purposes and mutual problems which they have every reason to work on together.

COMMITTEES

Most faculties are too large for intensive participation on a total group basis. They must be broken up into smaller groups for such purposes as conducting a problem census, active work on selected materials, or evaluation of the meeting. Such smaller groups may emerge quickly from the faculty meeting and dissolve after a brief period of work. Production committees or research teams are more likely to serve for an entire year or even for a longer period. Teachers should have an opportunity to work on such small teams, for several reasons. They are an indispensable means of carrying any concrete project to fruition. They can give an excellent opportunity for active participation. They furnish numerous challenges for new leaders to emerge. They may serve as a useful tool in breaking up undesirable faculty cliques by establishing working relationships that cross over older social ties. They can thus serve to unite and cement the faculty as workers engaged in a common enterprise. Such small research committees are a useful device in supervision.

SELECTING TEACHERS

The initial selection of teachers is an important function of supervision. In small schools this task falls on the superintendent of schools. In large urban schools it is likely to be assigned to a division of personnel, although some control of selection is often left with the principal. It is obviously important to select "good" teachers who will fit into the ongoing program, who are warm and understanding with children, who will be creative teachers and skillful in their relationships with their colleagues.

It is probable that a better selection of teachers would obtain if the present staff helped define the process and criteria for selection. The immediate colleagues of the prospective teacher should interview him and, if at all possible, should see him in action as a worker with youth. This can be done through observation of practice teaching in some cases. The development of extern plans and the more general use of prospective teachers as substitutes or as cadet teachers would also be helpful in the selection process.

SUPPLIES AND EQUIPMENT

One area in which the supervisory process can really be helpful to teachers is in the ready procurement of supplies, teaching aids, and equipment needed for classrooms. There is no simpler way to boost morale than by securing for teachers the materials and equipment they believe are important. Conversely, morale suffers a blow whenever there is cause for suspicion that teachers' requests are not given any serious consideration. A comparatively little money and effort invested in the area of supplies and equipment will go far to build morale. It should be added, however, that a district too poor to furnish adequate supplies can overcome this handicap if there is mutual respect and candor in the relationships between teachers and administrators. Teachers can forgive much if they feel that everything possible is being done to help them.

IMPROVING THE TEACHER'S LOT

Other things besides supplies contribute to teachers' happiness. They have a right to economic security. They deserve higher salaries, an assurance of reasonable tenure, and a sound policy for sick leave. It is a function of supervision to work hard to secure these things. Other protective plans such as group insurance, hospitalization, credit unions, and buying coöperatives will help ensure security. As such, they should be a goal of supervision. Even small things may help in this effort. For example, the practice of deducting holidays from the teacher's salary check is indefensible in the case of professional persons who are on annual salaries, and works hardship in many cases. The same is true of the ten-month contract. The principal who is interested in helping teachers as a means of improving instruction will work hard to achieve a reasonable degree of economic security for them.

RECOGNITION

Another contribution to morale, and one that costs no money, is the recognition of successful teaching. It is usually easy to spot the principal who uses teamwork in supervision. He talks readily enough about "our" program and seldom calls it "my" program. He is quick to give credit to teachers who have helped develop an activity. He never claims credit for himself but feels sufficiently rewarded when members of the team are mentioned in the newspaper. He gives praise sincerely when it is due. He tries to make it possible for every member of the faculty to have a chance to assume leadership and to receive public credit for successful projects.

Praise must be meant. Teachers are alert to insincerity and

reject efforts to buy their loyalty by fulsome, undeserved praise. It is highly probable, however, that most supervisors err on the side of too little, not too much, praise.

There is some hazard that public credit and praise may be heaped on the more active or on the allegedly "proadministration" teachers and withheld from others. Judicious distribution of credit may be necessary, with special attention directed to persons who seldom receive any recognition.

EVALUATING RESULTS

An earlier section of this chapter has stressed the importance of continuous, coöperative evaluation of the instructional program. It has been emphasized that such evaluation must be based on criteria that have been developed by teachers for the particular program under study. Students can share also in this process through evaluations of teachers, discussions of purposes desired for a high school education, and appraisal of their own progress. Indeed, the crucial evaluators in most schools are the students. In the long run the success of the program will be measured by their satisfaction and understanding of their own achievement. It is accordingly a vital part of the supervisory process to provide means for students to evaluate what is happening to them. Such discussions should not only be permitted and "respectable"; they should be encouraged and conducted with all possible skill and insight as a daily phase of good teaching.

Former students who have dropped out or graduated can be of great help through follow-up studies. Direct appraisal through alumni meetings has been successful in some schools.

Finally, parents and other local citizens have ideas about the purposes desired for the school, and about its effectiveness. Their evaluations will be actively and systematically sought and used by an alert school staff. The philosophy and techniques for such participation will be discussed in the chapter that follows.

FOR FURTHER READING

Association for Supervision and Curriculum Development, *Coöperation: Principles and Practices, Eleventh Yearbook,* Washington, The National Education Association, 1938.

Association for Supervision and Curriculum Development, *Group Processes in Supervision,* Washington, The National Education Association, 1948.

Association for Supervision and Curriculum Development, *Leadership at Work,* Washington, The National Education Association, 1943.

Ayer, Fred C., *Fundamentals of Instructional Supervision,* New York, Harper & Brothers, 1954.

Briggs, Thomas H., *Improving Instruction,* New York, The Macmillan Company, 1938, chaps. 13 and 15.

Cox, Philip W. L., and Langfitt, R. E., *High School Administration and Supervision,* New York, American Book Company, 1934, chap. XXVII.

Douglass, Harl R., and Boardman, Charles W., *Supervision in Secondary Schools,* Boston, Houghton Mifflin Company, 1934.

Edmondson, J. B., Roemer, Joseph, and Bacon, Francis L., *The Administration of the Modern Secondary School,* New York, The Macmillan Company, 1941, chap. XIX.

Foster, Herbert H., *High School Supervision,* New York, Thomas Nelson & Sons, 1939, chaps. II, III.

French, Will, Hull, J. Dan, and Dodds, B. L., *American High School Administration,* New York, Rinehart & Company, 1951, chap. 10.

Johnson, Paul, "A Community Plans for Better Schools," *Educational Leadership,* May, 1952, pp. 506–507.

Kelley, Earl C., "The Function of the Principal in a Modern School," *American School Board Journal,* June, 1947.

Koopman, G. R., Miel, Alice, and Misner, P. J., *Democracy in School Administration,* New York, Appleton-Century-Crofts, 1943.

Krug, Edward A., *Curriculum Planning,* New York, Harper & Brothers, 1950.

Miel, Alice, *Changing the Curriculum,* New York, Appleton-Century-Crofts, 1946.

Prall, Charles E., and Cushman, C. Leslie, *Teacher Education in Service,* Washington, American Council on Education, 1944, chaps. VI, VII.

Spears, Harold, *The Emerging High School Curriculum and Its Direction,* New York, American Book Company, 1948.

Spears, Harold, *Improving the Supervision of Instruction,* New York, Prentice-Hall, 1953.

Tyler, Ralph W., "Evaluation as a Function of Supervision," *Elementary School Journal, XLIV,* January, 1944, pp. 264–273.

Wiles, Kimball, *Supervision for Better Schools,* New York, Prentice-Hall, 1950.

C H A P T E R 6

Ꮮ

The Principal and the Community

THE SCHOOLS BELONG TO THE PEOPLE

One of the major obstacles to improving schools seems to be our fear of the people in the community. It is ironic that this fear has prevented us from effective use of those same persons, and of other resources outside the school, as aids to the process of planning for better schools. It is the unknown which causes us to be afraid. There is perhaps no more significant area of the unknown in American education than the opinions of lay citizens regarding education.

This condition is not the result of indifference or long-standing opposition to schools on the part of the public. On the contrary, the American people are keenly interested in public education, and have maintained that interest for a long time. The history of public support for education in the United States is an impressive one. Beginning with the colonial laws which devoted tax moneys to the establishment of a school in each colony, and continuing to strengthen with each expansion of our country, this emphasis on public education has been a significant part of the American tradition. Not only did public schools spread geographically as people moved westward; they also continued to extend upward on a tax-supported basis. The story of this extension of the common school upward has been told in Chapter 2. It represents one of the characteristic tenets of the American people—the belief that a democracy's success depends on the education of its citizens.

In some other parts of the world public education has been considered a function of the national government. In the United States it has always been thought of as a state responsibility, with extensive authority and powers delegated to local districts. The concept of community schools, maintained and controlled by the citizens of a city or a primary school district, is a deep-seated American tradition. Even today, when many local schools are chiefly supported by funds from state or federal governments, the idea still obtains that control of the schools is a local matter. The people not only own the schools; they also want to maintain control of their property. The interest which citizens generally show in their schools is well known. No issue will fire a community into action quite so readily as some problem concerning their schools. Schools and education are important news, as magazine and newspaper editors are well aware. Hundreds of thousands of citizens serve faithfully (and usually without pay) on local boards of education. Over six million people belong to local PTA chapters affiliated with the National Congress of Parents and Teachers. Perhaps an equal number are members of similar local groups without national affiliation. Athletic, musical, and dramatic affairs in the local school are attended by most of our people at one time or another.

OLDER CONCEPTS OF COMMUNITY RELATIONS

This interest in schools, and the sense of local ownership which underlies it, have often been maintained without much support from professional school persons. Indeed, some administrators and teachers appear to have forgotten who own the schools. Public interest in the school program is sometimes regarded as a threat to school officials or as an invasion of their province. This attitude was characteristic of an early stage in school-community relations, in which school people apparently wished the public to leave the schools alone. The lay citizens were expected, indeed required, to send their children to school, and it was assumed that they would continue to support the school by the payment of taxes. Any further manifestation of community interest in the schools was likely to be interpreted as interference. This attitude was, of course, more often found in urban areas or at least in school systems which were large enough to employ a professional superintendent. In many such school systems even the board of education was expected to rubber-stamp the superintendent's policies and acts.

In recent years this policy of "leave us alone" has become less general. Today it appears no longer possible to maintain such an attitude in times of increasing school costs, which mean increasing need for public support. We have moved into an era of selling the school to the public. This "public relations" kind of thinking may be just as authoritarian as the older isolationism. In some communities it means that all important decisions, including educational goals, will be settled by school leaders, and then the program will be sold to the community through the numerous publicity media now available. Public support will thus, it is hoped, be bought for the existing program which has been planned by professional school people. This public relations era is still generally characteristic of city school systems in the United States.

A third kind of policy is beginning to emerge today. In the face of widespread attacks on public education, school leaders are discovering that public support for a program cannot always be secured unless lay citizens really believe in the program. Some school leaders no longer believe that they have all the answers. They are beginning to turn to parents and other community citizens for help in (1) establishing the general purposes of education, (2) contributing resources for the effective realization of those purposes, and (3) appraising the achievements of the school in the light of these coöperatively established goals.

This third point of view has often been referred to as the "involvement" policy.[1] It rests its case on the fact of public ownership of the schools, and on the democratic thesis that better answers can emerge from coöperative planning by all persons concerned than from administrative decisions by a few leaders. This point of view is based on a fundamental faith in people, and in the processes of effective communication. It assumes that people are generally interested in the education of their children and that they have a contribution to make in helping good schools to become better ones. It assumes further that the chief obstacle to such involvement of lay citizens lies not in the incompetence or lack of interest of people, but rather in their common inability to communicate with each other, to express their judgments, to plan with others, to achieve consensus, to use resources in problem solving, and to appraise achievements in the light of purposes they help establish.

These and many other processes which are involved in group planning need desperately to be perfected by our citizens if local democracy is to be effective. The school program, in which all citizens have a natural stake, can furnish the motivation and the means of acquiring the skills of coöperative planning. In that process, better programs can be developed. On this thesis an entirely new approach to school-community relations is beginning to emerge in schools across the country.

THE JOB OF THE SUPERINTENDENT

During the era of public relations as such, the idea has become established that contacts with the community are the job of the superintendent of schools, or of a director of public relations appointed by him. This centralization of responsibility has tended to obscure and to diminish the role of the school principal in school-community contacts.

There are certainly important public relations functions which

[1] For a more detailed analysis of the problems and techniques of involving citizens in school planning, see J. W. Menge and Roland C. Faunce, *Working Together for Better Schools*. New York, American Book Company, 1953.

can be most effectively served by the central office. There is a need for system-wide publicity which can best be furnished by the superintendent's office. Overall school policies must be established as a basis for sound planning at the building level. The superintendent has a definite responsibility for furnishing professional leadership to the board of education and the community citizens commission on education, if such a group exists. He also has a co-ordinating role in respect to the various programs of community relations which operate at the school building level, and which should become integrated into an effective system-wide program.

On the whole, however, the superintendent's role has been overplayed and the principal's role ignored in this area of community relations. Many secondary school principals do not think of themselves as community-relations leaders. Indeed, some principals are prevented by local school policy from having any significant role in interpreting the schools or in reaching out to involve the community in the school's program. Even a program of school publicity must be based on data collected by and reflective of each school building and its curriculum. Unless each school's staff and administration are actively involved in establishing the purposes and directing the emphasis of such publicity, they cannot even be intelligent contributors of information. Publicity media such as newspapers, radio, television, posters, dioramas, or other exhibits, demonstrations, speakers' bureaus—these and a dozen other techniques for telling people about the schools must draw their material from an actual program which is presently operating in some building in the school system.

When we attempt to move beyond the realm of school publicity and involve lay citizens in educational planning, it becomes even more imperative that the program be decentralized into school building units. This is owing to the fact that the neighborhood school is the natural unit for curriculum development. Most successful curriculum programs today are based on the school building unit. There is a natural bond between parents whose children attend the same school—a bond which has often been established in neighborhood or church groups, even before these citizens had children in the school. The city school system is often too big, too complex, to permit people to feel any identification with it. Furthermore, the real curriculum only takes place in a given school, for it consists of the actual experiences which children have day by day as they live together in a school. These experiences may be quite different from those provided in a city-wide course of study.

Finally, the nearness of the school makes it possible for community people to become readily involved in the program, in contrast to the seemingly far-off central office of the school system. It is possible for citizens to think of the neighborhood school as their own project. This possibility makes the role of the building principal a crucial one in school-community planning.

SURVEYING THE COMMUNITY

The alert administrator will seek, first of all, to understand clearly the nature of the community which the secondary school serves. There are some special problems in this task for secondary school principals and staffs. The elementary school attendance area is small and compact. The numbers of parents involved are few, as compared with the high school's parent group. The agencies and resources are also few in number in comparison with those of the large area served by a senior high school. In spite of difficulties that exist, the modern principal realizes that it is important to know certain things about the community served by the junior or senior high school. He may not do all the surveying alone; indeed, it is highly important that the staff share in the study of the community. Such areas as the following will have significance for the planning of a better school by all the persons concerned:

1. The nature of the community:
    its type of housing, business and industrial concerns, economic potential, and future

2. The backgrounds from which spring the mores people hold: history of settlement, type of people, prevailing religious groups
3. The social structure of the community:
    the cliques or controlling groups which establish patterns, the leaders and the followers, the shifts in the leadership role, the patterns of social relationships in various neighborhoods, the factions and cleavages
4. The problems which seem to concern people in the community:
    their views on political and economic issues, their views in regard to education; the needs which exist for a richer life for all citizens
5. The resources which individuals and groups possess and which could be utilized for the improvement of the school
6. The birth rate and the migration trends which will have an impact on school enrollments
7. The organizations and institutions which people join, and their potential contribution to the school program; the groups to which various staff members of the school belong.

Such surveys are not simply conducted and soon terminated. They represent a continuous, never-ending challenge to the school administrator who realizes the importance of such information. When proper relationships with lay persons and groups are established, facts about the community will continue to flow into the school and enrich the understanding of the staff. This result tends to be achieved when citizens are brought into intimate contact with the school program. It also takes place as administrators and teachers join community groups and assume full status as citizens and neighbors. Further data with regard to particular community needs or resources can be secured by secondary school students who are engaged in studying their own community.

ADVISORY COMMITTEES

Many secondary schools are large enough to warrant the election or appointment of an advisory committee. Such committees usually include parents, teachers, and administrators. Their purpose is to give school leaders an accurate sounding board for community reactions, to represent certain constituents interested in helping plan a better program, and to channel all suggestions to the level at which action will be possible. As the name implies, advisory committees are expected to give suggestions and advice, not to frame official policies. If a real, grass-roots system of representation exists and the building advisory committee adequately reflects staff and community thinking, it may serve the role of policy making in an unofficial capacity. Such a group can supplement and enrich the thinking of the official board of education. It can also provide a direct channel to most citizens if it is sufficiently representative of all groups. It has the advantage of being smaller than the parent-teacher association and hence is likely to be a more effective working group.

THE PTA

The parent-teacher asociation is the most inclusive parent group, and one which can be of immense help in improving schools. It has been more generally effective in elementary than in secondary schools, for a number of reasons. The larger number of parents involved, the greater complexity of the program, and the absence of a single teacher, such as the elementary room teacher, have been factors of difficulty at the secondary school level. Perhaps a more significant cause lies in the diminishing of the responsibility which parents feel as children grow up, in combination with the adolescent search for independence. In spite of these factors, many junior and senior high schools have developed highly effective parent-teacher groups which have made a valuable contribution to school-community relations. Many secondary schools have a Parent-Teacher-Student Organization (PTSO) which brings students into an active role in planning with adults. No principal interested in community relations can afford to be without a parent organization of some kind.

THE ROOM PARENTS' CLUB

Some of the most successful PTA's, especially at the junior high school level, have been supported by a lively group of room parents' clubs based on the home rooms or the core classes. The room group forms a somewhat more efficient basis for participation of parents in planning. It has the advantages of unity of purpose and of compact size, which quickly enable members to get acquainted and to develop mutually accepted goals. It is probable that the larger, building-based PTA has some advantages also in terms of greater resources for carrying out a program. A combination of the two—room parents' clubs and a school parent-teacher group—would appear to be valuable.

GRADE-LEVEL PLANNING

Another type of organization which is halfway between the room and the building organization is the grade-level council or planning committee. This group has responsibility for setting the goals and developing plans for instruction and/or activities at a given grade level, such as the twelfth grade. Most grade-level committees are composed of teachers, including class advisers. Some schools have invited parents to work on such grade level councils, with good results.

STUDY COMMITTEES

Still another kind of organization involving lay citizens is represented by the special study committees. These may be set up to make a study of the growth characteristics of the early adolescent, to help plan a new high school building, or to develop a school camping program. In theory, such committees are often considered to be limited to the "why" of education—the goals or purposes of certain parts of the program—as opposed to the "how." In practice, however, such limitation appears to be artificial and unnecessary. As a matter of fact, special study committees in secondary schools have successfully tackled one or another of the following problems, which are offered as illustrative of their scope:

Athletic equipment	Nature of learning
Attendance areas	Orientation to new school
Audio-visual aids	Out-of-school jobs
Band uniforms	Recreation facilities
Bicycle care	Rules for use of cars
Birth rate	Salary schedules
Bond drives	School assemblies
Building plans	School excursions
Cafeteria menus	School camping
College guidance	Science program
Commencement	Senior trips
Daily time schedule	Social programs
Dropouts	Speakers' bureau
Fire drills	Special-day programs
Follow-up studies	Student welfare
Growth and development	Teacher tenure
Health examinations	Teaching reading
Health records	Testing program
Home-room program	Textbook selection
Homework	Vandalism
Improving school yard	Vocational guidance
Job opportunities	

Such a list could be extended almost indefinitely. Wherever a real problem can be identified, a parent-teacher committee in some school has worked toward its solution. It is important to note that such study committees have as members both parents and teachers, and frequently administrators too. Thus resources and specialized, technical help are either readily available or can be found. It is unnecessary for such study or action groups to mill about in confusion or mutual ignorance.

INVOLVING STUDENTS

Undoubtedly the most important public relations agents are the secondary school students. Any program which does not provide for their contributions or attempts to ignore their opinions will fail to establish sound community relationships. If students generally feel that they are attending a good school, parents will tend to feel that way too. If, on the other hand, they go home each day reflecting confusion or perplexity about the instructional goals set for them, parents are also likely to become confused. If students feel frustrated or resentful over treatment they believe teachers accord them, the seeds of resentment are being sown in parents too.

It is therefore of great importance that boys and girls have a part in the evaluation of their learning, and that they understand what the purposes of their experiences are. This understanding can be achieved if teachers work to develop the techniques of pupil-teacher evaluation, but it will not happen automatically.

At the building level, students can be selected from student council or classes to serve on grade-level councils or in the parent-teacher organization. Such associations are increasingly being called Parent-Teacher-Student Associations, with a constitution providing for student participants and one or more student officers on the executive board. Students are often called in to serve also on special study committees, such as those referred to earlier. The student council offers an excellent opportunity for the expression of representative student opinions about the school. Chapter 10 includes some suggestions on how the student council can serve this function.

THE CLASSROOM

One important function that parents and other community citizens can serve is to enrich the instructional program. This is an important goal of a community school and has been dealt with in some detail elsewhere.[2] Every community contains resource persons who can help in the secondary school classroom. Two tasks

[2] See, for example, Edward G. Olsen (ed.), *School and Community Programs,* New York, Prentice-Hall, 1949, Chapter 4; also James I. Quillen and Lavone A. Hanna, "Using Community Resources in Social Studies Instruction," *Education for Social Competence,* Chicago, Scott, Foresman and Company, 1948, Chapter XI.

to which the administrator should give attention are the stimulation of teachers and students to locate and use this kind of help, and the coördination of the program. Some citizens who could make a real contribution may never be located. Others may be approached so frequently that requests to contribute may finally come to be regarded as an imposition. These problems can be met if the staff plans wisely the use of community resources. A directory of available persons, agencies, and materials useful in the instructional program can be helpful. Constant communication throughout the staff will keep all members posted on what use is being made each week of such resources.

The student-activities program, too, can be enriched by community help. Parents have helped as chaperons at parties, gone to camp with groups of youngsters, visited school clubs to discuss their hobbies, and helped to make arrangements for school trips to see places of interest. They have supported certain school activities, such as athletics, band, and orchestra, in rather dramatic fashion. In many schools such activities could not continue without the active support given them by groups of interested parents.

Less frequent, but not less important, are the efforts made by some school staffs to involve parents and other citizens in policy making regarding the extent or direction of student activities and in appraisal of their contribution to pupil growth. If such involvement of parents in planning were more often employed, we would hear less talk about the "frills and fads" in education, and less tendency to regard the activities program as dispensable. Even more important, we would probably have better activities programs if lay citizens helped plan them.

THE PRINCIPAL'S TASK

The administrator of a secondary school faces a major dilemma in respect to involvement of the community in program planning. He is a status leader in the school system. He has had five years or more of professional training for his job. He is, in a sense, the captive of a tradition which holds him to be an expert. He is supposed to know all the answers.

Furthermore, the principal is a line officer of the school system. In popular theory the wishes of the community are supposed to be expressed by the legally elected board of education (no matter how unrepresentative of the citizenry it may be). The board in turn transmits those wishes to a superintendent of schools, who is responsible for executing its policies. In turn, the superintendent transmits the responsibility for a secondary school unit to the principal of that school, who is expected to transmit the policies of the school system to "his" staff through assistant principals or department heads. He is a link in a hierarchy.

In this chain of authority, what becomes of the people who live in the area served by the school? How are they supposed to help plan policies or programs which have been transmitted downward from the superintendent rather than upward from the people and their children? How can a building principal ask a teacher-parent group to help evolve answers if the tradition holds that he is the medicine man who already has the answers?

The answer is, of course, that the principal does not have the answers and must escape the shackles of those traditions which force upon him the medicine-man role. He may accept his delegated authority from the superintendent; he may, by the same logic, delegate some of his authority to a well-integrated, intelligent group of parents and teachers if he desires to do so. He may even delegate some powers to students. He is still responsible to the superintendent of schools, of course. He may believe, and others around him may share his belief, that those responsibilities will be performed even more ably by well-organized groups of those who are directly concerned with policies. In short, the principal may justifiably elect to share his leadership function with teachers, parents, and students. He may decide that

The effective administrator is he who challenges teachers and parents to develop into leaders by inspiring them and leading them to participate in planning, executing, and evaluating activities within a school.

Furthermore, the effective administrator is one who is himself continually inspired and guided into participating as one of the group, by the leadership which emerges from teachers, parents, and students.[3]

It is sometimes assumed that the democratic leader is the weak leader. This opinion stems chiefly from the long tradition of authoritarian administration which most principals inherit. Recent data indicate the crucial importance of leadership in achieving improvement in schools. The Midwest Administration Center recently interviewed 400 teachers and polled 1800 others in 43 states and 216 school districts. It found a significant relationship between teachers' ratings of their administrators and the extent of their satisfaction with their school.[4] It is highly probable that a similar correlation will generally be found between community attitudes toward their school leaders and satisfaction with their schools. Since administrators play such a crucial role in the achievement of an improved program, it becomes doubly important that the role be a democratic one. In working toward this desirable end, secondary school principals may find themselves in a variety of roles.

1. *Follower.* When leadership is genuinely shared, the status leader will frequently find himself in the role of follower. As ideas and leadership emerge from a group of parents and teachers, the principal must be sensitive and responsive to the situation and know when to slip "into the ranks." He must be able to shed the halo of his position, and be accepted by parents and teachers as a peer, when leadership has emerged for a time from the group. Kurt Lewin has pointed out the fact that leadership and followership in a democratic enterprise are but two sides of the same coin:

The democratic follower has to learn to play a role which implies,

---

[3] Michigan Department of Public Instruction, *Planning and Working Together,* Bulletin 337, Lansing, Mich., State Department of Public Instruction, 1945, p. 154.

[4] *Administrators' Notebook,* Midwest Administration Center, University of Chicago, I:8, March, 1953.

among other points, a fair share of responsibility toward the group and a sensitivity to other people's feelings.

What holds for the education of democratic followers holds true also for the education of democratic leaders. In fact, it seems to be the same process through which persons learn to play either of these roles and it seems that both roles must be learned if either one is to be played well.[5]

In achieving the role of full participator, the principal will find it important to learn the technique of becoming a follower when occasion demands.

2. *Stimulating group action.* The principal is not only a leader and a follower in action programs. He is also a stimulator of such programs, especially in situations where no one else can yet assume this role. He must understand the group's readiness for action, and he must be skilled in the techniques of presenting problems without accentuating existing barriers within the group. Again, there will also be other persons who stimulate initial group action. Perhaps a special responsibility rests with the principal to analyze skillfully the situation and the group's readiness, and to help them get started on problems which are real to them. Care should be taken to ensure that the problems are real ones; the principal is faced by myriad problems which cannot be really shared by parents or community groups until they have made a beginning in policy planning.

3. *Interpreting programs.* The community expects the principal to do more than propose action and participate in it. He is perhaps the major interpreter of the school, and he must be ready to assume this role when required. There is special need for interpretation when change is under way in the school and older values are being questioned. Of course, others interpret also. Teachers and students, as well as other parents, are constantly serving this role. The principal is assumed to be capable of spearheading the task,

[5] Kurt Lewin, "Dynamics of Group Action," *Educational Leadership,* January, 1944, p. 199.

as status leader of the program. He should never arrogate to himself the sole authority as interpreter of the school. He should seek constantly to share the role, but be ready to assume it when necessary. This means that he must be actively involved in the planning stage, and have some knowledge of the goals of the program and a great deal of faith in others involved in it.

4. *Analyst of group process.* In order to be of maximum help in initiating group planning, the principal must be a student of group process. He needs to know the structure of interpersonal relationships which characterize the group. He should know the leaders, whose views are likely to constitute an index of community opinions regarding the school.[6] He should also be aware of the process through which a group unifies itself, achieves consensus about a common problem, gathers data, reaches tentative conclusions, and evaluates its own work. He must understand and appreciate people and have faith in the value of their individual contributions. He should be aware of the barriers which already exist and of those which may develop as a group attempts to mobilize for action. He should also be able to help a group resolve those barriers and utilize its own resources.

In short, the principal and his way of operating are likely to be the crucial factors in any process involving group planning.

5. *Expediter of plans.* In any group including parents and other lay citizens the principal is likely to be the chief expediter of the group's recommendations or conclusions. It is he who will be called on to furnish information of a technical nature. He will serve as liaison with the central office and the board of education. He will be expected to help the group (1) secure help and data, (2) reach the proper group or person with its ultimate recommendations, and (3) get satisfactory action, if action is sought. Since most problems are the result of a breakdown in the lines of communication, this role of expediter is really a matter of ensuring

---

[6] T. J. Jenson, "Identification and Utilization of Opinion Leaders in School District Reorganization," doctoral dissertation, School of Education, University of Wisconsin, Madison, Wis., 1952.

that all channels are clear for ideas, suggestions, and facts to flow from the group to the appropriate agency and from administration to the group.

EVALUATING THE PRINCIPAL'S ROLE

How can these differing roles of the principal be evaluated? Perhaps questions such as the following may be helpful to the principal who seeks to appraise his own effectiveness as a leader, participator, stimulator, analyst, and expediter of group planning with community groups:

1. Do parents feel that their opinions really count?
2. Is there a free channel for the flow of ideas from the public to the school, and back?
3. Are decisions made in harmony with basic policies evolved by the total group?
4. Do others besides the principal receive public credit for ideas and achievements?
5. Does the principal speak of "our school," "our problems," "our staff," in preference to "my school," "my problems," "my staff"?
6. Can people disagree with the principal without risk of recrimination?
7. Are the powers and abilities of all persons in the group fully utilized?
8. Is the leadership role sometimes assumed by parents or others not on the school staff?
9. Are social relationships improving within the group?
10. Are many persons developing competencies and understandings which will make them useful leaders?
11. Do individuals increasingly tend to exhibit a concern for the welfare and achievements of the group?
12. Are individuals gaining increased confidence and courage?
13. Is the administrator able at times to assume a peer relationship (of equals) in parent groups?
14. Does every parent have the feeling that he or she is really needed in the improvement of the program?

15. Is community participation in planning becoming a right and a responsibility rather than a favor granted by the administration?

The principal who can honestly say "yes" to such questions as these is at least on the high road to realizing his roles in group planning with community groups.

SUMMARY

In this chapter an analysis has been made of the task of the principal as a leader in school-community planning. The older "leave-us-alone" policies of the schools appear no longer possible, even if they are desired by some school leaders. Even an intelligent program of school publicity can no longer suffice, *if programs are to change and adapt to new needs*. When programs are changed, maximum understanding must be sought from the people, who are the real owners of the schools. This understanding and support can come about only through involvement of more and more lay citizens in planning, implementing, and appraising the school's program.

In such a plan of involvement, no one has a more crucial role than the principal. It is probable that no such program will be achieved without his consent and support. Even more significantly, the program calls upon the principal for new roles involving new skills which the older, authoritarian roles did not demand of a school administrator. The recent attacks upon the public schools have conveyed a left-handed blessing; for they have brought home to us all a new realization of the need for courageous, skillful school leaders. Our administrators today must be ready and able to work with people in the community. They must believe in the power of the people to improve the schools, and they must develop the skills which democratic planning demands.

For Further Reading

American Association of School Administrators, *Public Relations for America's Schools,* 28th Yearbook, Washington, The National Education Association, 1950.

Association for Supervision and Curriculum Development, *Forces Affecting American Education,* Washington, The National Education Association, 1953.

Campbell, Clyde M. (ed.), *Practical Applications of Democratic Administration,* New York, Harper & Brothers, 1952.

Cook, Lloyd and Elaine, *A Sociological Approach to Education,* New York, McGraw-Hill Book Company, 1950, Part IV, chaps. XIII–XVII.

Gwynn, J. Minor, *Curriculum Principles and Social Trends,* New York, The Macmillan Company, 1950, chap. XIX.

Hanna, Paul R., *et al., Youth Serves the Community,* New York, Appleton-Century- Crofts, 1936.

Hand, Harold, *What People Think About Their Schools,* Yonkers, N.Y., World Book Company, 1948.

Hollingshead, A. B., *Elmtown's Youth,* New York, John Wiley & Sons, 1949, chap. XVII.

Hulburd, David, *This Happened in Pasadena,* New York, The Macmillan Company, 1951.

Hymes, James, *Effective Home-School Relationships,* New York, Prentice-Hall, 1953.

Melby, Ernest O., and Puner, Morton (eds.), *Freedom and Public Education,* New York, Praeger and Company, 1953.

Menge, J. W., and Faunce, Roland C., *Working Together for Better Schools,* New York, American Book Company, 1953.

Mort, Paul, and Vincent, William S., *A Look at Our Schools,* New York, The Ronald Press Company, 1946.

National Society for the Study of Education, *Citizen Co-operation for Better Public Schools,* Chicago, University of Chicago Press, 1954.

Olsen, E. G. (ed.), *School and Community,* New York, Prentice-Hall, 1945.

Olsen, E. G. (ed.), *School and Community Programs,* New York, Prentice-Hall, 1949, chap. 4.

Scott, C. Winfield, and Hill, Clyde M. (eds.), *Public Education Under Criticism,* New York, Prentice-Hall, 1954.

Stratemeyer, Florence B., *et al., Developing a Curriculum for Modern Living,* New York, Bureau of Publication, Teachers College, Columbia, 1947, chap. VIII.

Thayer, V. T., *Public Education and Its Critics,* New York, The Macmillan Company, 1954.

Yauch, Wilbur A., *How Good Is Your School?,* New York, Harper & Brothers, 1951.

Yauch, Wilbur A., *Improving Human Relations in School Administration,* New York, Harper & Brothers, 1949.

Yeager, William A., *School-Community Relations,* New York, Dryden Press, 1951.

CHAPTER 7

....

The Guidance Program

WHAT IS GUIDANCE?

In recent years a great number of words have been published about guidance; yet there is still widespread confusion about what it is, and about who should do it. Both professional literature and programs of educational conferences reveal a considerable variety of interpretations and emphases. There is still disagreement as to the kinds of guidance, and which should be dominant: vocational, educational, moral and ethical, or emotional and social. There are disagreements as to the respective merits of directive (either prescriptive or suggestive) guidance and non-directive guidance. We are not agreed as to the relative merits of individual and group guidance, or of periodic emphasis as compared with continuous emphasis. The general educators urge a generalized approach, the specialists a specialized program. There are earnest advocates, too, of the use of the classroom, the home room, and the counselor.

There is more agreement among authorities on a definition of guidance than there is on the direction of guidance programs. As a matter of fact, there is no substantial disagreement among guidance specialists with the definition of guidance presented by Hamrin and Erickson in 1939: "Guidance in the secondary school refers to that aspect of the educational program which is concerned especially with helping the pupil to become adjusted to his present situation and to plan his future in line with his interests, abilities, and social needs." [1]

It will be noted that this definition emphasizes adjustment to the pupil's present situation. The need for such adjustment is mainly created by the inadequacy of the pupil's "present situation"—that is, his program of studies in the secondary school. The history of the modern guidance movement indicates that it sprang up, and has enjoyed a phenomenal development in senior high schools, as part of an effort to help students understand and accept an unrealistic program of instruction. The typical high school student sees no relationship to his present needs in the various assignments he confronts in most high school classes. He may accept the teacher's word that it will sometime be helpful to learn:

The parts of speech
The parts of a sentence
The complete conjugation of verbs
The dates of the Norman invasion
The Pythagorean theorem
The Latin verbs that take the ablative
$X^2 - y^2 = (x + y)(x - y)$

He may accept these and a thousand other assignments like them as a part of going to high school, but he is not likely to see their bearing on his present needs. If he is not particularly successful in his classes, he may seek other experiences in which he can achieve success. Thus it is assumed by some authorities on guidance that boys and girls must adjust to existing programs that may be ill adapted to needs, and that the role of guidance is to facilitate this process.

---

[1] Shirley A. Hamrin and Clifford E. Erickson, *Guidance in the Secondary School*, New York, D. Appleton-Century Company, 1939, pp. 1–2.

GUIDANCE AND INSTRUCTION

Some of these writers point out that guidance and instruction cannot be the same processes, because the teacher has certain other functions besides pupil adjustment. For example, the teacher is said to be responsible for imparting information, for making assignments, and for checking the mastery of certain areas of subject matter. The teacher may also spend part of his time in maintaining control of "his" classroom. All of these are deemed to be functions apart from, or even foreign to, the guidance process.

The trouble with this point of view is that it assumes the worst about instruction. Not all teachers consider it their basic task to impart information to their pupils; some help the learner to acquire his own information as a part of fulfilling his own purposes. Not all teachers make assignments or check the mastery of subject matter; some have learned to help boys and girls to develop their own assignments and to evaluate their own progress. Not all teachers spend their time in controlling the classroom; an increasing number guide young people in the techniques of individual and group self-control. Teachers who use such techniques as the following are exemplifying good guidance methods in the regular classroom:

1. Studying the needs, interests, abilities, and problems of each individual in a class
2. Analyzing the relationships that exist between individuals and subgroups in a class
3. Helping groups of students to discuss, analyze, and define problems of current interest that they need to solve for themselves
4. Guiding students in working on the solution of real-life problems in the classroom
5. Deepening their insights and enriching their interest in the world about them
6. Helping students to evaluate their own growth
7. Guiding students in the techniques of group self-control
8. Giving students insight into their own behavior

9. Helping them to make increasingly wise choices among alternatives
10. Helping them to learn from their own mistakes
11. Helping them to respect themselves and others
12. Helping them to get along well with others

Classroom instruction that is geared to the real developmental tasks of adolescents is likely to be "guidance-centered." As both the curriculum and methods of the secondary school become geared to the task of meeting actual needs of individuals and groups, the distinction between guidance and instruction will tend to disappear. The basic task of guidance is to discover the emerging needs of boys and girls and then to adapt the instructional and activities program to meet these needs. As Stiles and Dorsey have stated: "Guidance is a process of helping individuals to make choices relative to recognized problems, the solution of which will lead to continued adjustment." [2]

The supposition that guidance is a different function than instruction is thus based on the most limited (and some day they will be obsolete) concepts of instruction. These concepts limit the teacher to such processes as assignment, drill, examination, and classroom control, which are minimized to an increasing degree by the modern teacher. It is true that not all teachers are free from traditional methods; but any movement that assumes the immutability of older methods as its reason for being is on unsound ground. If guidance must be defined as a function separate from instruction, then instruction will have to remain static and uninspired. Should that condition obtain throughout a school there would, in turn, be little good resulting from guidance efforts of counselors. One soon runs out of places to send maladjusted students. They can eventually manage to fail or get into trouble in almost any phase of a program that is not in gear with either their interests or their needs.

[2] Lindley J. Stiles and Mattie Dorsey, *Democratic Teaching in Secondary Schools,* Philadelphia, J. B. Lippincott Company, 1950, p. 238.

Alberty has stated: "To the extent that the high school conceives its function as that of helping the adolescent meet his needs and solve his problems it organizes its curriculum for this purpose, and again the distinction between education and guidance tends to disappear." [3] He goes on to pay tribute to the guidance movement, however, for certain contributions to the modern theory of learning:

1. It has stressed the need for continuous study of individual differences among students in terms of capacities and interests.
2. It has emphasized the importance of the physical and mental health aspects of development.
3. It has centered attention upon the need for better personnel records, to replace the barren records of subjects taken and marks received.
4. It has developed and popularized the use of interest and aptitude testing, as a supplement to the standardized subject-matter tests which are often the only kind of tests given in a school.
5. It has emphasized the need for individual counseling and has provided much help in the refinement and use of counseling techniques.

It is possible to recognize these contributions and still to insist that the above contributions *ought* to be part and parcel of the modern curriculum and utilized by the teacher in the day-to-day work of the classroom. [4]

STUDENT ACTIVITIES CAN HELP

As secondary schools have gradually modified their programs of instruction, a kind of supplementary or auxiliary program has developed that is much more directly geared to the interests and purposes of students. This is the extracurricular activities program which is, for many students, the real heart of the school. There is more student interest in the activities program in most schools

[3] Harold Alberty, *Reorganizing the High School Curriculum*, rev. ed., New York, The Macmillan Company, 1953, p. 324. Reprinted by permission of the publisher.
[4] *Ibid.*, pp. 324–325.

than in the regular classes. Here students' social needs are better met, their interests in hobbies developed and enriched, and their leadership encouraged. Curiously enough, many a high school that has a highly traditional program of instruction has developed a lively and functional activities program, perhaps as a partial antidote for what goes on in the classrooms. Student activities constitute a real opportunity for good guidance practices. This opportunity will be capitalized only as teachers are involved actively in the program and support it with enthusiasm. Discussion of this point will appear in Chapter 9.

THE HOME ROOM

As one phase of the student activities program the home room was developed for guidance purposes during the 1920's and 1930's. It was usually set up as a daily period of 20 to 45 minutes, with almost every teacher assuming sponsorship of one section for guidance purposes. High hopes were expressed by early advocates of the home room,[5] and organization of home rooms spread at a phenomenal rate until about 1940. Its goals were not generally realized, however, and the amount of time assigned to the home room has diminished in most schools. Some recent surveys indicate that it has become chiefly a record or roll-taking device in many senior high schools.

The junior high school has generally retained the home room. Lounsbury's study of 251 junior high schools in the Midwest in 1954 revealed that 93 percent had home-room periods averaging 28 minutes in length.[6]

The home room still persist in other schools and occasionally serves some desirable functions:

> A convenient administrative unit
> A unit of a large school community

[5] See, for example, Harry C. McKown, *Home Room Guidance,* New York, McGraw-Hill Book Company, 1934.

[6] John H. Lounsbury, "The Role and Status of the Junior High School," doctoral dissertation, George Peabody College, Nashville, Tenn., 1954.

A supplementary instructional agency

A means of counseling and group guidance

A device for developing better parent relationships

A means of improving human relations with the school.[7]

The home-room period was generally reduced or eliminated during the emergency educational programs of World War II. The recognition of its value had started to fade before 1940, however. It failed to measure up to early expectations because of two major factors: (1) there was not enough time allowed for the home room; (2) it bore no particular relationship to the total program of instruction or student activities. McKown had stated the case for the home room as follows in 1934:

The home room, with its main emphasis upon the education of the student rather than the passing along of a body of subject matter, epitomizes the very soul of the modern conception of education; that the pupil himself is far more important and sacred than any information he may ever accumulate. In reality the home room creates a situation in which the pupil himself becomes the subject studied, worked with, and learned about. *He* and *his* activities, experiences, and interests compose the curriculum. He *is* the curriculum. And all subjects, courses, knowledges, and informations are justifiable only if they contribute definitely and directly to *his* development.[8]

This statement is an excellent one. It might be considered to be descriptive of a good program of instruction in general education instead of being limited to the home room. At any rate, these goals are more often achieved today in core classes employing two or three periods each day than in the "extracurricular" home-room period. Perhaps the home room was never really recognized by school people as a focus or integrating factor for the entire curriculum. Perhaps teachers never understood or really accepted it. The rapidity with which it was adopted would indicate that it was

[7] Adapted from Edgar G. Johnston and Roland C. Faunce, *Student Activities in Secondary Schools,* New York, The Ronald Press Company, 1952, Chapter 4.

[8] By permission from McKown, *op. cit.,* p. 20.

generally organized by administrative fiat rather than as a result
of careful study by the faculty of each school.

THE CORE CURRICULUM

At any rate, the excellent purpose and philosophy of the home
room have reappeared in recent years, under various titles, as the
basis for the core curriculum. As described in Chapter 3, the core
curriculum represents an effort to organize learning around the
real problems and needs of youth, which are also likely to be at
the same time the needs of our democratic society. Thus its basic
purpose is the same as that ascribed by McKown to the home
room. The chief difference is that core classes are a part of the
basic curriculum instead of remaining on its fringe as the home
room did; thus the core is, by definition, more integral and central
in the student's program. It also enjoys a longer block of time,
ranging from two to six periods daily. As a result of this longer
time block the core teacher is usually limited to two sections of
students, a factor which concentrates his guidance functions on
fewer persons than he would have in his classes in a departmentalized program.

OTHER CLASSES

Examples can be found of other (single-period) classes, too,
that are guidance-centered. The study of vocations is frequently
offered as a one or two semester class in ninth or tenth grade.
Classes in orientation, personal-social adjustment, and home and
family living represent a guidance emphasis in the regular classroom. Many high schools have classes called "guidance" for one
or two semesters.

As an example of how any one of these areas can be built into
the regular curriculum of the secondary school, a United States
Office of Education monograph reports as follows on education
for home and family life:

Secondary schools are providing education for home and family living through different schemes of organizations. Such instruction is being offered through separate courses; units and parts of units within courses; core curricula or common learnings offerings; total school programs of family life education; other total school programs, such as guidance and health education; special school activities such as assembly programs; and programs of youth organizations.

1. Separate courses which have as their main focus education for home and family living. They include such courses as homemaking, home economics, home and family living, personal-social problems, family relations, personal problems, boys' home living. . . .

2. Units within other courses which contribute to education for home and family living. Units are integrated in such areas as English, social studies, health education, agriculture, distributive education, industrial arts, and consumer education. Some units being introduced are: psychology of group living, human relations, understanding ourselves and others, our manners and social customs, boy-girl interests, choosing a mate, approaching marriage, personal and family finance, housing the family, caring for the sick in the home, nutrition, family recreation, and legislation which affects the family.

3. Core curricula or common learnings courses. Such courses offered in a limited number of schools are designed in part to prepare pupils for family living. In one school students taking the seventh, eighth, and ninth grade core may select from such problem areas as: managing my personal affairs, understanding my body, living in the home, and improving personality. Students taking the tenth, eleventh, and twelfth grade core have opportunity to work on such areas as: problems of the family as a basic social unit and problems of producer-consumer economics.

Another school offers freshman problems as the common learnings requirement. It enables students to become acquainted with the human body and problems of keeping it healthy, and to learn the nature of growth and development of personality, adolescent development, boy-girl relationships, and sex education.

4. Total school programs of family life education. These are being planned and developed cooperatively by teachers, administrators,

students, and parents in a few schools. Within one school program of family life education the areas of child guidance, human relationships, and planning for the future are stressed. In some schools there is effort to integrate home and family living into all classes.[9]

Similar descriptions could be cited of other "life adjustment" areas that are being learned about in American secondary schools. These programs represent a direct guidance emphasis. If pupil choices and self-direction are used in such instructional programs, they would appear to be examples of both guidance and instruction. Such courses might be described as guidance-centered instruction. It should be noted, however, that the initial use of content that appears life-centered will not ensure that guidance, in the sense of efforts to improve adjustment, will continue to take place. A course in home and family living can be taught in such a way that it is more monotonous than the Punic Wars. The teacher will not help individuals to make an effective adjustment unless he sets out to find out "what makes him tick" and is willing to adapt instruction to emerging pupil needs. He will do well to ask himself such questions as the following, suggested by Elizabeth Brady, as he approaches a new experience with young people:

Has he (the pupil) had a chance to learn what the school takes for granted—especially language, manners, ways of playing with others, obeying rules, concepts like "cooperation"? If not, what has he learned in these and related areas?

What particular expectations and pressures has he had to meet thus far, particularly in his family and play group? To what special pressures has membership in a minority group subjected him?

What values has he taken on? What does he consider success?

What kind of self does he value? What does he expect of others?

What concepts has he acquired about everyday realities—what a family is, or what a community is?

[9] United States Office of Education, *Vitalizing Secondary Education,* Bulletin 1951, No. 3, Federal Security Agency, Washington, 1951, pp. 79–80.

What ways of expressing feelings has he developed? How does he feel about the things which happen to him?

How has he learned to relate himself to others? What does he expect in his relations with others? [10]

It is thus possible to center guidance in the classroom through introducing new required or elective courses in which the content or the methods used contribute to the goal of helping students to make successful adjustment and wise choices among the issues and problems that confront them. It is also possible to introduce appropriate units into English, social science, science, and other classes as a means of helping these required areas of the departmentalized school to become guidance-centered. Modern text materials in English and social studies, especially, reflect the trend toward actual youth problems.

Because of its relative freedom from subject-matter patterns, the core or common-learnings class is possibly in the most favorable position of all to give help on real adjustment problems. Alberty quotes a resource unit developed for core classes in Maryland that has numerous guidance implications. Examples of learning activities included in this resource unit developed in Worcester County, Maryland, follow:

Think of some adult with whom you get along very well. List the characteristics of this person. Check those which you believe that you also possess. Then add some of your traits which are not exhibited by this adult. Compare these with the qualities which he or she possesses but you do not find in yourself. How do you explain the fact that these differences do not interfere with your friendly relations?

Prepare a similar list for an adult with whom you do not get along well. You and this person must have some traits in common as well as some in which you differ markedly. How do you explain that in

[10] Elizabeth Hall Brady, "Children Bring Their Families to School," Association for Supervision and Curriculum Development, *Fostering Mental Health in Our Schools,* 1950 Yearbook, Washington, The National Education Association, 1950, pp. 27–28.

your relationship with this person, your differences are so much more significant than your likenesses?

To what extent are you responsible for your friendly relations with one person and your disagreement with the other?

Recall a recent incident in your association with each of these adults which illustrates your ability or inability to get along. To what extent did your own attitude affect your own behavior and that of the other person?

Use the filmstrip and recording "Meet Your Mind" by Dr. William Menninger (Lewellyn's Productions, 8 South Michigan Avenue, Chicago, Illinois) in classes to help students review visually the information they have learned about behavior.

Construct cooperatively a rating scale which lists 8 or 10 traits such as consideration for others, facial expression, poise, etc. List interpretation of each from one extreme to the other. Have everyone rate himself and have everyone rate someone else. Pool the values to see if there are differences. (Avoid making this a popularity contest or a matter dealing with individuals in the class. Keep project on a level of comparing total values within the class.)

A group may present "The Ins and Outs," a dramatic sketch for and about teenagers. This skit tells the story of a student who is not accepted into the social life of his school and the effects on his behavior. You may obtain the script from the Southern California Society for Mental Hygiene, 600 South Hobert Boulevard, Los Angeles, California.

Write a short skit dramatizing introductions. Include in your cast one person who knows nothing of correct social usage. Contrast this person with one who is familiar with the customs governing greetings and introductions.

Divide the class into groups. Let them first practice by themselves in different corners of the room. Then each group should give an introduction before the class in order to receive constructive suggestions from the other students. To judge the introduction ask these questions:

Was the introduction scene gracious, friendly, cordial?

Were the people at ease?

Was the scene a happy one or was it rather solemn?

Was the introduction hurried or awkward?

Were the names spoken distinctly?

Was anyone shy or embarrassed?

Was a suitable conversation clue given?

Write short character sketches of two girls (or two boys). Do not write about people whom others will recognize. Choose girls or boys who are very different from each other. What do you admire in each? What must you overlook?

Plan a dinner and an evening party for the class in the school. Show the movie "Are You Popular?" (Coronet Films, 65 E. South Water Street, Chicago, Illinois). Afterwards have pupils discuss it. In planning the dinner and evening party, arrange for groups to practice conventional projects, such as setting table, writing letters, etc.

Organize a panel (or several panels) of class members to discuss "Teenage Problems" at a PTA meeting or to provide a program for other organizations of adults in your community.[11]

INDIVIDUAL COUNSELING

Not all problems that a group selects for study will have equal value for every individual pupil. There are individual problems that are not readily or easily expressed in a group. These offer the teacher a challenge to create opportunities for individual counseling. Interviews with students can be arranged before or after school, at noon, or during a free period. Just as often, however, a skillful teacher will find time for such counseling during class periods while group work or individual projects such as creative writing are under way. The core teacher usually has a smaller total number of students and is better able to locate those individuals who need some special help. He also has the group for longer periods daily and for more than one semester, so he can afford to use the time-consuming nondirective approach. The teacher has an immense advantage over the principal or a special counselor in that he can watch the operation of the group, follow up directly his suggestions, and analyze outcomes. The techniques needed for

[11] Selected from Snow Hill Board of Education, *Getting Along With Others,* Snow Hill, Md., 1952. Quoted from Alberty, *op. cit.,* pp. 332–333.

most counseling situations can be learned by any interested teacher who has opportunities to try them in actual practice.

There appears to be an excellent case, therefore, for teacher-counselors. In particular, the core program seems to offer special advantages for both individual and group guidance. Not all teachers, of course, are equally qualified or even equally interested in helping youth to make successful adjustments in coping with their problems. Some teachers appear to fit into the guidance function from the start. Others have to learn it by experience, with someone's help. A few are unfitted by temperament to deal with the real problems of others, and must be reassigned to some less strategic role.

There are differences in the types of problems that youth present, too. Some of these can be predicted because they come up perennially as a phase of developmental tasks. These problems are "normal" in the sense that they are shared by a great many youth of the same age. Other problems are the product of acute emotional disturbance which cannot be handled effectively by most teachers.

ROLE OF COUNSELORS

Because of the need for direction and coördination, for in-service education in guidance techniques, and for a resource when the problem is too difficult for the teacher, there is genuine need for special counselors. No school can have too much help. Most schools need counselors who are qualified to give leadership in developing a program, who have control of some techniques that help special cases, and who can coördinate the program through liaison with resources in the school as a whole and in the community.

Alberty cites the following functions that appear to require specialized personnel:

1. To co-ordinate the group and individualized instruction which is the principal responsibility of the classroom teacher.

2. To administer programs for promoting a better understanding of the student, through the securing of adequate data.

3. To aid in vocational placement of students both in the part-time work program of the school and in full-time employment at the end of the period of formal education.

4. To deal with difficult cases of physical or psychological mal-adjustment which require special training and skill of a psychiatric nature.

5. To maintain a follow-up of graduates and dropouts and to interpret data regarding such a follow-up for the purpose of improving the guidance program, and the total school program.[12]

Chisholm lists substantially these same responsibilities of the guidance specialist and adds two: "stimulate teacher interest and efficiency in guidance, and . . . assist in developing a better understanding of guidance throughout the community and in securing a more effective cooperative relationship with parents and other laymen in the community."[13] Needless to say, counselors will not undertake deep psychotherapy. Where such treatment is indicated they will refer cases to the appropriate place where help can be given.

The special counselors discussed above would be useful in every school. It is desirable that they be selected with an eye to their major task, which is probably not counseling students but helping teachers. In terms of the hours available and the typical number of students per counselor, it is unlikely that they can be expected to deal effectively with many students.[14]

They can, however, affect practices throughout the school by giving skillful leadership to the process of developing a total program. This means that their primary work is likely to be with

---

[12] *Ibid.,* p. 335.

[13] Leslie L. Chisholm, *The Work of the Modern High School,* New York, The Macmillan Company, 1953, p. 458.

[14] The average number of pupils per counselor in schools having counselors in the United States was 524.1 in 1951–1952; U.S. Office of Education survey reported in *Bulletin of the National Association of Secondary School Principals,* 38:200, February, 1954, p. 234.

teachers. The chief justification (though not the only one) for employing special counselors lies in the need for help by teachers. A counselor who can work effectively with students but not with his colleagues would be relatively ineffective in improving guidance practices throughout a school. The teacher is the heart of a good program. Any important changes in the program must involve helping the teachers to change their points of view and their methods of dealing with students.

Unfortunately, some counselors have been ineffective in helping teachers. Part of their ineffectiveness results from their status in the school. The counselor is usually paid a higher salary than the classroom teacher. He has less classes, if he teaches at all. He has a private office, he is free to come and go during school hours, and he may be regarded as "in line" for promotion to the principalship. Any person enjoying special status must overcome the barriers that such status imposes between himself and the persons with whom he must work—through whom, in fact, he can become effective. Some teachers will resent his favored status to the point of criticism and attack. Others will use him as a scapegoat when things go wrong. Still others will simply expect all guidance problems to be solved by this superior member of the staff, and will thus absolve themselves of all responsibility for guidance activities. In some schools the counselor is actually prevented from giving any leadership to the guidance program because of the load of clerical or disciplinary functions that land at his door.

A few counselors have, perhaps unwittingly, contributed to the barriers that prevent them from becoming effective. They sometimes act as though they welcomed these differences between themselves and ordinary teachers. They may behave like members of a favored (and mysterious) cult who know the answers to problems of human behavior. The words they use may not be understood by other faculty members. They may speak blandly of the ego and the superego, of aggression and withdrawal, of phobias and sublimation. Not only their specialized vocabulary but also their attitudes toward teachers may contribute to the very barriers they must remove in order to become effective.

Probably few counselors today make all the mistakes mentioned above. But all counselors who have a favored status must bridge the gap between themselves and teachers if they wish to improve the guidance program. (Like any supervisor, the counselor must earn the right to work with teachers by becoming a valued resource for them.) It will usually help the counselor in this effort if he has one or more classes of his own. It is helpful to be able to talk about "our" kids instead of "your" kids. It will also help him enormously to act always as though he believed that teachers are important. When his actions give teachers clear evidence that he regards them as the central agents in the guidance process, and himself as helper, he will begin to bridge the gap between himself and others. He can then be instrumental in improving the program.

ROLE OF TESTING

There was a period not too many years ago when "guidance" was mainly concerned with administering tests and interpreting their results. Many people believed that at last the problem of improving education had been solved with the widespread adoption of standardized testing programs. They assumed that educational goals could be defined and objectified, their achievement measured accurately, and that changes in method would then readily be made by teachers in light of the outcomes of the tests.

Fortunately, this initial faith in testing has given way to a more realistic understanding of the partial contribution that test scores can supply in learning more about pupil growth. We now know that many important educational goals cannot be measured by the so-called objective tests. We have discovered further that blind faith in a testing program will usually lead teachers to ignore individual differences among students and to establish the norms given for certain tests as their standard goal for an entire class. As Travers has stated: "Attempts to measure school achievement solely through the use of a few typical objective tests represent an outmoded view of evaluation. Currently available objective tests and teacher-made tests are valuable for measuring certain limited aspects of achievement, but they should not be considered to measure a major fraction of the important outcomes of education." [15]

With the growing conviction that a testing program must not be permitted to establish the goals of instruction, the emphasis is shifting to a more realistic use of tests. Certain kinds of test data can give us helpful information about boys and girls, and can serve a function in counseling and instructional improvement. These outcomes will obtain only when such data are regarded as just a part of the total picture.

Standardized tests used in secondary schools are generally of four types. These are achievement, intelligence, personality, and aptitude or diagnostic tests. A comprehensive listing of published tests of these four types may be found in the successive editions of *The Mental Measurements Yearbook.*[16]

Besides the standardized tests the quality of teacher-made tests has improved as we have learned more about the techniques of measurement. There is still an unfortunate tendency for tests to establish the real goals of instruction. We say, for example, that our goals in the social studies relate to such things as helping students to learn how to understand themselves, to get along better with others, to assume responsibility, to make wise choices in civic matters, etc. Then we give them periodic tests on their mastery of dates and personages in history. There is a dual need to develop and use methods of appraisal that measure other areas of growth, and to diminish the emphasis on memory testing. Above all, there is a need to help youth to evaluate their own growth, both individually and in groups.

[15] Robert N. W. Travers, *How to Make Achievement Tests,* New York, The Odyssey Press, 1949, p. 2.

[16] Oscar K. Buros (ed.), *The Third Mental Measurements Yearbook,* New Brunswick, Rutgers University Press, 1949.

OTHER SOURCES OF DATA

The program of evaluation need not consist solely of test scores. There are other resources for learning about students, and for helping them learn more about themselves. In a school where guidance is effective the staff will be collecting and studying data from a number of sources:

> Scores on achievement, aptitude, intelligence, and personality tests
> Health data
> School marks
> Student-activities participation record
> Work record, employer's appraisals
> Anecdotal records
> Work samples
> Autobiographies
> Self-analysis paragraphs
> Wishing-well test
> Opinions of other teachers
> Sociograms
> Judgments of other (individual) pupils
> Interview records
> Interest inventories
> Questionnaires about study habits, hobbies, jobs
> Attendance record
> Letters to and from parents
> Group appraisals by peers
> Statements of pupil regarding school or life plans
> Results of parent conferences
> Student self-appraisals
> Student appraisals of others
> Student appraisals of class progress
> Data on family and home
> Attendance record
> Case studies by teachers
> Court records

Report from church or other community groups
Time budgets
Follow-up data

It should be noted here that the teacher, who is the central figure in any guidance program, should have an adequate file of data about pupils in his own possession. It is not enough to ensure that teachers can have access to materials in the office of the counselor or principal. If they are expected to use data, they must have it at hand in their own rooms. This is necessary not only for convenience of ready access; it is important also because of the additional status that is conveyed to teachers by such decentralization of guidance data. Copies of all important records should be on file in the teacher's room. Counselors should come to teachers for data rather than teachers having to go to the counselor. The faith in teachers which this practice clearly implies will pay off in terms of better guidance.

STUDY OF GROUPS

Further development of the matter of pupil records will appear in the chapter that follows. At this point it may be appropriate to discuss the teacher's responsibility for study of a group, as distinguished from learning about individual students. Much has been learned in recent years about relationships that develop within a class group, and the impact of these relationships on both behavior and general development. The teacher who is interested in guidance will analyze his group in many ways. He will be interested in such factors as the following, which form the Table of Contents of Redl's *Know Your Group*.[17]

I. Group Composition
II. Group Organization, Group Structure, Group Roles
III. Group Code and Popularity Patterns
IV. Friendships, Hostilities, and Group Spirit

[17] Fritz Redl, *Know Your Group, an Instrumentation for the Analysis of Discipline Problems and of School Morale,* Wayne University, Detroit, 1943.

V. Reaction to Your Leadership
VI. Routine and Discipline
VII. Interest Distribution and Work Behavior
VIII. Group-Dangerous Behavior of Individuals
IX. Group-Favorable Behavior of Individuals
X. Special Assets
XI. Problem Traits
XII. Background Transparence

The alert teacher will study his group in respect to such factors as these, using observations, sociometric tests, sociodrama, discussion, and group appraisal. He will seek to learn in advance about his group's background and what relationships have developed. He will be interested in the cliques that exist, the shifting patterns of leadership, the isolates and rejected students. He will want to know their stage of acceptance of each other and of the teacher. He will study evidences of their readiness to plan, to assume responsibility for what goes on, to assess results.

All these matters affect the "guidance climate" of the room. They help the teacher determine what help is needed and at what points it can be most effective. They help him, too, in setting up the structure of the room in such a way as to promote interaction and group solidarity or morale. The group climate significantly affects the adjustment of every individual in the group. Not only group discipline but also the effective development of every student is influenced directly by the nature of group relationships. For such intensive study as this, it is desirable to keep a teacher and a class together for more than one semester. In many schools the core classes or the home rooms remain with the same teacher for at least two or three years.

ORGANIZATION FOR GUIDANCE

An earlier chapter [18] has outlined the current trend toward the core curriculum and has suggested that the central agent in the

[18] See Chapter 3.

guidance process might be the core teacher. The teacher of a core class not only continues with the class for two years or more, but is with it for two or three periods daily. If an entire school, or even one entire grade level, is thus organized, each core teacher could become chiefly responsible for one or two sections. If the entire faculty is assigned at least one core class, the system will resemble the home-room plan but with considerably greater time available. In most core programs, however, a group of general-education teachers are in charge of core classes, with each one having two sections totaling four to six periods daily. The rest of the teacher's assignment may be a counseling hour or a one-period class in a special subject field. The rest of the staff may have a conventional assignment of five one-period subjects in the fields not included in the core class. In most senior high schools these would include music, foreign languages, mathematics, laboratory science, commercial subjects, industrial arts, practical and fine arts, and advanced courses in speech, writing, and other fields of special interest to some students.

In schools where there is this division of responsibility between the core and special-interest subjects, the coördination of the guidance activity would be the task of the core teacher for perhaps two sections of students. This does not mean that other teachers would have no interest in guidance, or would contribute nothing to the guidance program. On the contrary, a chemistry or Spanish teacher will collect much significant data about his students if he regards himself as an effective leader of youth instead of a purveyor or checker of subject matter. He will report these data occasionally to the core teacher as a means of helping the latter to know more about the adjustment of his students in various special subjects. The core teacher will take initiative in collecting information from other teachers, studying it, building it into the personnel file, and using it in interviews with students and parents. He will also be responsible for helping the special-subject teachers learn about individual students in their classes. Means would be developed in such a school for constant sharing of information about students both in written and oral form.

It should be noted that there will probably be less of these special-subject teachers in the junior high school because of the longer block of time usually employed for core classes at that level. The sharing process is much simpler when fewer persons are involved. Even at the senior high school level, however, the process is not too difficult when it is undertaken by core teachers at each grade level. Students from any particular core class will not usually be enrolled in more than eight or ten classes taught by special-interest teachers.

Attention has been paid in the preceding section to the organization of a guidance program around core classes. The same procedures could be used with a school-wide home-room program, with the exception that there is less time for guidance and more persons involved in the home-room plan. A further possibility is a series of one-hour courses required at every grade level, on which the guidance function can be based. A few schools are attempting this approach with homemaking, agriculture, or social science classes.

THE PRINCIPAL AS COUNSELOR

The typical small school as yet employs no special counselors. The principal in such schools may find himself frequently cast in the role of counselor. Even in larger schools the principal is likely to have some counseling contacts with students. In these contacts the principal may have to overcome certain handicaps of his position in order to do effective counseling. As head of the school he inspires a certain (normal) amount of awe which presents a barrier between himself and students. The authority of his position may prevent students from discussing their problems freely with him. The impression created in students by the principal's office does not inspire their confidence. Finally, if they are already in trouble they may be emotionally disturbed or aggressively disposed toward the whole business of "seeing the principal."

In spite of these handicaps, many principals engage successfully in counseling interviews because of their readiness to see the student's point of view and listen to his problems. If a principal seeks to apply the techniques of the good counseling interview to his conferences with students, he will find it possible to overcome the initial obstacles that result from his position in the school. Robinson has listed the following "basic orientations" in counseling that should be considered by the principal: (1) acceptance of the client, (2) dealing with the core of the client's remarks, (3) division of responsibility, (4) amount of lead in counseling.[19]

Thus, if the principal really accepts the student who is in his office for help, he will be more apt to get his confidence. It is not necessary, obviously, to accept all his actions, but the student must really feel that the principal regards him as important and that he is fully accepted as a member of the school. He should view the principal as one who is interested in him and in his problems, who understands the core of his remarks, who is fair in assigning and accepting responsibility in the interview, and who is able to help him make up his own mind about what he should do. Even when students have run afoul of school rules or are seriously upset, they can recognize and accept fair treatment. If the principal keeps his temper and listens for clues to constructive action, most students can be helped to see how they can adjust to a situation. Often the student who is thus encouraged to analyze his own situation will come up with an acceptable solution of his own—one that he might have rebelled against if it had been earlier offered by the principal. This is the essence of good nondirective counseling.

Happily not all the principal's counseling contacts are with students who are in trouble. Indeed most of the individual interviews he has with students may be with leaders who are respon-

[19] Francis P. Robinson, *Principles and Procedures in Student Counseling*, New York, Harper & Brothers, 1950, pp. 72–80.

sible for various student activities. The principal's counsel may be needed on projects being planned or undertaken by the student council or the senior class. The assembly committee may meet with him to plan a future program. Student leaders may wish to discuss the conditions of the halls or parking lot, or to plan with the principal ways of improving school spirit. These contacts with student leaders are a source of real pleasure to the secondary school principal. They make his job worth while. Further discussion of these kinds of counseling contacts will be presented in Chapter 10. Other types of counseling interviews that the principal may frequently have with students are:

Counseling regarding the selection of a college
Helping students decide on a course of study
Counseling regarding the selection of a life work
Helping students get part-time work
Giving help on evaluating a student's progress in school
Helping students elect a club
Getting help for a student on a personal health problem
Giving advice on study habits
Helping a new student get started in school
Helping a student get a loan
Arranging a student's schedule so as to permit half-time employment

THE PRINCIPAL AS COÖRDINATOR OF GUIDANCE

Whether or not the principal is called on to do actual counseling, he is sure to have a definite and important role as leader and coördinator of the whole guidance program. Either directly or indirectly he will have contacts with community agencies and resources that relate to the school's guidance program. These include churches, youth-serving agencies such as the YMCA and YWCA, recreation department, probate court, police or sheriff's department, United States Employment Service and other job-placement agencies, social workers, etc. They may also include persons from nearby universities or government agencies who can serve a resource role. He will be responsible for marshaling the resources and coördinating the whole program. It will be his task to provide inspiration and leadership to the whole staff toward a better guidance program. He will help define the need, assemble and organize resources, and direct their use. He will have to iron out occasional squabbles and differences of opinion. He will look constantly for wasteful overlapping and for omission of important emphases. He will lead the staff in evaluating the effectiveness of the program.

Perhaps most important of all, the principal will furnish an example for the whole school in his treatment of people and in his basic interest in their successful adjustment. Since he is aware that people usually live up to our expectations of them, he will act sincerely as though he expected the best from students and teachers. He will be counted as their friend and colleague, who enjoys being with them every day, and to whom they know they can turn for help. He will be able to answer in the affirmative such questions as Kelley has suggested for the principal's self-appraisal:

Do I realize that even my own success and well-being, in the long run, depend on the success and well-being of students and teachers?

Do I feel the unique worth and dignity of the most unpromising student in the school?

Do I seek ways of making him feel that he can share in the project?

Do I look for and encourage teachers to assume a share in leadership? [20]

The principal who sets the kind of example implied in these questions will presently find that the school where he works is guidance-centered. This means that adults who serve on its staff are effectively aiding students to make wise choices, to assume increasing responsibility for their own acts, and to adjust successfully to new situations.

[20] Earl C. Kelley, "The Function of the Principal in a Modern School," *The American School Board Journal,* June, 1947.

For Further Reading

Alberty, Harold, *Reorganizing the High School Curriculum*, New York, The Macmillan Company, 1947, chap. XI.

American Council on Education, *Helping Teachers Understand Children*, Washington, the Council, 1945.

Arbuckle, Dugald, *Teacher Counseling*, Cambridge, Mass., Addison-Wesley Press, 1950.

Association for Supervision and Curriculum Development, *Fostering Mental Health in Our Schools*, 1950 Yearbook, Washington, The National Education Association, 1950.

Baxter, Edna D., *An Approach to Guidance*, New York, Appleton-Century-Crofts, 1946.

Chisholm, Leslie L., *The Work of the Modern High School*, New York, The Macmillan Company, 1953.

Cunningham, Ruth, *et al.*, *Understanding the Behavior of Boys and Girls*, New York, Bureau of Publications, Teachers College, Columbia University, 1951.

"Education Is Guidance," *Educational Leadership*, *V*:481–548, May, 1948 (entire issue).

Faunce, Roland C., and Bossing, Nelson L., *Developing the Core Curriculum*, New York, Prentice-Hall, 1951, chap. 9.

Fedder, Ruth, *Guiding Home-Room and Club Activities*, New York, McGraw-Hill Book Company, 1949.

Hamrin, Shirley A., and Erickson, Clifford E., *Guidance in the Secondary School*, New York, D. Appleton-Century Company, 1939, chap. 1.

Johnston, Edgar G., *Administering the Guidance Program*, Minneapolis, Educational Publishers, 1942.

Johnston, Edgar G., and Faunce, Roland C., *Student Activities in Secondary Schools*, New York, The Ronald Press Company, 1952, chap. 4.

McKown, Harry C., *Home-Room Guidance*, New York, McGraw-Hill Book Company, 1934, chap. 1.

Rasey, Marie, *Toward Maturity*, New York, Hinds, Hayden & Eldridge, 1947.

Sheviakov, George, and Redl, Fritz, *Discipline for Today's Children and Youth,* Association for Supervision and Curriculum Development, Washington, The National Education Association, 1944.

Stiles, Lindley J., and Dorsey, Mattie, *Democratic Teaching in Secondary Schools,* Philadelphia, J. B. Lippincott Company, 1950.

Strang, Ruth, *Pupil Personnel and Guidance,* New York, The Macmillan Company, 1940.

··

CHAPTER 8

Pupil Records

IMPORTANCE OF RECORDS

In the preceding chapter attention was directed to the "guidance-centered" kind of instruction, which begins with the study of students' individual needs. For this kind of instruction, it has been suggested, a great deal of information is needed about individual learners. More than hunches or guesses is required if learning is to be guidance-centered. Close at hand in the teacher's room must be a growing body of information about each student. The process of studying the learner will produce data; the adaptation of learning to individual needs and abilities will demand that the data thus collected be available. A new emphasis on pupil records has resulted from needs-centered teaching. Indeed, a visitor could learn much about trends in any school by examining the kinds of pupil records that are kept there. They constitute an index of the educational goals of the school. No matter what goals the official statements of the school's philosophy may stress, the purposes that are really functioning are revealed by the kind and quantity of information collected about pupil growth. It is occasionally true that growth data are being collected on a broad base for younger students and not for upper grades, if a systematic program of personnel records has only recently been launched. It is also sometimes true that lack of time, personnel, or funds may have temporarily delayed the inauguration of a thorough program of data collection. Such delay is unfortunate, for adequate information about students is needed in the secondary school for several important purposes. Teachers need such information as they begin to work with students in terms of their needs, interests, abilities, and problems. Facts are also needed for recommendation of students to jobs or colleges. Data about pupil growth are also of significance in the evaluation of the school's program, which will be carried on continuously by an alert staff.

TYPES OF DATA NEEDED

Records of pupil growth should go back several years if trends are to be revealed. This means that the gap must be bridged between elementary and junior high school. There is little excuse for the frequent failure of secondary schools to make use of information collected in the elementary school.

The base should be broad, in harmony with the modern trend toward study of the whole child. There was a period when the secondary schools were concerned with little more than the academic skills of youngsters. An instructional program as limited as that could get along with no information beyond marks "earned" in various subjects and credits accumulated. Today's school staff seeks to know a great deal more about students because teachers are concerned with their total development. Accordingly, they need information about many aspects of growth:

1. Vital data: age, birthplace, home address, number and sex of siblings, age and occupation of parents, educational level of parents, etc.
2. School record and attendance, achievement level in academic skills
3. Health record
4. Intelligence
5. Personal-social adjustment: to peers and to older persons; in school, home, and community

6. Personal problems and fears
7. Interests and hobbies
8. Vocational goals
9. Aptitudes that may affect vocational choice
10. Participation in group activities: in neighborhood, community, and in school activities
11. Image of self: personal goals and standards
12. Insights about social, civic, and economic problems

Some suggestions of techniques for collecting information in respect to these aspects of growth were included in Chapter 7. Some of these techniques are widely used and relatively simple. The collection and filing of test scores and questionnaires, for example, pose no serious problem once the decisions are made as to which instruments are most useful and who is to keep the file. (On this last issue the modern use of carbon-copy forms may help solve the problem of how to make data available in more than one place.)

Other techniques suggested in Chapter 7 have not been widely adopted, perhaps because no one staff person has had time to interest himself in the growth of particular individuals. For example, the collection of samples of a student's work in writing and art çan be very helpful in revealing growth over a period of years, but it presents certain problems that someone must solve. The file can become burdensome in size unless materials are summarized and the originals discarded at intervals. Someone who has responsibility for the individual over a period of time must assume control of the file.

ANECDOTAL RECORDS

The anecdotal record is a useful device, both in its own right and as a means of periodic summary of other data. For various reasons the anecdote has not enjoyed general use above the elementary school level. This has been mainly due to the fact already alluded to: that a workable assignment of responsibility for individual students has not been achieved in departmentalized schools. It is a very different matter to assume responsibility for thirty pupils than for two hundred. In secondary schools where teachers have five or six classes each day, no single teacher has time to study the behavior of any individual pupil. With the development of the core program a more promising base has been provided for developing and using anecdotal records.

The anecdotal record is a written narrative of a single incident or a closely connected series of incidents that reveal significant behavior traits about the person. It differs from the case study in that it is more narrow and specific, dealing with a single episode or incident. It is different from unguided reactions of teachers to pupils in that it is objective and free from judgment, with the possible exception of the process of selecting the incident for the anecdote.

The incident selected for narration could be one that reveals either positive or negative traits of the child. It should be an incident that reflects significant behavior characteristics. Judgment or interpretation should not be included, but left instead to the reader who is to use the record. If one or two sentences of interpretation are included they are often added in a separate paragraph at the end of the anecdote.

Helen stood quiet before the principal's questions. Repeatedly she was asked to state her side of it, but she only shook her head. I was nearly certain it had not been she, but had to bide my time. When it had all been cleared up, I said to Helen: "You knew you were not to blame. Why didn't you say so?" A shrug was the major part of her answer, but after a moment she added: "What's the use of wasting my breath? No one from my block ever got anyone to listen to them and neither will I. Get it in the neck anyway." [1]

TEACHER: If you really want to move, I'll try to arrange it. Why do you want to?

[1] Marie Rasey, *Toward Maturity*, New York, Hinds, Hayden & Eldridge, 1947, p. 109.

JERRY: It's awful hard to keep from looking . . . like in spelling.

TEACHER: I haven't noticed you do that much; in fact, I've been proud of your depending on yourself. Anyway, you seemed to be so happy when you were moved to this table that I don't like to move you away, for I like you to be happy.

JERRY: Well.

TEACHER: When you feel tempted, move to another table of your own accord. Then you could come back here. Would that help?

JERRY: I think so.

TEACHER: Shall we try this for a while?

JERRY: Okeh.[2]

Often the anecdotal record is a developing, growing report consisting of a series of dated entries that add up to a better understanding of the pupil. The ASCD yearbook from which the sample anecdote was quoted has this to say about the criteria for good anecdotal records:

A criterion for recording skill is the extent to which the teacher lets the child tell his own story. A good record is one which included specific details, a wide selection of behavioral incidents, actual conversations, samples of written or other creative expression, descriptions of behavior in formal and informal situations, behavior with friends and relatives, and behavior in and out of the classroom. A good anecdotal recording is specific, factual, descriptive of what was actually seen to occur, devoid as much as possible of subjective terms. The recorder should indicate time of day, central focus of the incident, beginning, middle, and end. The data so introduced give more meaning when later interpreted for the bearing they have on one or more phases of the child's development.[3]

The chief objection to the use of anecdotal records is that the teacher is alleged to have neither the time nor the skill to develop and use them. The time would be available if the teacher were

---

[2] Association for Supervision and Curriculum Development, *Fostering Mental Health in Our Schools,* 1950 Yearbook, Washington, The National Education Association, 1950, p. 197.

[3] Helen Bieker, "Using Anecdotal Records to Know the Child," *ibid.,* p. 185.

recording anecdotes, not on two hundred students, but on fifty or sixty, and over a period of two years instead of one semester. It is probable that extensive use of this device will have to await the development of core programs or effective home rooms. Given the time, teachers can develop the skill. With some help from persons experienced in the use of anecdotal records, teachers have become highly skilled with this device.[4]

As in the case of pupils' work samples, anecdotal records can accumulate over the years until they constitute a filing problem. They should be sampled and summarized periodically by the teacher responsible for the group so that many anecdotes can be destroyed. Some that show significant stages in the pupil's development should be retained. Others may be summed up in a brief case study for the file. Care should be exercised at this point to insure that the file contains an adequate summary of significant data that will help the next teacher gain a better understanding of growth trends and overall pattern of behavior.

Teachers are finding anecdotal records helpful. Jones and Galbraith studied the use made of anecdotal records in the Plainfield, New Jersey, High School, where nearly seven hundred anecdotes were developed during a ten-week period. The study indicated that anecdotal data abstracted for inclusion in the cumulative record were more useful to teachers than marks or test scores.[5]

It has been suggested earlier that the staff member who is expected to use the data about a pupil should have the basic file in his own possession. This will usually mean that teachers who have home rooms or core classes should be furnished with locked, fire-resistant files for this purpose. There are, of course, some materials that a student should have available to him. Other materials in the file should be confidential, since no good purpose can be served by sharing them with students. This is true of anecdotal records and

[4] See American Council on Education, *Helping Teachers Understand Children,* Washington, the Council, 1945, pp. 1–41.
[5] Galen Jones and Adria Galbraith, "An Experiment With Anecdotal Records," *Guidance in Public Secondary Schools,* Educational Records Bulletin No. 28, New York, Educational Records Bureau, October, 1939, pp. 189–202.

case studies. It is generally true also of intelligence test scores, unless they are skillfully interpreted to the student. It should be possible for the teacher to lock up one set of files while at the same time he gives the student free access to his own collection of work samples, creative writing, etc.

CUMULATIVE RECORDS

The cumulative record is usually considered as confidential. It is often printed on a 9-by-12-inch cardboard folder with name exposed, within which such materials as anecdotal records, correspondence with the home, absence excuses, and test scores are filed. Lounsbury's study of 260 junior high schools revealed that 99.2 percent used cumulative record forms, which were used and added to regularly by teachers in 73 percent of the schools.[6] Segel reports that at least 30 percent of all public elementary and secondary schools in the United States make use of cumulative records.[7]

The "CA-39" form, widely used in Michigan schools, is presented here as Form 1. It is one example of a cumulative record form that is nearly state-wide in adoption. Improvements can be made in any form that is in current use.

FORM 1.

MICHIGAN CUMULATIVE RECORD FOLDER CA-39

SUGGESTIONS FOR ADDITIONAL DATA WHICH MAY BE FILED IN THIS FOLDER:

1. Correspondence with Parents.
2. Records of Home Visits, Parent Interviews, etc.
3. Records of Pupil Interviews or Counseling.
4. Anecdotal Records or Behavior Journals.
5. Diaries, Autobiographies, etc.
6. Copies of Pupil's Long-Range Course Elections.
7. Special Data on Health, Attendance, Discipline, etc.
8. Profile Sheets from Interest Inventories.
9. Personality Rating Sheets.
10. Vocational Themes, Career Booklets, etc.

RECORD OF TRANSCRIPTS SENT:

DATE	TO WHOM SENT	REASON

MEMORANDA:

[6] John H. Lounsbury, "The Role and Status of the Junior High School," unpublished doctoral dissertation, George Peabody College, Nashville, Tenn., 1954.

[7] David Segel, "Occurrence of Items in Cumulative Records in Use in the United States," *Handbook of Cumulative Records,* Bulletin 1944, No. 5, U.S. Office of Education, Federal Security Agency, Washington, 1944, p. 1.

PAGE 1

NAME _____
NO. OF CHILDREN IN FAMILY
*ECONOMIC STATUS OF THE HOME ___ GOOD ___ MODERATE ___ LOW ___ UNKNOWN
*TOTAL *BOYS *GIRLS *OLDER CHILDREN IN FAMILY *BOYS *GIRLS *YOUNGER CHILDREN IN FAMILY *BOYS *GIRLS
MALE / FEMALE
PLACE OF BIRTH
RACE ___ WHITE ___ NEGRO ___ OTHER
DATE OF BIRTH
CHURCH PREFERENCE
CODE

ELEMENTARY SCHOOL RECORD

SUBJECTS		YEAR						
	KDG.	1ST GRADE	GRADE	GRADE	GRADE	GRADE	GRADE	GRADE
ENGLISH	ARITHMETIC							
	READING							
	LANGUAGE GRAMMAR							
	HANDWRITING							
	SPELLING							
SOCIAL SCIENCE	HISTORY							
	GEOGRAPHY							
SCIENCE	GENERAL SCIENCE							
	AGRICULTURE							
	PHYSIOLOGY HYGIENE							
ARTS AND CRAFTS	HOUSEHOLD ARTS							
	INDUSTRIAL ARTS							
	ART							
	MUSIC							
DAYS PRESENT								
DAYS ABSENT								
TIMES TARDY								
REMARKS								

SECONDARY SCHOOL RECORD

7TH GRADE · 8TH GRADE · YEAR · YEAR

YEAR WEEKS IN SCHOOL YEAR SUBJECTS MARK 1ST 2ND GRADE POINTS 1ST 2ND

UNITS FOR THE YEAR
HALF DAYS ABSENT

YEAR WKS. IN SCH YR. SUBJECTS REL. PER WEEK MARK 1ST 2ND GRADE POINTS 1ST 2ND

UNITS AND POINTS FOR YEAR
UNITS AND POINTS TO DATE

PHOTOGRAPH

FAMILY DATA

	FATHER	MOTHER
NAME OF PARENTS		
HOME ADDRESS		
COUNTY OR STATE OF BIRTH		
NATIONAL DESCENT		
OCCUPATION		
LANGUAGE IN HOME		
EDUCATIONAL STATUS		
DATE NATURALIZED		
CAUSE OF DEATH		
STEPPARENT		
GUARDIAN		
MARITAL STATUS WITH WHOM DOES CHILD RESIDE		

GRADUATION DATE
NO. IN CLASS
RANK IN CLASS

GRADUATION FROM SENIOR HIGH SCHOOL

DATE TAKEN AGE GRADE
NAME OR SIGNATURE OF HIGH SCHOOL PRINCIPAL
NO. OF RANKS COURSE COMPLETED

CODE FOR BIRTH INFORMATION — CERTIFIED COPY OF BIRTH CERTIFICATE ... BC CHURCH RECORD ... CR FAMILY BIB. ... FB SCHOOL RECORD ... SR PASSPORT ... P PARENT'S STATEMENT ... PS LIFE INSURANCE POLICY ... LI IMMIGRATION CERTIFICATE ... IC

* RECORD IN PENCIL

CONSECUTIVE ADDRESSES AND SCHOOLS ATTENDED

DIST. NO.	TOWNSHIP, VILLAGE OR CITY	COUNTY	DATE ENTERED	DATE LEFT	CODE

EXTRA CURRICULAR ACTIVITIES

	EL.	EL.	7	8	9	10	11	12	PG

INTELLIGENCE TESTS

DATE	GRADE			C. A.	M. A.	I. Q.

ACHIEVEMENT TESTS

DATE	GRADE			C. A.	SCORE	NORM.

INTEREST AND APTITUDE TESTS

DATE	GRADE			C. A.	RAW SCORE	COM. SCORE

HEALTH APPRAISAL—AS RECOMMENDED BY MICHIGAN DEPARTMENT OF HEALTH

CHECK—GIVING
DIPHTHERIA   SCARLET FEVER   MEASLES   WHOOPING COUGH   CHICKEN POX

YEAR OF SICKNESS
MUMPS   SMALLPOX   TYPHOID   FREQUENT COLDS   TONSILITIS

WHEN POSSIBLE
PNEUMONIA   T. B. (FORM)   OTHERS

DATE	GRADE	HEIGHT	WEIGHT	HEARING R.	HEARING L.	VISION R.	VISION L.	EYES	EARS	NOSE	ORAL HYGIENE	OCCLUSION	DECIDUOUS TEETH	PERMANENT TEETH	TONSILS	LYMPH GLANDS	THYROID	HEART	LUNGS	SKIN	NUTRITION	POSTURE	ORTHOPEDIC DEFECTS	NERVOUS SYMPTOMS	SPEECH	OTHER DEFECTS	EXAMINER

CODE   O—NORMAL   OO—CORRECTED DEFECTS   X—TO BE WATCHED   XX—NEEDS MEDICAL ATTENTION   X X X—NEEDS IMMEDIATE ATTENTION
CIRCLE THE X, XX, OR XXX WHEN THE CONDITION IS CORRECTED

REMARKS:—(EXPLAIN ALL DEFECTS NOT COVERED BY CODE)

DATE

IMMUNIZING AND DIAGNOSTIC PROCEDURES RECORD—FOR RESULT INDICATE POSITIVE (+) OR NEGATIVE (—)

YEAR AND RESULT	DIPHTHERIA	SMALLPOX	WHOOPING COUGH	T. B. TESTS	X-RAY	RESULT OF X-RAY

GR.	EDUCATIONAL PLANS	VOCATIONAL PLANS	INTERESTS AND HOBBIES	SPECIAL TALENTS		
7						
8						
9						
10						
11						
12						
PG						

CODE FOR REASON FOR LEAVING SCHOOL
TR—TRANSFERRED   OA—OVER LEGAL AGE   D—DEAD
EP—EMPLOYMENT PERMIT   UA—UNDER LEGAL AGE   M—MARRIED
PI—PERMANENT ILLNESS   INST—INSTITUTION

	SPECIAL RECOGNITION	GR.
		7
		8
		9
		10
		11
		12
		PG

NAME _____ MARRIED NAME _____ ADDRESS _____

EDUCATIONAL FOLLOW-UP RECORD

DATE	NAME OF INSTITUTION	COURSE OF STUDY	REPORTED PROGRESS

EMPLOYMENT RECORD (WHILE ATTENDING SCHOOL AND AFTER LEAVING SCHOOL)

GRADE IF IN SCHOOL	AGE	YEAR	LENGTH OF JOB	NAME AND ADDRESS OF EMPLOYER	TYPE OF WORK	WAGES OR SALARY	REMARKS

OTHER SIGNIFICANT EXPERIENCES

OTHER WORK EXPERIENCES

YEAR	TYPE OF WORK	TIME SPENT

HOME DUTIES

YEAR	TYPE OF DUTY	YEAR

EXCEPTIONAL EXPERIENCES (TRAVEL, ETC.)

YEAR	PLACES, ETC.

Another form adopted for state-wide use is the "Cumulative Record" for California junior and senior high schools. The form contains fifty-two headings and was adopted by the Association of California School Principals after a study of the items needed in a cumulative record form. A manual of instruction for its use was also distributed to secondary schools of California.

Other states also have developed their own cumulative records that differ in number or title of the headings from the forms used elsewhere. A nationally recommended cumulative record form was developed by a committee of the National Association of Secondary School Principals. It devotes less space to anecdotal entries and more space to achievement records. A thirteen-year cumulative form has also been prepared by the Association for Supervision and Curriculum Development of the National Education Association.

A local school faculty should examine and compare various cumulative record forms in order to decide whether to adopt one of those available or develop their own. The cumulative record is too useful a device to neglect. Teachers who wish to develop instructional programs that are guidance-centered will need some version of the cumulative record.

DEVELOPMENTAL RECORD

In some schools the cumulative record assumes the form of a book, sometimes thirty to forty pages long, within which is space for the periodic summaries of anecdotal records. The records are filed temporarily inside the book until the summaries are made. This "developmental record" accompanies the pupil from kindergarten through the twelfth grade.

The Ann Arbor, Michigan, developmental record book is kept at the secondary level by home-room teachers. It is simply titled "Cumulative Personal Data Form." The covers of the book resemble the cumulative record form included earlier, in that they are of heavy cardboard with exposed flap for name, address, and

I.Q. Inside are such headings as Family Data, Schools Attended, Intelligence Test Data, Personality Test Data, Interest Inventory Data, Vocational Aptitude Test Data, and Secondary School Achievement Test Data. On the back cover are the following headings: Extra-curricular Activities, Vocational Plans, Educational Plans, Employment Record. The front cover is used for instructions to teachers, with a separate mimeographed manual expanding these instructions. The outside covers are reproduced as Form 2.

Inside the covers appear the forms presented as Forms 3, 4, 5, and 6, titled "Health Record," "Elementary School Achievement Test Data," and "Elementary School Classification Record."

The rest of the twenty-two pages of the book are used for a "Developmental Record," with a page of instructions to teachers. These instructions begin as follows:

The remaining space in this booklet is devoted to a developmental record of the child. The developmental record is a very essential part of the total data about the child's growth and his progress through school. Its special contribution is that of describing the wholeness of his changing personality; this by contrast with the more specific types of information such as test scores, club memberships, or illnesses which are recorded elsewhere. As a record of personality growth it has value and meaning for every child, however normal his development may be. The bases on which the record is to be kept are as follows:

1. At least once each year it is required that a summary paragraph concerning the child's current adjustment and his progress during the period be written by the teacher.
2. Each teacher is urged to accumulate in the developmental record during the year brief, descriptive anecdotes for each child in his group. Further suggestions appear below regarding this procedure.
3. Each teacher who does not accumulate descriptive anecdotes or incidents about all the children in his group is expected to do so at least for those pupils who in his judgment deviate significantly from "normal." [8]

[8] Published by permission of the Ann Arbor Public Schools.

FORM 2.

Cumulative Personal Data Form
Grades K to 12

SUGGESTIONS TO GUIDE TEACHERS IN KEEPING THIS RECORD

I. Census and

II. Family Data, p. 2
1. Page 2 should be filled in at the time of the child's entrance to school. Annually, each teacher should bring this page up to date. Certain items are recorded in pencil because they change from time to time. All other entries are in ink.
2. Intelligence quotient, page 2, should be the latest one given on page 23. The actual intelligence quotient should be preceded by the number "18" to disguise it.

III. Schools Attended, p. 2

IV. Health Record, pp. 3 and 4
1. Teacher's Health Observations are recorded during the year by entering check (√) marks.
2. Absence Record is kept by writing in the current grade placement of the child and his absence record for the year.

V. Elementary School Achievement Test Data, p. 5
1. Entries should be made each time an achievement test is given. Include results from all tests, individual as well as group.
2. The column "Composite" should contain the composite score computed from results of all tests given at any one time. A bracket should be used to combine the names of those tests which have been used for securing the composite score. For example, if a Gates Reading, a Woody-McCall Arithmetic and an Iowa Spelling Test are all given at one time, those names in column one should be bracketed and the composite grade level score should be entered on a line with the last named test. If, however, a battery is given, such as Progressive Achievement, all scores, including the composite score, may be entered on the same line across the page.
3. The column "Achievement Ratio" should be computed for the entire battery of tests given at one time. The achievement ratio is found by dividing age level by mental age.

VI. Elementary School Classification Record, p. 6
1. An entry is made at each time of regular promotion, semi-annual or annual.
2. Some children may have additional entries. This would happen when re-classification occurs within the year. In this case the column "Remarks" should contain a statement of the reason for re-classification. There should also be entered here explanation at other times of any special conditions relating to classification decisions.

VII. Developmental Record, pp. 7 to 22
Suggestions are given on page 7.

VIII. Intelligence Test Data, p. 23
1. Group or individual test scores are entered here.
2. The teacher should request a summarizing statement from the examiner whenever an individual test is given. Significant notes should be entered.

IX. Personality Test Data, p. 23

X. Interest Inventory Test Data, p. 23

XI. Vocational Aptitude Test Data, p. 23
Equally important with test scores are the interpretations. In some instances a fuller statement than the space provided for interpretive remarks should be prepared and included in the folder.

XII. Secondary School Achievement Test Data, p. 23
1. The school should provide a routine so that test results are forwarded to the teacher who keeps this record.
2. Because age and grade level scores are decreasingly useful in the secondary school grades, rank in group or percentile rank are better comparative indices.

XIII. Extra-Curricular Activities, p. 24

XIV. Interests and Activities, p. 24

XV. Vocational Plans, p. 24

XVI. Educational Plans, p. 24
1. Entries in the junior high school grades are significant even though they are deemed not to be lasting choices.
2. If more extended remarks are desirable than space allows, they should be made and enclosed in the folder.
3. The participation of parents in the making of these plans is an important phase of the record.

XVII. Employment Record, p. 24
Discretion will have to be exercised in deciding to enter the odd-jobs type of employment especially peculiar to earlier years.

XVIII. Post-School Record, p. 1

By permission of The Riegle Press, Flint, Michigan.

XVIII. POST-SCHOOL RECORD

DATE OF LEAVING	IF GRADUATED, WHAT CURRICULUM?	IF NON-GRADUATE, WHAT GRADE?	TO WHAT COLLEGE OR SCHOOL?	TO WHAT JOB OR ACTIVITY?

FURTHER FOLLOW-UP DATA:

I. NAME | DATE OF BIRTH | PLACE OF BIRTH | ADDRESS (PENCIL) | SEX | COLOR | PHONE (PENCIL) | I. Q.: (PENCIL) DATE: (PENCIL)

II. FAMILY DATA

	MOTHER	FATHER
NAMES OF PARENTS		
COUNTRY OR STATE OF BIRTH		
NATIONAL DESCENT		
OCCUPATION — DATE		
PLACE OF OCCUPATION		
OCCUPATION — DATE		
PLACE OF OCCUPATION		
OCCUPATION — DATE		
PLACE OF OCCUPATION		
OCCUPATION — DATE		
PLACE OF OCCUPATION		
OCCUPATION — DATE		
PLACE OF OCCUPATION		
LANGUAGE IN HOME		
EDUCATION (LEVEL ATTAINED)		
DATE NATURALIZED		
DATE OF BIRTH (OPTIONAL OR APPROX.)		
DATE & CAUSE OF DEATH		
STEP PARENT (CHECK)		
GUARDIAN		
MARITAL STATUS		
WITH WHOM CHILD LIVES		

SIBLINGS

NAME	BIRTH DATE	REMARKS: SCHOOL, PERSONALITY, OCCUPATION, ETC.

OTHERS LIVING IN THE HOME

NAME	AGE (APPROX.)	REMARKS: RELATION, OCCUPATION, ETC.

HOME ENVIRONMENT

DATE	FAMILY RELATIONSHIPS, ECONOMIC STATUS, ADEQUACY OF DWELLING

III. SCHOOLS ATTENDED

TOWNSHIP, VILLAGE OR CITY	DATE ENTERED	DATE LEFT	REASONS FOR LEAVING

VIII. INTELLIGENCE TEST DATA

DATE	NAME OF TEST	C. A.	M. A.	RAW SCORE	I. Q.	NOTES	EXAMINER

IX. PERSONALITY TEST DATA

DATE	NAME OF TEST	PARTS OF TEST AND SCORES FOR EACH										INTERPRETIVE REMARKS	EXAMINER
		I	II	III	IV	V	VI	VII	VIII	IX	X		

X. INTEREST INVENTORY DATA

DATE	NAME OF TEST	WEIGHTED SCORE	SCORE	NORM	RANK IN GROUP	REMARKS

XI. VOCATIONAL APTITUDE TEST DATA

DATE	NAME OF TEST	WEIGHTED SCORE	REMARKS

XII. SECONDARY SCHOOL ACHIEVEMENT TEST DATA

ENGLISH

NAME OF TEST	DATE	GRADE	SCORE	NORM	RANK IN GROUP

OTHER TESTS

MATHEMATICS

NAME OF TEST	DATE	GRADE	SCORE	NORM	RANK IN GROUP

OTHER TESTS

XIII. EXTRA-CURRICULAR ACTIVITIES

GRADES	COMMITTEES; SPORTS; CLUBS; DRAMATICS; FORENSICS; OFFICES HELD; OUTSIDE ORGANIZATIONS. HONORS AND AWARDS. ETC.
EL	
EL	
EL	
7	
8	
9	
10	
11	
12	

XIV. INTERESTS AND ACTIVITIES

GRADES	HOBBIES; SKILLS; TALENTS; HOME DUTIES; CAMP; TRAVEL; OUTSTANDING ACCOMPLISHMENTS. ETC.
EL	
EL	
EL	
7	
8	
9	
10	
11	
12	

XV. VOCATIONAL PLANS

GRADE	VOCATIONAL CHOICE	REMARKS; EVIDENT APTITUDES; RELATED EXPERIENCES; NEEDED TESTING OR COUNSELLING; REASON FOR CHOICE; ETC.

XVI. EDUCATIONAL PLANS

GRADE	CURRICULUM CHOICE	REMARKS; BASIS OF CHOICE; EVIDENT APTITUDES; NEEDED TESTING OR COUNSELLING; WHAT SCHOOL AFTER HIGH SCHOOL?; ETC.

XVII. EMPLOYMENT RECORD

AGE	YEAR	DURATION OF JOB	NAME AND ADDRESS OF EMPLOYER	TYPE OF WORK	WAGES	REMARKS

FORM 3.

IV. HEALTH RECORD

DEFECTS	TEACHER'S HEALTH OBSERVATIONS GRADE															ABSENCE RECORD—(HALF DAYS)			
	N	N	K	1	2	3	4	5	6	7	8	9	10	11	12	GRADE (GIVE NO.)	TOTAL ABSENCE	ABSENCE FOR ILLNESS	ABSENCE FOR OTHER CAUSES
EYES																			
Styes or Crusted Lids																			
Inflamed Eyes																			
Crossed Eyes																			
Frequent Headaches																			
Squinting																			
EARS																			
Discharge from Ears																			
Earaches																			
Fails to Hear Questions																			
TEETH—Need Care																			
GENERAL CONDITION																			
Very Thin																			
Very Fat																			
Does Not Appear Well																			
Tires Easily																DATE		TEACHER'S REMARKS	
Poor Muscle Coordination																			
Bad Posture																			
BEHAVIOR SYMPTOMS																			
Emotional Disturbances																			
Speech Defect																			
Twitching Movements																			
Nervousness																			
Unduly Restless																			
Nail Biting																			
Excessive Use of Toilet																			
Poor Sleep Habits																			
Poor Food Habits																			

Courtesy of Mr. Russell West, Assistant Superintendent of Schools, Ann Arbor, Michigan.

177

HEALTH RECORD

TESTS AND MEASUREMENTS

DATE	GRADE	HEIGHT	WEIGHT	VISION RT.	VISION LT.	HEARING RT.	HEARING LT.

PREVIOUS ILLNESSES

	AGE		AGE
MEASLES		HEART DISEASE	
MUMPS		OTHERS (SPECIFY)	
CHICKEN POX			
WHOOPING COUGH			
GERMAN MEASLES			
SCARLET FEVER			
RHEUMATIC FEVER			

DISEASE PROTECTION

	DATE
DIPHTHERIA	
SMALL POX	
TETANUS	
WHOOPING COUGH	
TYPHOID FEVER	
DATE	

TUBERCULOSIS HISTORY

CONTACT WITH KNOWN TBC?	
TUBERCULIN SKIN TEST?	
X-RAY OF CHEST?	

PHYSICIAN'S RECOMMENDATIONS

NURSE'S REPORTS

DATE	

V. ELEMENTARY SCHOOL ACHIEVEMENT TEST DATA

NAME OF TEST	DATE	GRADE	GRADE LEVEL SCORES											ACHIEVEMENT RATIO
			READING		ARITHMETIC		LANGUAGE				OTHERS	COMPOSITE		
			PARTS	AV.	PARTS	AV.	SP.	PEN.	AV.					

Courtesy of Mr. Russell West, Assistant Superintendent of Schools, Ann Arbor, Michigan.

179

VI. ELEMENTARY SCHOOL CLASSIFICATION RECORD

DATE	GRADE	SCHOOL	TEACHER	PRINCIPAL	REMARKS

The instruction page continues with suggestions for writing (1) summary statements about children at the end of each year or at any time when a pupil is about to transfer, and (2) anecdotes. The remaining fifteen pages are reserved for entering these summaries and anecdotal records throughout the thirteen years of the child's school life. The summaries are set aside from the anecdotal entries by the word "Summary" in the date column. (All entries are dated.)

This developmental record has been found useful and effective in the Ann Arbor Schools.

MARKS

One major purpose of personnel records is to provide descriptive information for future employers or college registrars. For this use there has been much dependence on the marks the student has attained in various classes. Indeed, at the time of recommendation some schools have very little in their files but marks and attendance data. The chief reason why symbol marking is retained in high schools is that administrators and teachers have assumed that marks are needed by colleges and employers. It is ironic that symbol marks, on which such dependence has been placed, should be such notoriously poor predictors of success in life or in employment. For college admission purposes, marks are a somewhat more reliable guide, but even here the best that can be said of them is that they are better than nothing. The so-called registrar's rating, largely based on grade point average earned in high school, is a better predictor of college success than the pattern of subjects pursued in high school. This, however, is faint praise indeed, since the patterns of subjects have been shown to bear little relationship to success in college.

The facts are that symbol marks are invalid (in that they do not measure what they purpose to measure), are unreliable (in that they do not agree and cannot be compared), and are nondescriptive (in that they convey no useful information about the person marked). Wrinkle, after citing various research studies showing that symbol marks cannot be compared, lists the following fallacies about marks:

FALLACIES ABOUT SYMBOL MARKS

1. Anyone can tell from the mark assigned what the student's level of achievement is or what progress he has made.
2. A student can achieve any mark he wishes if he is willing to make the effort.
3. The student's success in his after-school life compares favorably with his success in school.
4. The student's mark is comparable to the worker's pay check.
5. The competitive marking system provides a worthwhile and justifiable introduction to competitive adult life.
6. School marks can be used as a means to an end without their becoming thought of by students as ends in themselves.[9]

Basically, the inability of marks to serve the various functions which they are supposed to serve lies in the fact that they do not represent fixed values in terms of which they may be interpreted. The assumption that you or I or anyone else, except the person who gives a mark, can look at it and tell with any degree of accuracy what it means is the No. 1 fallacy involved in the conventional marking system.[10]

The employer who wishes to know the degree of skill in typing attained by a candidate will find his actual achievement in typing more helpful than his marks in typing class. Similarly, the data most needed by a college admissions office are descriptive and specific records of skills and of behavior in situations comparable to those encountered in college. These records can be collected and ways can be found to summarize them for the use of the college counselors. The only persons who have the opportunity to collect, analyze, and sum up these kinds of information about a student

[9] William L. Wrinkle, *Improving Marking and Reporting Practices* in *Elementary and Secondary Schools*, New York, Rinehart & Company, 1947, pp. 36–49.
[10] *Ibid.*, p. 35.

are the teachers who have worked with him in high school. Better ways must be found than marks given in various subjects to describe a student and to predict his probable future adjustment.

PREDICTIONS OF ADJUSTMENT

One high school faculty developed a series of forms to be used in making predictions of post-school success. Teachers could estimate on these forms the degree of "adjustment skills" and abilities that a student had developed in each class and file these estimates with the counselor.

The latter could then summarize the estimate and fill out a summary of them in connection with the student's application for college. The "adjustment skills" form included such items as the following:

1. Social adjustment and acceptability:
    To others own age
    To adults and adult society
    To authority
    To social responsibility. Respect for property
2. Health adjustments (Care of self):
    Physical
    Mental
    Emotional
3. Adjustments to work habits and procedures:
    Attendance
    Punctuality
    Problem solving
    Initiative, self-control, self-appraisal
4. Adjustment to the home situation:
    To stability of residence
    To socioeconomic conditions
    To general conditions
5. Adjustment to a purpose of life (philosophy)

Opposite each skill the teacher was asked to check such columns as "highly successful," "generally good," "has difficulties," "serious trouble," "no basis for prediction." There was also a column for exploration of deviation in the student's behavior.

The form for evaluation of abilities included the following items:

Intellectual
    Creativeness
    Intellectual curiosity
    Inquiring mind
    Ability to appraise and to use evidence
    Independent thinking
    Faces facts and situations objectively, open-mindedly

Physical aptitude
    Physical skill
    Energy output
    Stamina

Special abilities
    Ability to organize
    Leadership—ability to influence others
    Sense of humor—proportion

Teachers rated these abilities on a conventional scale of superior, above average, average, below average, very limited.

The application for college admission, based on these estimates of adjustment skills and abilities plus test data and other materials in the cumulative record file, included a series of columns headed: "On the basis of work done in this course, the student should do college work in the area indicated." The separate columns were then headed "with distinction," "very well," "with passing grades only," "with serious difficulty," "should not attempt college work." Columns for grade level of each class, number of units, and explanation of any deviations in the student's program of work completed the application form.

Over one hundred college admissions officers reacted to this form with enthusiastic acceptance. It was their judgment that the "prediction" forms offered them more data about students than the conventional credit transcript. It appears probable that some such device would be useful as interpretation of the traditional marks, if not as a replacement for them.

MARKS MAY HINDER INSTRUCTIONAL IMPROVEMENT

Employers and college admissions officers are looking for more descriptive data about candidates than are afforded by symbol marks. This is one excellent reason for developing "something better" than marking systems. But there are other reasons, too. The following comparison of instructional goals and marks may sharpen the need for developing better evaluative devices:

THE MODERN SCHOOL SEEKS:	SYMBOL MARKING TENDS:
To teach skills of cooperative planning	To encourage competition
To teach skills of self and group appraisal	To place evaluative responsibility solely on the teacher
To help students to adjust more successfully to their peers	To erect barriers between peers
To provide a well-rounded learning experience	To place undue emphasis on subject mastery
To make evaluations continuously, as a part of group planning	To emphasize terminal evaluation
To help students to grow from where they are	To force all to meet minimum standards, or quit
To provide learning experiences deriving from the intrinsic needs and desires of the learner	To serve as an extrinsic motivation, thus helping to perpetuate poor teaching.[11]

It appears that the use of symbol marks not only fails to provide valid evidence about pupil growth, but also interposes certain

[11] Adapted from Roland C. Faunce and Nelson L. Bossing, *Developing the Core Curriculum,* New York, Prentice-Hall, 1951, pp. 282–283. Reprinted by permission of the publisher.

obstacles to the improvement of instruction. The traditional system of A-B-C-D-E-marks lies close to the roots of those things that are wrong with secondary education. Symbol marking supports (and in turn is supported by) the outmoded concept of absolute grade standards, the concept of mastery for its own sake, the ideas of extrinsic reward and punishment as a means of motivating individual effort. It is tragic that the concept of marks has become so well established in our secondary schools that teachers (and students) cannot visualize any other motive for effort than getting a mark. It is even argued that marking based on effort is unfair to the student of higher ability who needs to make no effort in order to surpass the achievement of his peers. Thus the use of absolute achievement standards becomes justified in order to spare the superior group from having to make an effort!

In spite of much study and discussion that have been devoted to the problem of our inadequate marking system, it is still generally with us at the secondary level. This is probably due to the fact that we have thus far failed to develop a method that parents, students, and teachers agree is better than symbol marks. Even the "predictions of adjustment" forms described earlier were not adopted for use by the faculty that developed them.[12]

CHECK LISTS

In recent years, however, some promising devices have gained favor as supplements to the marking system. As these methods prove successful and are extended, it may become possible to rely less and less on marks as a means of reporting growth. One such device is the descriptive report or check list. Widely used in elementary schools, the check-list report has recently gained many adherents in the junior high school. Senior high school use of the check list is chiefly as a "citizenship" supplement to the academic marks.

---

[12] Similar techniques have been used in a few high schools, chiefly laboratory schools connected with universities.

The check list is usually composed of specific behavior traits or skills, with a space for comments by teachers and parents. Such items as "command of numbers," "growth in vocabulary," "improvement in writing," "working in a group," "courtesy toward others," "being able to direct his own activities," are characteristic of the check-list type of home report. To the extent that it is specific and descriptive, the check list represents an improvement over symbol marks. Even the check list, however, is an impersonal device that provides no direct contact with parents in the reporting process. Its descriptive power is limited also by the ingenuity of those who select items for inclusion in the check list.

LETTERS TO PARENTS

Some secondary schools have begun to use personal letters to the parents as a means of reporting growth. The letter has certain important advantages over the check list. It is more direct and informal, and it encourages a direct reply. It is considerably more descriptive and offers an opportunity to include anecdotal data. The letter device also provides more scope for describing and interpreting the work of the class. An example of a teacher's report by letter is as follows:

DEAR MR. AND MRS. JONES:

Since my last letter to you, Mary has made some important gains which will interest you. She has made improvement in her silent reading rate, as our last test shows. Her art work and penmanship are both improving. I know you have seen the design she made for her group mural during the unit on transportation.

As a result of a suggestion you made in your last letter, we managed for her group to put on a play about safety last Friday. Mary was active in all the arrangements, and actually took a part herself in the play. She did the part fairly well and we were all encouraged to see this effort on her part to overcome her shyness.

If it is possible for her to entertain her friends occasionally at home, I think this will help to give Mary additional poise.

I am glad the dental appointment is almost due. She complained of pain in her tooth yesterday.

In summary, Mary is making good progress.

If you could manage to visit the room the last hour next Tuesday you'd see her in action as a Teachers' Aide. She performs this responsibility very well.

Most sincerely,[13]

Other examples of letters to parents are much longer than this one, and more descriptive of the work of the class. In some schools the various teachers for a given student forward to the core teacher their notes on the student's recent progress, which are then all incorporated in one letter by the core teacher. Two examples of such summary letters to parents are included in a handbook published and distributed at Ohio State University School.[14] One of the letters begins with an explanation of how often such a letter may be expected, and includes several pages of description of procedures and recent achievements of classes in core, English workshop, home arts, American history, and physical education. Each section describes the role played by the student with whom the letter is concerned and reports his actual participation, achievements, and growth in such areas as oral and written language, discussion, social adjustment, reading, craft activities, interests, attitudes, and physical skills. The letters thus constitute a rather complete report of the growth of the student, and an interpretation also of the school's program to the parents.

The letter is vastly more descriptive than symbol marks. It need not involve the comparison with other students implied by marks. Instead it enables both teachers and parents to look at each student

[13] J. W. Menge and Roland C. Faunce, *Working Together for Better Schools,* New York, American Book Company, 1953, p. 107.

[14] *A Handbook for University School Parents,* College of Education, Ohio State University, Columbus, Ohio, 1954.

as a unique individual, to appraise his strengths, and to invite coöperation in overcoming any weaknesses. It is a channel also for two-way communication between teachers and parents. Continued use of letters will usually result in visits to the school by parents.

The use of letters has not become widespread in secondary schools because of their departmentalized character. A teacher can hardly give serious consideration to writing letters to parents of 150 to 200 different students in his classes. It is possible, however, for the core or home-room teacher to be responsible for collecting data from other teachers and writing such letters for thirty or thirty-five students in his section once each semester. The provision of stenographic help, either from the school office or from senior shorthand classes, will greatly facilitate the task. Dictaphone machines are also a possibility. Schools might well set aside school time for this purpose. It is at least as useful as other clerical tasks connected with closing a semester, for which time is allowed in many schools.

It is important that time be spent in helping a faculty learn how to write effective letters to parents. In some schools a period is set aside during preschool conferences for this purpose. Parents have been brought in to help develop criteria for effective letters.

Students should be encouraged to write letters to their parents, too. Such letters can consist of reports of recent group activities in a class, evaluation of the student's own role in these activities, and estimates of his recent progress in terms of goals he has helped establish for himself. Such student letters are not a substitute for letters from teachers, but rather a supplement to them. They provide an excellent motive for self-appraisal by students.

PARENT-TEACHER CONFERENCES

Perhaps the most effective reporting device of all is the conference between one teacher and the parent or parents of each student. This device has been widely used in elementary schools for many years. Recently it has been adopted by junior and senior high schools, usually as a supplement to the marking system. In some schools the parent-teacher conference is used as a substitute for one of the three marking periods each semester.

Most schools set up the schedule of conferences after school or in the evening. Some schools dismiss early on conference days. A few schools close for an entire day and bring parents in by school bus for the conferences and other activities.

The core or home-room teacher may be chiefly responsible for arranging the schedule of conferences, with special teachers also available in their rooms. Special teachers may also supply information to the core teacher on regularly used report forms. A committee of teachers and parents may serve as guides and receptionists on conference day. In one high school a committee of parents sent out the letter of invitation to the conference,[15] including in it a request for nominations for the committee for the coming year:

DEAR PARENTS:

We hope that you have already made arrangements to visit the Wayne High School next Tuesday or Wednesday for a conference with your son's or daughter's teachers. We of the Parents Committee feel that this is a worth-while project and we trust that every parent will make an appointment for the conference.

Members of the Parents Committee will be at the high school during the entire conference period. We hope to be able to talk with you and learn your suggestions for improving the program of the high school. We also ask you to suggest one or two individuals whom you consider educational leaders in this community who could work on a committee with the high school staff to make the plans for improvement. A new high school parent steering committee will be selected from the suggested list.

Will you please fill out the lower part of this page and bring it with you to the parent-teacher conference?

(Signed by members of Parents Committee)

---

[15] Faunce and Bossing, *op. cit.*, p. 295.

List suggestions for
improvement:

List names for new committee
members:

....

....

....

....

....

....

....

....

Over three-fourths of parents in this school attended parent conferences. Participation in other schools has approached 100 percent. Teachers and parents report the following advantages they see in the parent-teacher conference:

1. The parent-teacher conference provides the opportunity for a clear, descriptive report of pupil progress.
2. It brings teachers and parents into contact, and provides a chance for them to get better acquainted.
3. It encourages parents to ask questions and get satisfactory answers.
4. It permits reporting to be made on the basis of the individual's own development in terms of his own potential, instead of forcing automatic comparisons with other pupils.
5. It enables teachers to find out more about their pupils.
6. It strengthens the school-home tie, and thus makes a significant contribution to "public relations."
7. It challenges the teachers to do real evaluation. One cannot effectively participate in such conferences without first knowing something about pupils.[16]

The last point mentioned above is a significant one, to judge by the frequency with which teachers mention it. They report that they would be reluctant to enter in such conferences without feeling reinforced by having a considerable amount of data about pupils—data that can be made understandable to parents. The approaching conference is thus a direct challenge to teachers to accumulate facts about the development of their students. The marking system presents no such challenge because marks do not

[16] *Ibid*, p. 296.

have to be based on facts—and cannot usually be reliably interpreted.

The Glencoe, Illinois, *Bulletin on Preparation for the Conference* suggests seventeen questions that teachers should seek to answer about pupils in preparing for an interview with a parent. It then suggests that teachers enrich the cumulative record by adding the results of the parent conference to it, immediately following the interview.

Trytten has described the preparations for parent conferences in the University High School of Ann Arbor, Michigan:

> The homeroom teacher . . . schedules the interviews, each with the parents of his group, about thirty in number. The homeroom teacher in the University High School system continues with his group until they graduate and so, through successive years of observation and continuous home and school contact, he becomes acquainted with the pupil, his family, and his developmental history. These accumulated resources made the homeroom teacher the logical person to represent the school in these conferences and the arrangement reduced the interviews to a workable number.
>
> The homeroom teachers were briefed by the other teachers in several ways. Continuous, informal reporting by all school personnel is standard practice. This reporting may be oral or written. These reports cover observations of significant achievement, behavior, or attitudes. Thus, preceding the conferences, the homeroom teacher met with all of the teachers of his grade and got an over-all picture of each pupil, supported by oral observations, and also by check-sheets available from most of the teachers.[17]

A general form of the check-sheets used by teachers in reporting progress to the home-room teacher is reproduced here as Form 7. Forms 8, 9, and 10 are examples of more specialized check sheets developed for the same purpose by some departments of the University High School staff.

[17] John M. Trytten, "Parents Like the Conference Plan," *Bulletin of the Michigan Secondary School Association,* XVI:3, March, 1952, p. 18.

```
                    UNIVERSITY HIGH SCHOOL
                      Ann Arbor, Michigan
Report on_____for period ending_____
To_____From_____Class_____
     Homeroom Teacher

Comments:




On the whole, (his) (her) achievement to date in this class entitles
(him) (her) to a mark of:
              A    B    C    D    E
```

Courtesy of Dr. John M. Trytten, University of Michigan.

The conferences in this high school were scheduled during two school days reserved for them each semester. Any classroom teacher could be included in a given conference at the request of a parent or a home-room teacher. In summing up the advantages of the plan, Trytten reports:

1. Communication was established with more parents than by any other activity—94 percent of all parents of the six grades.
2. The parents expressed almost unanimous appreciation of the procedure. About 85 percent of the parents returned for the second series of conferences.

FORM 8.

```
┌─────────────────────────────────────────────────────────────────┐
│                     UNIVERSITY HIGH SCHOOL                        │
│                       Ann Arbor, Michigan                         │
│                                                                   │
│ Report on_____for period ending_____   │
│                                                                   │
│ To_____From_____Class: Chemistry     │
│       Homeroom Teacher                                            │
├─────────────────────────────────────────────────────────────────┤
│                                          Low    Average    High   │
│  1.  Functional understanding of                                  │
│      basic chemical concepts          _____   │
│                                                                   │
│  2.  Ability to solve problems                                    │
│      using ideas                      _____   │
│                                                                   │
│  3.  Skill in laboratory techniques   _____   │
│                                                                   │
│  4.  Skill in reporting results of                                │
│      laboratory experiences           _____   │
│                                                                   │
│  5.  Reading thoroughness and compre-                             │
│      hension                          _____   │
│                                                                   │
│  6.  Ability to solve problems                                    │
│      using numbers                    _____   │
│                                                                   │
│  Comments:                                                        │
│                                                                   │
│                                                                   │
├─────────────────────────────────────────────────────────────────┤
│  On the whole, (his) (her) achievement to date in this class      │
│  entitles (him) (her) to a mark of:                               │
│                          A   B   C   D   E                        │
└─────────────────────────────────────────────────────────────────┘
```

Courtesy of Dr. John M. Trytten, University of Michigan.

3. The homeroom teachers, without exception, said that the conferences had been very valuable, though strenuous.
4. The teachers made every effort to define their objectives and to observe behavior in order that their comments might be valid and specific enough to be helpful.[18]

It seems clear that teachers must do careful planning for conferences with parents. They do not always know how to present

[18] *Ibid.,* p. 18.

FORM 9.

UNIVERSITY HIGH SCHOOL
Ann Arbor, Michigan

Report on_____for period ending_____

To_____ From_____ Class: __Spanish__
    Homeroom Teacher

	Needs attention	Average	Outstanding
Elements affecting grade directly:			
1. Skill in speaking Spanish			
2. Understanding spoken Spanish			
3. Skill in reading Spanish			
4. Skill in writing Spanish			
5. Knowledge and understanding of Spanish peoples, customs, and countries			
6. Application beyond minimum requirements			
Elements affecting grade indirectly:			
7. Effective use of class period			
8. Homework done carefully and promptly			
9. Regular attendance at classes			

On the whole, (his) (her) achievement to date in this class entitles (him) (her) to a mark of:

        A   B   C   D   E

Courtesy of Dr. John M. Trytten, University of Michigan.

FORM 10.

UNIVERSITY HIGH SCHOOL
Ann Arbor, Michigan

Report on_____for period ending_____

To_____From_____Class: <u>American History</u>
   Homeroom Teacher

Course objectives: Understanding and appreciation of our democratic heritage; of the major social and economic trends in American History; of the role of government in a democracy; of the responsibilities and the rights of the individual in a democracy; and of how and why the democratic way of life should be maintained and strengthened.	Consistently outstanding work	Consistently good achievement	At times above average	Average	Performance often below average	No evidence of effort or ability
1. Pupil's achievement to date in so far as the above objectives are concerned						
Acquisition of skills:						
2. Memorization of factual information						
3. Integration of factual information						
4. Reporting – oral and writing						
5. Analytical reading						
6. Note taking						
7. Use of library aids						
8. Group discussion skills: listening and contribution						

On the whole, (his) (her) achievement to date in this class entitles (him) (her) to a mark of:

               A   B   C   D   E

Courtesy of Dr. John M. Trytten, University of Michigan.

data, how to deal with certain questions that parents raise, or how to maintain a reasonable schedule for the interview. These problems, and others related to the effective use of parent-teacher conferences are important enough to warrant study in faculty meetings and workshops. Analysis of successes and failures will be helpful in such study. The parent-teacher conference is so valuable a device for reporting growth that it is well worth the time and effort required to master its techniques. As more and more secondary schools make use of the conference plan, it may be discovered that it is a better way than symbol marking. Meanwhile, it is at least a valuable supplement to the marking system.

The check list, the letter, and the parent-teacher conference have been considered as supplements to or as substitutes for the conventional system of reporting to parents by symbol marks. The marking system, it appears, is not really needed for home reporting purposes. The prediction-of-adjustment device described earlier may possibly prove superior to symbol marks for purposes of recommendation to college or employment.

MARKS AS RECORDS

Marking systems are often justified, however, as a means of briefly recording achievement in various classes, simply for record and transfer purposes. It is certainly easier to place a B on a student's permanent record opposite the word English than to record all the possible graduations of a student's progress in respect to interests, skills, knowledge, appreciation, understanding, social adjustment, and other areas of growth in which modern teachers are interested. The trouble is, of course, that the B does not mean what people think it means. Indeed, it is likely to mean little beyond the momentary, personal reaction of a teacher to a student in one situation. If we are to describe the growth of students, we must do much better than marks. In fact, we must do so much better that it will become obvious to all that marks are almost useless in contrast to all the other data we have.

Cumulative records must provide space for at least a summary of some other data besides marks. There should be space for test scores, educational and vocational plans, interests and hobbies, talents and achievements, outstanding personal strengths and weaknesses, physical growth data, and many other facts about each student. When adequate data are collected in the cumulative record, the actual symbol for summarizing achievement tends to lose its significance. It could become a mere record of "satisfactory" or "unsatisfactory" *if enough data of a more pertinent nature are readily available in the file.* On the other hand, if other data are not adequate, a change from A-B-C-D-E to S-U will represent no advantage to teachers or parents. It may even appear to be a move toward collecting less instead of more information about students. This may explain why the S-U marking plan has sometimes been opposed by parents. Even though the A-B-C-D-E marks are pitifully inadequate and tell us little about students, the S-U mark may appear even less adequate *unless everyone is aware that the volume of significant data has increased.* In short, we must come to depend more on facts and less on symbols. This trend calls for adequate means of collecting and recording facts. It calls also for intelligent use of these facts in sharing information with parents, employers, and college registrars, as well as among teachers and counselors within a school.

NEED OF COÖPERATION

The development of such a system of pupil records as this is a total-faculty task. It cannot be achieved by the principal or counselors, or even by a committee of the faculty, unless the whole staff is interested in collecting and using facts about pupils. Many a school has collected thousands of test scores that teachers generally do not know how to use. These data are collecting dust in some administrator's file. Unless teachers share, as a group, in deciding what data are needed about students and how such information can be used, it is unlikely that the time and money needed for collecting it will be justified. This task is a professional one that cannot be assigned to clerical workers. Those who must *use* information must share in *collecting* it after they have *helped decide* that it is needed. The process of planning and working together that is involved in such a total-faculty approach to pupil records is a vital challenge to administrative leadership. Many a curriculum improvement program has begun with anlysis by the faculty of information needed about pupils and how such information can best be used. One faculty group began a three-year program by examining in its preschool conference the techniques of writing and using anecdotal records. This project led the group members to analyze the whole cumulative record file and to make some modifications in it. They next studied the testing program and changed the instruments they had been using. They decided that use of pupil files would be accelerated if each home-room teacher kept the files. The short home-room period appeared inadequate for guidance purposes and was lengthened by combination with certain required subjects. Out of this change emerged a core program, about three years after teachers had first decided they needed help on anecdotal records.

Thus the coöperative development of usable pupil records is often a good point at which to begin programs of school improvement. The principal can stimulate such study by simply asking the staff what information should be collected about pupils. This approach will be most promising when teachers are aware that they are to be the collectors and users of pupil records.

For Further Reading

Aikin, Wilford M., *The Story of the Eight Year Study,* New York, Harper & Brothers, 1942, chap. 4.

American Council on Education, *Helping Teachers Understand Children,* Washington, the Council, 1945.

Association for Supervision and Curriculum Development, *Fostering Mental Health in Our Schools,* 1950 Yearbook, Washington, The National Education Association, 1950.

"Counseling and Guidance in the Secondary Schools," *Bulletin of the National Association of Secondary School Principals,* XXXV, January, 1941 (entire issue).

Douglass, Harl R., *Modern Administration of Secondary Schools,* rev. ed., Boston, Ginn and Company, 1954, chap. 18.

French, Will, Hull, J. Dan, and Dodds, B. L., *American High School Administration,* New York, Rinehart & Company, 1951, chap. 21.

Johnston, Edgar G., *Administering the Guidance Program,* Minneapolis, Educational Publishers, 1942.

Meek, Lois H. (ed.), *The Personal-Social Development of Boys and Girls with Implication for Secondary Education,* New York, Committee on Workshops, Progressive Education Association, 1940.

Smith, Eugene R., and Tyler, Ralph W., *Appraising and Recording Student Progress,* New York, Harper & Brothers, 1942.

Smith, Glenn E., *Principles and Practices of the Guidance Program,* New York, The Macmillan Company, 1951.

Spears, Harold, *The High School For Today,* New York, American Book Company, 1950, chap. XI.

Strang, Ruth, *Pupil Personnel and Guidance,* New York, The Macmillan Company, 1940.

Strang, Ruth, *Role of the Teacher in Personnel Work,* New York, Columbia University Press, 1946.

Traxler, Arthur E., *Techniques of Guidance,* New York, Harper & Brothers, 1952.

U.S. Office of Education, *Handbook of Cumulative Records,* Bulletin 1944, No. 5, Washington, Federal Security Agency, 1944.

Wrenn, C. Gilbert, and Dugan, Willis E., *Guidance Procedures in High School,* Minneapolis, University of Minnesota Press, 1950.

Wrinkle, William L., *Improving Marking and Reporting Practices in Elementary and Secondary Schools,* New York, Rinehart & Company, 1947.

CHAPTER 9

Student Activities

In the two preceding chapters analysis of the guidance function of the secondary school has been presented. In the process of developing and interpreting data regarding pupils, it is important to consider their all-around growth in all kinds of situations. The student activities program can make a valuable contribution here. The total picture of a boy or girl may alter in significant ways when data are studied regarding his or her adjustment to other students in the relatively informal situations which student activities offer.

The term "extracurricular" used to be generally applied to all student activities which took place outside the doors of the classroom. This word derived, of course, from the origin of the activities program in the out-of-school lives of adolescents. In recent years most secondary schools have lifted student activities to a position of acceptance and respectability. They are now generally given credit in one form or another, sponsored by regular members of the staff, and scheduled, at least in part, on school time and in school facilities. Yet the term "extracurricular activities" is still widely used, perhaps for want of a better one. There is certainly valid objection to the prefix "extra," which relegates activities again to some outside area and which implies that they are nonessential if not hostile to the fundamental goals of the school.

Because of the trend toward making such activities a basic part of the total educational program, the term "student activities" has recently gained general favor.

PURPOSES OF ACTIVITIES

We hear a great deal about meeting the needs of youth. School leaders are rather generally committed to this goal as a criterion for measuring the effectiveness of the school program. "Needs" may be interpreted in various ways. They may be immediate or ultimate, specific or general. They made be expressed directly by youth, or inferred by adults.

The Educational Policies Commission has classified youth needs into the well-known four categories of self-realization, human relationships, economic efficiency, and civic responsibility. A somewhat different approach is represented by the term "developmental tasks" which are imposed by the bio-social demands on a person in the particular environment in which he lives. Havighurst identifies nine of these developmental tasks as characteristic of adolescents:

1. Accepting one's physique and accepting a masculine or feminine role
2. New relationships with age-mates of both sexes
3. Emotional independence of parents and other adults
4. Achieving assurance of economic independence
5. Selecting and preparing for an occupation
6. Developing intellectual skills and concepts necessary for civic competence
7. Desiring and achieving socially responsible behavior
8. Preparing for marriage and family life
9. Building conscious values in harmony with an adequate scientific world picture.[1]

[1] Robert J. Havighurst, *Developmental Tasks and Education,* Chicago, University of Chicago Press, 1945, Chapter V.

It is interesting to note that many of these developmental tasks are performed by young people in a rich, well-administered program of student activities. This is particularly true of programs wherein students have had a share in planning and administering their own activities. In such schools, there are many rich opportunities for youth to learn how to meet and solve the real problems involved in growing up. Indeed, in some schools the activities program appears to be the only area in the school where real help is given in these vital developmental tasks of adolescence.

Dewey pointed out over a half-century ago that education is "the stimulating of the child's powers by the demands of the social situation in which he finds himself."[2] This conception of education casts the teacher in a new role, that of the architect who plans a challenging setting for the educational process. To the extent that the classroom itself presents a lifelike, creative social situation in which learning is inevitable, a lesser burden is placed on the student activities program. In many schools, however, classroom instruction still tends to emphasize verbal, academic mastery of subject matter without much apparent relationship to real life functions. In such schools, the social situations to which Dewey referred are usually discovered in the realm of student activities. For many students, the only genuine challenge to learning is provided by some student activity; such students often privately consider the classroom experiences as a necessary evil which must be endured in order to make the real business of the school—i.e., the activities program—possible and available. This attitude is more typical of high school students than is commonly supposed. It represents an ironic contrast to the point of view which the faculty of such a school is likely to hold regarding the respective importance of the classroom and student activities. Thus it is not uncommon to observe schools whose curriculums are limited, verbal, and academic, but whose activity programs are rich, lively,

[2] John Dewey, *My Pedagogic Creed, op. cit.*

and challenging. This curious contradiction might eventually disappear if careful evaluation were made by the staff of the purposes and effectiveness of the activities program.

These purposes, in summary, should include the establishing of a lifelike, social situation which will challenge the learner's powers by its intrinsic appeal to his interests. It should provide opportunity to perform real developmental tasks which can contribute directly to the adolescent's growth and development in constructive directions. To this end, the program must recognize the validity of individual hobbies, cultural interests, and recreational needs. It must equally recognize the social and civic needs which youth confront as they live, work, and play together.

In the light of these purposes, it appears of utmost importance that young people be actively involved in planning their own activities. If such involvement occurs also in the classrooms, so much the better. If it occurs nowhere else in a school, at least student participation is basic to the planning of an effective student activities program.

ORGANIZING THE ACTIVITIES PROGRAM

The shadowy line which separates student activities from the classroom curriculum may be observed in any one school. For example, courses in safety have grown out of safety projects in the home room. Field experiences may be tried out in a science club, and subsequently used to enrich instruction in science classes. The athletic program may meet partly on school time and partly after school. The band may receive "regular" credit but the choir none. These discrepancies are perhaps natural symptoms which characterize a transitional process in which activities are gradually gaining greater respectability. They may also result from the fact that various activities originate in different ways. Some are traditional and perennial. A high school without a basketball team, for example, is a rarity. Other activities persist from year to year because of the interest of certain teachers who sponsor them. Still others are introduced by the principal or faculty in the effort to emulate other schools. In some schools, efforts are made at regular intervals to discover what new activities the students themselves want. Sometimes an evaluation of the program may produce some new activities and eliminate some traditional ones.

The program of student activities may cover a large scope. This fact is emphasized by the classifications suggested over twenty years ago by a committee of the North Central Association:

Type One: Participation in the organization, management, and control of the school. The first type includes the cooperative activities of pupils in such organizations as student associations, student councils, senates, executive committees, cabinets, boards of control, congresses, squad patrols, classes, and other administrative groups. It includes also such individual activities as those of monitors, assistants, guards, elected leaders, voluntary workers, and special administrative appointees. This type is the most broadly inclusive of all, and consequently the most difficult to keep separated from other types.

Type Two: Drives and community activities. Drives and campaigns: such activities as are necessary to carry on drives and campaigns in clean-up and paint-up week, health week, anti-litter week, bird week, education week, anti-noise week, community chest campaign, and school bond campaign. General improvement activities: junior foresters, conservation club, junior citizens' club, junior association of commerce, junior booster club, community playgrounds, opportunity school, and the like.

Type Three: Religious and social welfare clubs and organizations of relief. Religious clubs: Hi-Y, Girl Reserves, religious education groups, social and welfare clubs, Boy Scouts, Girl Scouts, Campfire Girls, boys' brotherhood, thrift clubs, etc. Organizations of relief, Junior Red Cross, first aid groups, social service clubs, national safety, Near East relief, hospital auxiliaries, bands of mercy, red star league, etc.

Type Four: Purely social activities. Parties, dances, mixers, picnics, social dancing clubs, etiquette clubs, dinners, banquets, receptions. Illustrative activities for which the home is directly responsible. Activities under school influence and for which the school is indirectly responsible. Incidental conduct activities such as meeting and talking with pupils in the corridors, in the classroom, in the lunchroom, in the auditorium, in the gymnasium. Social activities of pupils, informal but purely social in nature, such as mixers, afternoon school parties, picnics, and informal affairs in the gymnasium. Social activities of pupils in more formal gatherings of pupils, such as dinners, receptions, and banquets, social and etiquette club activities.

Type Five: Athletics and other physical training activities. Mass play and physical activities common to an unlimited number of participants: e.g., cage ball, etc. Activities for the larger group games; e.g., football, basketball, etc. Activities for the small group games; e.g., wrestling, tennis, etc. Activities for individual participation games; e.g., golf, archery, etc. Activities for managers, captains, etc.

Type Six: School publications. Newspapers, magazines, annuals, and handbooks. Activities of members of a board of publication. Activities of managing editors and assistant managing editors. Activities of reporters. Activities of business managers, circulation managers, or assistants in either case. Activities of students not officially connected with the publication.

Type Seven: Dramatics and public speaking. Plays, pageants, operettas, movies, folk songs, and dances; debating, oratory, extemporaneous speaking, school forums. Activities common to dramatics and public speaking. Activities common to various forms of dramatics. Activities peculiar to specific dramatic forms or to described individual participants. Activities peculiar to debating. Activities peculiar to other kinds of public speaking.

Type Eight: Musical activities. Chorus, glee clubs, quartets, operas, operettas, cantatas, appreciation clubs, band, orchestra, and other musical organizations.

Type Nine: Subject clubs. Agriculture, commercial, English, mathematics, social science, science, trade and industrial, and other subject clubs.

Type Ten: Miscellaneous clubs (not included in Type Nine). Aircraft, travel, radio, camera, collection, rifle, etc.

Type Eleven: Assemblies. Talks by principal, teachers, pupils, or outsiders. Dramatics by staff, pupils, outsiders, or combination. Demonstration, musical entertainment, public speaking, school forum, recognition assemblies. Programs or recitals of entertainers. Movies. Radio programs, special day programs.

Type Twelve: Homeroom activities.[3]

In recent years some additional student activities have been developed, most of which can be classified in one or another of these twelve types. Perhaps school camping should be added as a separate category.

Not all of these activities will be needed in any given school. Larger schools will obviously require a richer and more extensive program than small schools. Urban and rural schools may differ in some ways as to the kinds of specific activities which will be most useful and appealing to students. It is important to survey student opinion on this point and involve students in the planning of an enriched activities program. This may be accomplished continuously through an effective school council organization. It may be helpful also to make a formal survey at least once a year to discover new trends in students' interests, and to evaluate the adequacy and effectiveness of present activities.

In most schools the organization of the activities program is the direct responsibility of the principal. In large high schools a teacher or counselor usually serves part time as director of activities.

SCHEDULING ACTIVITIES

The importance of scheduling is recognized by every experienced principal. The extent of participation by students depends in no

---

[3] L. W. Webb, *et al., High School Curriculum Reorganization,* Ann Arbor, Mich., The Ann Arbor Press, 1933, pp. 359–362.

small measure on scheduling. When most activities are held after school hours, they are not available to students who work at part-time jobs or must leave on the school bus. The schedule must take account, too, of various needs for special facilities or equipment for certain activities.

In the effort to schedule activities in such a way as to permit all students to participate, schools are more and more often reserving a time for them during the school day. This is sometimes accomplished by the use of study-hall periods and noon hours.

An increasing number of secondary schools have gone farther in this direction and adopted an activities period which is scheduled every day. Some schools use the home-room period on certain days of the week for clubs and assemblies. Others have both a home-room period and an activities period daily.

In an effort to provide flexibility and freedom of choice, many activity periods are scheduled after the last "regular" period. Unfortunately, this device usually means in practice that school is over a little earlier for those youngsters who must work, with the result that those for whom the period was devised are still unable to make use of it. For this reason there appears to be a trend toward the insertion of the activity period into the middle of the day.

A number of secondary schools have adopted one version or another of the floating, or rotating, activity period. This device has been used for many years in schools across the country. It was recently featured in a United States Office of Education monograph.[4] This pamphlet described a program followed in East Hampton, Connecticut, High School, which developed a schedule composed of five periods of sixty minutes each per day. One of the five periods each day was devoted to electives and to student activities:

[4] U.S. Office of Education, *Education Unlimited,* Bulletin, 1951, No. 5, Washington, Federal Security Agency, 1951.

	Monday	Tuesday	Wednesday	Thursday	Friday
1	■				
2		■			
3			■		
4				■	
5					■

The rotation of the activity period in this plan contributed some flexibility to the total program, since it could be reversed or alternated if special circumstances demanded a change in the time of the activity period.

Another plan which has met with favor in some schools is the double or triple noon period. A rich program of activities can be combined with, and built around, the noon luncheon, with alternating periods for different groups of students. This permits a large student body to make efficient use of limited cafeteria facilities and still effectively employ the remaining noon time, some before and some after lunch.

The activities period has been rather widely adopted in senior high schools. It has more recently spread to the junior high school also. Lounsbury's study of 251 junior high schools in the area of the North Central Association revealed that 39 percent of the schools provided an activity period in addition to the home-room period. This activity period averaged forty-three minutes in length.[5]

Thus, there are many variations of the student activities period. The plan developed in each school should be adapted to local factors and specific needs. The scheduling of activities during the "regular" school day seems wise as a means of making possible a more general participation. It is probable, however, that after-

[5] John H. Lounsbury, "The Role and Status of the Junior High School," unpublished doctoral dissertation, George Peabody College, Nashville, Tenn., 1954.

school time will also continue to be used for activities which require longer periods. Every effort should be made to ensure that such after-school activities do not penalize teacher and students, and that opportunities are also available for similar kinds of activities during the school day.

FINANCING THE PROGRAM

Another factor which often prevents students from participating in activities is their cost. A study in Illinois [6] recently revealed that boys and girls in the upper socioeconomic group participated in school activities about twice as much as those in the lower group. In another study the Illinois program revealed typical "hidden tuition costs" for student activities which may help explain why the less favored socioeconomic group does not participate. Median costs were as follows for certain activities, selected at random from a long list:

Baseball	$12.25	Senior Band	3.50
Basketball	12.80	Orchestra	2.25
Football	2.10	Clubs	0 to 19.30
Golf	50.00	Athletic events	5.05
Class dues, 11th-12th		Graduation	13.35
grades	1.00		

Dolan's study of hidden tuition costs in the LaSalle-Peru, Illinois, Township High School revealed that the average annual total of student expenditures in that school was $72.75 for freshmen, $90.75 for sophomores, $164.45 for juniors, and $189.50 for seniors.[7] It is not surprising that boys and girls from poor families do not generally take part in student activities. Yet these activities are as deserving of status and attention as any other phase of the

[6] Harold C. Hand, *How to Conduct the Participation in Extra-Class Activities Study*, Bulletin No. 5, Illinois Secondary School Curriculum Program, Springfield, Ill., State Superintendent of Public Instruction, 1949, p. 26.

[7] Francis H. Dolan, "Hidden Tuition Costs," doctoral dissertation abstract published in *Bulletin of the National Association of Secondary School Principals*, 36: 188, October, 1952, p. 142.

school program. Fees, assessments, and admissions which place the financial burden on the individual student are likely to have a discriminatory effect. They often result in the selection of participants in activities on a basis of their parents' wealth.

In practice, the activity program is usually financed by some combination of the following sources:

1. *Individual student payment*
   Assessments, fees, dues, admissions, purchase of equipment or awards, purchase of school annual, paper, or handbook
2. *Sales and drives*
   Tag days, sale of pies, candy, etc., advertising space in school annual, raffles, bingo games, lotteries
3. *Public admission fees*
   Basketball, football, swimming, baseball, debates, plays, operettas, concerts
4. *Subsidy by school budget*
   Funds raised from public school taxes

Most high schools employ all four of these sources of funds, although limited use is made of drives and sales. The Bloomington, Illinois, High School finances school activities by a direct subsidy from the board of education. This has made it possible for students to attend all home athletic, dramatic, and music events without charge. They also receive the school paper and annual, and they attend parties and assemblies without charge.

Most high schools have not gone this far in the matter of board-of-education subsidies, but it is rather common for such subsidies to be available to cover deficits incurred by various school activities. Many high schools use an activity ticket plan which reduces the cost of all school activities to a manageable sum and then spreads that amount in installment fashion over the school year. This plan has certain advantages, as a recent volume on school activities points out:

1. It reduces total costs to the individual, thus encouraging participation.
2. It reduces the need for numerous, competing drives for funds by all-school organizations.
3. It enables revenue-producing activities to help carry non-revenue activities which have educative value.
4. It provides a business-like basis for compiling an activities budget.
5. It furnishes valuable financial, sales, and accounting experiences to students.[8]

Such an activity ticket, priced low enough to permit every student to participate in all school activities, can furnish a supplement to board-of-education financing. It can also supply valuable experiences in the budgeting, handling, and accounting of funds. Some further development of this point will appear in Chapter 12.

The activity ticket plan is widely used in secondary schools but not always with "blanket" coverage of all activities in a school. Sometimes the athletic events are separately financed by season ticket sales. In some schools the activities sponsored for fund raising by grade-level classes (junior carnival, senior play) are not included in the activity ticket. In other schools the dances or noon movies are excluded.

Such exclusions have a tendency to weaken the effectiveness of the activity ticket and to restore the emphasis to individual student admissions. In light of the convincing evidence on the exclusion of youth from low-income families from participating in activities, it appears that dependence on individual admissions is discriminatory. If student activities are really an integral part of the "free" educational program for all youth, the selection of participants on the basis of their parents' wealth can hardly be justified.

Dependence on tag days or ice cream sales is also inequitable as well as unbusinesslike. Sales or drives should be limited to projects that can meet such criteria as the following:

[8] Edgar G. Johnston and Roland C. Faunce, *Student Activities in Secondary Schools,* New York: The Ronald Press Company, 1952, p. 328.

1. The project should have definite educational value as experience in production, marketing, accounting, and financial planning.
2. The product should have a legitimate character and intrinsic value.
3. The product should not be such as to undermine health or morals.
4. The sales should be so distributed as to avoid competition between school groups and too frequent dislocation of the school's routines.
5. Participation in the project should be so distributed as to give many students the experience.
6. The project should not disrupt the economy of a local community.[9]

In summary, the cost of student activities has often been one factor in limiting participation in them. It seems legitimate to raise some funds from well-controlled sales and admissions to interested adults. The cost to students should be kept low through some plan for spreading payment and giving students experience in budgeting and accounting. The use of public tax moneys to insure a rich activities program for all students is entirely justified, and is probably increasing in American secondary schools.

CREDITS AND AWARDS

High schools have passed through certain stages in the transition from activities which had neither school recognition nor awards to a policy of regular credit for "curricularized" activities such as music. In that process certain kinds of extrinsic awards have been used. Some of these, such as pins, letters, or certificates, are still in use for certain activities, although their use appears to be diminishing. Some schools award a full credit for certain activities, half or quarter credit for others.

An increasing number of schools use some type of "activity points" (a special kind of school credit) for activities. This plan of activity credit is designed, in general, to achieve one or more of the following purposes: (1) to provide incentive for students to

[9] *Ibid.*, p. 329.

participate in activities; (2) to limit the overzealous student who so often dominates every school activity; (3) to form a basis for translating student participation in activities on some quantitative basis, and an aid to the guidance program; (4) to supply a minimum requirement in schools where participation in activities is compulsory.

Some point systems simply place a numerical limit on the number of activities permitted each student per semester. Others use a major-minor plan, with some such limitation as one major and two minor activities per student per semester. A third and more common plan rates each activity on a scale such as 1–6 or 1–10 points and imposes a limit of the total number of points a student may carry each semester. Conversely, a few schools set a minimum number of such activity points required for graduation.

Careful survey is required in a given school to determine what point value to use for each activity. The whole faculty and student body can help set such a scale on the basis of time required by the activity, opportunities and importance of each activity, and its relation to the curriculum.

Extrinsic awards have perhaps had their heyday. An increasing number of schools have gradually eliminated gold pins, keys, cups, and similar synthetic awards. The athletic letter is still with us, but it tends to be an all-school award based on some point system, at least in junior high schools. As student activities become more and more integral with the "regular" school program, there will probably be less and less reason for special awards as an extrinsic incentive. Instead, the trend appears to be in the direction of some type of point credit. This trend is in harmony with the concept of making available to every student some avenue toward success and recognition.

One other trend might be noted in connection with awards. Provisions regarding eligibility which once prevailed for most activities are becoming less generally required. It is now recognized that scholastic eligibility has been one more factor limiting the participation of boys and girls in the activities of their choice. Such provisions appear indefensible in that they are likely to ban the very student who most needs the experience of student activities. It is quite possible that the most significant experiences some students have in high school are in the realm of activities. To cut them off from the one functional experience in their school day will serve no good purpose. It is recognized, of course, that eligibility rules may be necessary in interscholastic activities to ensure that participants are bona fide students in the school which they represent.

EVALUATING ACTIVITIES

In our efforts to guide students constructively, we need evaluative evidence of their growth as individual members of an activity or team. Much helpful information about boys and girls can be derived from a careful evaluation of their experiences in clubs, sports, or other activities. We are also concerned with another kind of evaluation—that of the various student organizations and of the program as a whole.

It is not easy to measure growth in personality or character development. Techniques are needed for studying and interpreting behavior in informal situations, and for sharing these data with counselors and with other teachers. The following principles of evaluation seem to have significance in this area:

1. Evaluation should be continuous.
2. Students should help appraise their own growth.
3. Parents should share in evaluating experiences.
4. Measurement should be in terms of clearly stated goals.
5. All teachers should coöperate in the evaluative process.
6. Observation techniques can be helpful if they are objective and anecdotal.
7. Instruments and techniques should be developed and applied in the areas of pupil interests, personality development, and social adjustment.

Both individual and group self-analyses are useful in appraising progress. If these are oral appraisals a record should be kept of them. Teachers' and parents' judgments are too valuable to be left to memory; they should be recorded regularly and kept as an aid to the guidance process, and as a means of improving the activity.

Relationships between students may be revealed by sociograms, conversations, judgments regarding each other, and significant choices of leaders or partners. Anecdotes involving these kinds of items should be kept by coaches, class advisers, and club sponsors, as well as by all classroom teachers.

Evaluation of the program itself may take the form of faculty discussions based on data collected by each staff member. Such instruments as the "Student Activities" section of the *Evaluative Criteria* [10] may be helpful. This is a check list of analytical statements about each school activity, which can provide a springboard for faculty and parents' discussions. A longer check list is provided in the last chapter of the Educational Policies Commission volume, *Learning the Ways of Democracy*. In this final section questions are used to classify a program according to three levels—the "routine," the "imitative," and the "constructive":

Student life: routine level

Did you set up a plan of student government in your high school and then leave it to run itself? Do you regard student life outside of regular class hours as no particular business of the school? Is the one really big and important student activity the interscholastic athletic contests? Do most of the members of your faculty regard student clubs as a waste of time that might better be spent in home study? Do they regard student government primarily as a useful accessory for securing conformity to school regulations? Are your school social functions chiefly for the social elite of the school and the community? . . .

[10] Cooperative Study of Secondary School Standards, *Evaluative Criteria*, rev. ed., Washington, The American Council on Education, 1950.

Student life: imitative level

Have student activities grown up rapidly in your school, but grown without plan or purpose? Do you introduce new student activities because other schools have them rather than because your students need and want them? Do you swing between the extremes of a benevolent dictatorship over student life (in the name of efficiency) and complete abdication of responsibility (in the name of democracy)? Are your student elections primarily beauty or popularity contests, lacking real issues and exhibiting the seamy campaign practices of adult politics at their worst? Are your student courts concerned with punishment, careless about prevention? Are you constantly trying to modify the rules and by-laws so as to make your student activities more valuable, and are you constantly disappointed by the results obtained in this way? . . .

Student life: constructive level

Have you developed out-of-class activities in terms of the needs of your students and your communities? Is the student activity program a fully recognized, prestigeful part of your school's work? Do you use student activities as laboratories of civic education so that the line between curricular and extracurricular is indistinguishable? Is the school paper a means of forming and informing public opinion on school and community problems? Are your student elections conducted with high standards and based on real issues in the work of the school? Do you extend to student organizations all the freedom they can take, stopping, however, before the point where practice is given in undemocratic procedures? Are your student clubs conceived and operated in terms of service to the group and enrichment of individual lives? Do you protect your student activities from exploitation by commercial or other special interests? [11]

Rating scales and check lists are also available for most types of activities, and can be profitably developed by students and teachers for their own use.

[11] Educational Policies Commission, *Learning the Ways of Democracy,* Washington, The National Education Association, 1940.

The following example of a check list for evaluating a club sponsor's effectiveness was developed by a group of teachers in a graduate class:

CHECK LIST

(Rate yourself on the following points placing the appropriate number in the column at left of question: *3* for always, *2* for sometimes, *1* for never.)

....	Will my group function adequately in my absence?
....	Does my group disintegrate in face of crisis?
....	Do all members share the group interest?
....	Are goals common to the group?
....	Is the motivation toward these goals realistic?
....	Is there mutual respect for all expressed points of view?
....	Is the group able to come to a friendly conclusion?
....	Is discipline self-imposed rather than imposed from without?
....	Does the situation permit the evolution of real in-group leadership?
....	Is evaluation of group membership and group activities on an objective and continuous basis?
....	Is there self-evaluation as well as group evaluation?
....	Is participation on a willing, interested basis?
....	Does the handling of the group tend to promote social and emotional maturity?
....	Good group handling tends to promote group continuity. Do your group members tend to remain with the group?
....	Is there carry-over into other activities of the group members?

Benerd has suggested the following questions for faculty members to ask themselves about the activity program:

1. Do the students receive instruction and practice in sharing responsibility?
2. Do they have opportunities to deal with tensions that arise?

3. Do they have a part in planning the discussion activities of the group meetings?
4. Is the over-social pupil kept from overdoing?
5. Is the unsocial pupil, who is in need of the influence of a club, encouraged to find the group in which he can be at ease? [12]

A faculty interested in evaluating student growth will not overlook interest inventories, opinions of graduates and dropouts, problem check lists, interview records, case studies, and other techniques for assessing the development of students in the informal climate of social activities. Without continuous and careful evaluation it is unlikely that a program can continue to contribute maximally to the growth of young people.

RELATIONSHIP TO THE CURRICULUM

Many activities have become a part of the classroom curriculum. This is generally true today of physical education, music, speech, and journalism. In another sense it is true also of camping programs which "grow out of classroom experiences and return to enrich them," [13] of home rooms which really serve the function of unifying instruction in various classes, and of science clubs which are an extension of the experimental work of the science class.

It has been pointed out earlier in this chapter that the curriculum, defined broadly, is designed to meet the needs and to provide an opportunity for the necessary developmental tasks which adolescents face in growing up together. These tasks are the business of both classroom and extraclass experiences. These two phases of the school are really two sides of the same coin, designed for the same ends. They are mutually complementary, not rivals for the time and energy of students.

It is probable that we shall always have some total-school activi-

[12] Gladys Benerd, "How Can We Evaluate the Co-curricular Program?", *Bulletin of the National Association of Secondary School Principals,* 37:197, November, 1953, p. 61.

[13] Elbert K. Fretwell, *Extra-Curricular Activities in Secondary Schools,* Boston, Houghton Mifflin Company, 1931, p. 2.

ties which will be scheduled apart from the classroom program, either because they cut across the total school or because they are time-consuming. Even these activities can, however, become a part of the curriculum in the large sense. This will occur to the extent that:

1. Time provision is made for both students and teachers.
2. Recognition is adequately accorded in terms of credits and status.
3. Teachers generally accept the activities as an important part of the school program.
4. Attention is paid to their contribution of guidance data.
5. Techniques of sponsoring and directing activities are studied and developed.
6. The administration and community recognize the value of the activities program.
7. Evaluation of results achieved is conducted continuously with the purpose of constant improvement of the program.

The time is now past when student activities can be regarded as a necessary nuisance, a frill, or a fad. Modern school leaders recognize that one important test of a good school is the richness, vitality, and variety of its activity program. That program can become a vital force in helping to meet the needs of boys and girls.

The principal plays a crucial role in this business of developing an effective activities program. Student enthusiasm will ebb and faculty support will be lacking in schools where the administrator does not furnish leadership. This does not mean that he must "run the show." It does mean that he must do his best to stimulate its development, provide conditions promising for its success, and coördinate the numerous activities into a sound program. In these efforts he will seek constantly to use the resources of the whole school as well as of parents in the planning and evaluation of the program. There is perhaps no more natural challenge to the democratic school leader than the administration of the activities program.

FOR FURTHER READING

Benerd, Gladys, "How Can We Evaluate The Co-curricular Program?" *Bulletin of the National Association of Secondary School Principals.* 37:197, November, 1953.

Cooperative Study of Secondary School Standards, *Evaluative Criteria,* rev. ed., Washington, The American Council on Education, 1950, Sec. E.

Dolan, Francis H., "Hidden Tuition Costs," *Bulletin of the National Association of Secondary School Principals,* 36:188, October, 1952.

Educational Policies Commission, *Learning the Ways of Democracy,* Washington, The National Education Association, 1940.

Fedder, Ruth, *Guiding Home-Room and Club Activities,* New York, McGraw-Hill Book Company, 1949.

French, William, Hull, J. Dan, and Dodds, B. L., *American High School Administration,* New York, Rinehart & Company, 1951, chap. 13.

Fretwell, Elbert J., *Extra-Curricular Activities in Secondary Schools,* Boston, Houghton Mifflin Company, 1931, chap. I.

Hand, Harold C., *How to Conduct the Participation in Extra-Class Activities Study,* Bulletin No. 5, Illinois Secondary School Curriculum Program, Springfield, Ill., State Superintendent of Public Instruction, 1949.

Hand, Harold C., *Principal Findings of the 1947–48 Basic Studies of the Illinois Secondary School Curriculum Program,* Circular Series A, No. 51, Springfield, Ill., State Superintendent of Public Instruction, May, 1949.

Havighurst, Robert J., *Developmental Tasks and Education,* Chicago, University of Chicago Press, 1945, chap. V.

Hopkins, Ellsworth, *The Activity Period in Public High Schools,* Bulletin 1951. No. 19, Washington, Federal Security Agency, Office of Education, 1951.

Johnston, Edgar G., *Point Systems and Awards,* New York, A. S. Barnes and Company, 1930.

Johnston, Edgar G., and Faunce, Roland C., *Student Activities in Secondary Schools,* New York, The Ronald Press Company, 1952.

Jones, Galen, *Extra-Curricular Activities in Relation to the Curricu-

lum, New York, Bureau of Publications, Teachers College, Columbia University, 1935.

McKown, Harry C., *Extra Curricular Activities* (rev. ed.), New York, The Macmillan Company, 1952.

Strang, Ruth, *Group Activities in College and Secondary School,* New York, Harper & Brothers, 1941.

"Student Activities in Secondary Schools," *Bulletin of the National Association of Secondary School Principals,* No. 119, January, 1944.

"Vitalizing Student Activities in the Secondary School," *Bulletin of the National Association of Secondary School Principals,* No. 102, December, 1941.

....

CHAPTER 10

Student Participation in School Government

BACKGROUND OF STUDENT PARTICIPATION

The idea of student government is not a new concept. Plato's Academy and Aristotle's Lyceum had student "scholarchs," elected for the purpose of helping govern the school. Vittorino da Feltre introduced student government of the activities program into his "Pleasant House" in Mantua in 1428. Trotzendorff, in sixteenth-century Germany, developed a student monitor plan and a school court. Further contributions to the monitor system were made by Lancaster, Bell, and Hill in English schools of the early nineteenth century. The teaching and writing of Pestalozzi and Rousseau had earlier contributed to the concept of learning to govern as a part of school instruction.

In America the William Penn Charter School had an elected "school assembly" with governing powers before 1800. The first real public high school, founded in Boston in 1821, had a student council which was based upon certain pioneer experiments in colonial schools. Yet these, and some other experimental programs which might be cited, were but tiny rays of light, chiefly notable because of the general darkness. Despite a number of successful experiments in the late nineteenth century and the first two decades of the twentieth century, less than half of our high schools had organized student councils in 1925.[1] Yet in 1940 two separate national surveys of student participation revealed that 81 to 92 percent of American high schools had some organized form of student participation.[2]

It is clear that the student council movement captured American high schools with a suddenness that is unusual in the history of educational change. Many reasons have been cited for this rapid extension of the student council. Among these are the leadership of the National Self-Government Committee, under the chairmanship of Richard Welling; the organization of the state and national associations of student councils; the growth of the extracurricular activities movement; the influence of the evolving junior high school; and the cumulative effect of many speeches, articles, and books on the subject by educational leaders. In any case, the student council movement assumed during the years 1920–1940 the aspects of a popular trend, and any high school principal who wished to be in the swim had to develop one in his school.

AN EXTRACURRICULAR MOVEMENT

Whatever the cause or causes of its sudden extension, it appears certain that the student council did not appear in the typical American high school as the fruition of a general democratization of the high school. On the contrary, the student council was introduced into our secondary schools during a period when these institutions were still generally autocratic in their administrative organization, paternalistic in their pupil-teacher relationships, and authoritarian in their patterns of classroom instruction. The extracurricular domain was, in theory, organized as a means of giving students some voice in school affairs and it was precisely here that

[1] Much of the material presented in this chapter appeared in Chapter 3 of the volume *Student Activities in Secondary Schools,* by Edgar G. Johnston and Roland C. Faunce, New York, The Ronald Press Company, 1952. Acknowledgment is made to the publishers for permission to republish certain material.

[2] Harry C. McKown, *The Student Council,* New York: McGraw-Hill Book Company, 1944, p. 14.

the student council became classified and organizationally based. The early councils were even elected either as representatives of the school interest clubs and social organizations or of the grade-level "classes" whose functions were also extracurricular in nature. Later, with the rise of the home room, the student council commonly consisted of home-room representatives. Thus it tended to have little direct connection with or influence upon the classroom.

Classroom instruction has not, indeed, been a fertile ground for action democracy until recently. Teachers have too often been the goal determiners, assignment givers, sole evaluators, and controllers of group discipline in the classroom. There has been all too little opportunity, in most high school classes, for boys and girls to learn the difficult techniques of decision making, evaluation, and group planning upon which successful democratic action rests. Indeed, the persistent practice of having the adults set the purposes for the "learners" has resulted in an ironic shift of the students' real interests to the extracurricular domain. The high school student commonly accepts and achieves the teacher's goals for the class in a purely superficial way, and reserves his real enthusiasm for the things that matter to him—which may be football, dates, hobbies, or a job outside of school. Over half of our young people of high school age still reject the high school before graduation in favor of jobs, marriage, or just fun.

These facts have been pointed out many times before. The purpose of citing them here is to help to clarify the reasons why the student council movement made so little impact on the total school program, in spite of its ready acceptance by administrators. The really important aspects of the high school—the part for which credit was given and a generous time allotment made—were not only beyond the scope of the council but were so conducted as to defeat the purposes of democratic learning. Thus the student council entered the high schools during a period when the high school classrooms were not in gear with the goals which the student council sought to achieve—namely, the learning of the hard tasks of democratic citizenship through actual civic participation.

How about the total school, aside from the classroom? Here, too, the idea of democratic participation had not made any important impact. The line-and-staff administrative scheme centralized responsibility and discouraged group policy making. Even teachers were not generally encouraged to share in making important decisions, to say nothing of students. The basic pattern of human relationships was a paternalistic one which led from superintendent to principal, from principal to department head, from department head to teachers. At the bottom of this hierarchy sat the student, going through the motions of learning and being treated in paternalistic fashion by all the adults in the school. Any attempt on his part to organize the students for the purpose of assuming real responsibilities would probably have resulted in his expulsion!

Into such a basically undemocratic institution, then, the student council was introduced during the 1920's and 1930's as a carefully controlled, extracurricular gesture toward democracy. What were the results of this widespread experiment?

CONFUSION EXISTS ABOUT THE STUDENT COUNCIL

In the first place, wide misunderstanding about the purposes and legitimate scope of the student council has resulted from its general introduction into an unsympathetic milieu. High school principals, council advisers, professors of education, and others have debated vigorously for thirty years about the proper function of the student council. Professional literature is full of articles about the student council, arguing about its organizational framework, its scope, its purposes, and its proper field of activities. How can it be fitted into our typically line-and-staff administrative pattern, we ask? Should there be a veto power, and who should exercise it? Should we exclude some students from it, and if so, on what basis? How far dare we allow student councils to go? What should be the relationship of teachers to the council? Should school time be permitted for the school-wide discussion of council matters? All of these questions, and scores of others like them, have plagued the profession throughout the period of the student council's rapid extension, and are still before us. There is, even today, a vast misunderstanding of the purposes of student participation in school government. This confusion arises, in part, from the fact that our school organization is not traditionally a democratic one, and thus offers no clear basis for democratic student planning and action.

As a plan for civic training through civic participation, the student council has not been notably successful. Through scholastic eligibility restrictions, we have often limited participation in the council to those fortunate students who can be trusted, as evidenced by their marks in our classes. In some schools, the candidates for the council are first screened by the faculty. In a few schools, the faculty does the nominating. Perhaps even more serious is the degree to which participation tends to be limited to the elected representatives rather than extended to every student in school. Ideally, the council should be the voice of all the people. The youngest, poorest, least articulate, and least influential student in the entire high school should firmly believe, with all of his fellows, that he may present an idea which will affect the whole school through its transmission to the floor of the student council. Actually, as a result of our typically extracurricular base, little time is ever spent on school-wide discussions and group decisions by the constituents themselves. The identity of the council members is seldom remembered by the average student. He feels little concern about their decisions, or the reasons which prompted them—for they are not *his* decisions, *his* reasons.

Under these conditions, the student council tends more and more to become another school club, perhaps even a notch or two below some of the others in influence and importance. Members of the council, out of touch with the thinking of their constituents, tend to become oligarchs or members of a ruling clique instead of servants of the people.

Another factor helps to diminish the importance of the council. As a result of their confusion about its real function, high school principals and council advisers are still trying to frame up a limited field of legitimate activities for the council to assume. Many of us are not gifted with the faith in young people or the skill in working with them which is vitally needed in this process. Some of us are not above attempting to control the council's decisions by what we call "careful guidance." A few of us have so controlled and circumscribed the council's activities that it has acquired among the students a reputation as a group of stooges and rubber stamps. Under such conditions as these, the problems tackled by the council will rarely be real ones to students, and this unreality or artificiality will further diminish the council's usefulness as an instrument for democratic education.

To sum it all up, we have not always had a real faith in our students. We have not always acted as though we believed that young people are fundamentally good, that they, like us, want the good and well-ordered life, and that they can achieve it through actual participation as citizens of their school community. It is this faith in the people which lies at the root of democracy, and without this faith the tree cannot bear any fruit. Where student participation has achieved results, it was because someone believed in it. As we examine the history of the student council movement, it becomes evident that the student council has not usually had a real chance as an instrument of civic education. Yet, in spite of the limitations imposed by the structure and philosophy of the schools in which it must operate, the student council has persisted and even extended as a movement. Thousands of worthy achievements testify to the fact that our students want to be full citizens; that they have high ideals and the energy to pursue them; that they can, in short, be trusted to assume a significant role in their own group government. These achievements, this growth, have been possible only because someone in the school had faith in the basic goodness of students.

A TREND TOWARD DEMOCRACY IS NOW APPEARING

During the past fifteen years, while student participation was still maintaining a somewhat peripheral role as an extracurricular device, certain changes have gradually made an impact on the total philosophy of the school. These changes may have a far-reaching significance for the student participation movement; for the high school, which the student council entered at a period when it was still thoroughly authoritarian in its philosophy, is gradually and recently becoming conscious of the democratic way of life.

Beginning with successful experiments in the 1930's, the teacher-pupil planning motif has entered the classroom. In newer curricula, such as homemaking and agriculture, the change in the whole approach to instruction is so sharp as to be clearly noticeable. English, social science, mathematics, and science teachers have been slower to investigate and experiment with classroom democracy, but the recent trend toward removal by colleges and universities of their sequence requirements has encouraged the trend. Meanwhile, the core curriculum, under various titles and with various introductory stages, has made a considerable impact on the teacher-pupil relationship. Those who have visited high schools over the years agree that a new goal is evident in the classrooms. High school students are actually making choices in the instructional process. Teachers are becoming aware of the new science of group dynamics, and its implications for high school classes. Larger blocks of time, a characteristic of the core curriculum, are making possible a real constituent base for the student council. Some council representatives are discovering that there is not only time, but a real encouragement from their core teacher, to report council affairs to their constituents and to become true "servants of the people." In the schools where the skills of group planning and evaluation have become a classroom goal, the possibilities for the student council are almost unlimited. In such schools there is no problem of interesting the home room in the student council report. The council representative often finds instead that he must be on his toes in order to keep up with the plans for school betterment that are going forward in his own room. The climate of democracy obtains in the place where it can really affect things—namely, the classroom.

This same spirit of inquiry into the ways of democracy has also invaded the realm of administration. Some high school principals no longer find it necessary or desirable to make all of the decisions for the faculty. In many schools, policies are increasingly being developed by the coöperative planning of the whole staff, and even of community representatives. Administrators are beginning to be concerned about such things as the role of the status leader in a democratic planning situation, the development of the techniques of reaching consensus, the evaluation of growth in group-planning skills. Such concern for the techniques of democracy cannot help but influence student participation favorably. Democracy has a certain contagion about it. Teachers who are challenged to share in school planning are quite apt to challenge students to share, too. The ground for democracy is growing more fertile, and the effect of this more promising milieu upon student participation is already evident in many schools.

There are those who will warn us that we must not be too optimistic. Old ways change slowly. The high school is still a fundamentally authoritarian institution. The concern for group process referred to earlier has not penetrated all high school faculties or administrations. Indeed, the number of schools where teacher-pupil planning and the other processes of democracy are evident is still discouragingly small.

Yet the beginnings which we have reported appear to have truly dynamic possibilities. The war, and the stalemate which has since ensued, have served to sharpen the democratic values in our thinking as educators. The rapid growth of the science of group dynamics and the discoveries of modern educational psychology have given a tremendous boost to those who would help young people learn democracy by living it. We are teaching school in an era of basic transition from old to new—from the authoritarian to the democratic way of living and learning. Out of this era we are certain to emerge with better student councils, now founded strongly on a grass-roots kind of democracy.

STEPS TOWARD STUDENT PARTICIPATION IN GOVERNMENT

Meanwhile, the average secondary school principal will probably not discover such an ideal state of affairs in the school he serves. He is more likely to find the student council lacking in prestige and status in the school, as a result of several factors. The organizational base is likely to be rather unrepresentative, in the sense that council members seldom meet with their constituents to discuss school problems. The kinds of problems discussed in the council may appear unreal or unimportant to most students. The faculty may neither understand nor support the work of the council. There may be a long-standing tradition in the school that the council is only a glorified debating club for a few students who have good marks and a "stand-in" with the principal. Perhaps no effort has been made by anyone to discover the purposes or to evaluate the effectiveness of the student council.

It is to be hoped that the situation confronting a new principal will not be as bad as this; yet it is a fair description of too many school councils. What should be done in such a school? Where can one begin in the effort to develop representative democracy in a school where the status of the council has fallen so low that no one, student or teacher, appears to know or to care who is on the council or what they are doing?

1. FACULTY SUPPORT

The first step is to secure the support of the staff for a student participation program. No improvement can be permanent without the understanding and enthusiastic backing of the faculty. The purpose of student participation in school government should be clarified in discussions at faculty meetings. Some teachers may visit a neighboring school wherein a successful plan is operating, and report what they found to their colleagues. They may also attend one or more of the many student council conferences, where they may hear and observe the effects of the assumption of real responsibility by student leaders. The faculty may appraise the government plan of their own school to discover what roles students are presently playing. In this effort, the faculty may invite in representatives of the student body and of the parent group to discuss their views on what needs to be done to improve the situation. Eventually a faculty-student committee might be established to review the problem, and perhaps to propose needed changes in the constitution.

2. A REPRESENTATIVE BASE

One of the first tasks which must be faced in such a faculty and student appraisal is that of securing an adequate representative base. No plan of student participation can function without a real opportunity for contact between council members and their constituents. In the very small high school of one hundred students or less this may be achieved by weekly open-forum assemblies in which problems are presented by the officers and discussed by the entire student body. In larger schools a functional representative group must be established.

A common plan is to provide an extension of the homeroom period on at least one day each week, immediately following the student council meeting. This plan may work in schools which have a lively home-room program. Other schools have based the election of representatives on a given period of the school day, such as the first period, and devoted to council business one meeting per week of all classes meeting that period. In other schools a subject required of all students, such as English, has been selected for the representative groups and time provided at least one period each week. Another plan is to combine a class period with the following home-room period, thus giving a flexible time block which can be extended when needed for discussion of school problems. As has been suggested earlier, the core or unified-studies classes make an admirable base for electing council representatives in schools which have these groups with a time block of two or three periods daily.

Whatever the plan, it is essential that some kind of organization be developed which will provide an adequate, continuing contact between the representative of the council and his constituents. This is important, not only for referral to the entire school of important issues under discussion in the council. It also serves the vital function of permitting the initiation of plans or ideas throughout the school—of giving every citizen a voice and a channel for getting his ideas to the action level. Contact with the room groups is essential if any total school participation is desired.

3. TOTAL PARTICIPATION

It is highly desirable that all school citizens have a voice in the government. Most "student councils" are representative of but one group—the students themselves. This situation reflects an older era in which we used the term "student government," referring to a plan of complete autonomy by students over certain designated areas of responsibility. Naturally, adults were excluded under such plans. The principal and faculty, thus excluded, immediately tended to narrow and delimit the realm of responsibility of the council, hedge its operations about by prohibitions and warnings, and emphasize the power of the principal to veto its acts. Pupil participation, on the other hand, implies a system of coöperative planning in which both students and adults join in a democratic attack on the real problems of the school.

There are other citizens in the school besides the students. There are teachers and administrators and janitors and clerks. There are also, it is to be hoped, parents active in the PTA or in leadership roles in similar organizations. It is desirable that the council represent all these citizens directly, with the most numerous (student) constituents in a significant majority in the council. Such a "school council" might be composed thus:

1. Student officers elected by the school at large
2. Student representatives elected by home-room or core classes
3. One teacher representing and elected by the faculty
4. One janitor and one office clerk, appointed by the principal
5. One or two parents selected by the executive board of the PTA or by the school advisory council
6. The principal, or his appointed representative

In a total school council composed in some such manner as this, the walls of suspicion and hostility which have hampered the progress of student participiation will tend to disappear. There will be no necessity to wave the veto power before students as a threat, for the council will act only when all the facts are known and all aspects of the issue have been considered. Students will not have to wonder what "Mr. ——— will think of this" because Mr. ——— will be on hand to present his views. Parents, teachers, and other adults in the school will be continuously involved in planning with students, in contrast to remaining outside and wondering what mischief they are up to. Under such a plan of real civic participation, students can assume far greater authority and responsibility than under the student government concept.

Besides merely representing all citizens, the council must try to involve all citizens in its work. The cornerstone of this program is the effectiveness of the discussions that go on each week in the home rooms. These discussions must become so general, so interesting, and so informal that every student and every teacher will really have a chance to help solve problems or develop a plan. In the effort to improve the discussions in the home rooms, some councils have launched a total school study of speech techniques, aimed at securing effective reports by the council representative and a good discussion by his constituents. Speech or English teachers can devote some special effort to this problem. In one school all the core teachers spent an hour each week for a whole semester on the teaching techniques involved in securing effective reporting and discussion. This rather intensive in-service study resulted from the school council's efforts to secure total school participation.

The council should not "do" everything. Some projects can be farmed out to home rooms, classes, or clubs which volunteer. Perhaps a still better device for involving more school citizens in school projects is the "commission plan." In this plan, all the functions commonly undertaken by the council are assigned to various commissions, each of which has one member (usually the chairman) on the council, with the rest of the commission made up of volunteers from the total school. Each commission has a different faculty adviser.

One six-year high school with an enrollment of 700 established the following commissions, each reporting weekly to the council:

Study Hall Commission. This group made regular observations of the six student-governed study halls and rated them, basing the ratings on criteria established by the council.

Social Commission. Made arrangements for all school parties and picnics.

Assembly Commission. Received and booked programs for weekly assemblies. Planned some assemblies as needed.

Club Commission. Received annually petitions for charters from all school clubs. Considered petitions and issued charters.

Budget Commission. Received all requests for activity funds and estimates of revenues expected for the year. Assigned available funds after thorough discussion by all home rooms and the board of education.

Hall Commission.   Evaluated hall traffic conditions and suggested improvements. Conducted locker inspections and fire drills.

School Lunch Commission.   Appraised condition of school cafeteria and made proposals for improving any aspect of lunch hour, including recreational program.

Grounds Commission.   Responsible for suggestions regarding landscaping and traffic on school grounds.

Athletic Board.   Discussed and developed schedules, policies regarding equipment, increasing student participation, conduct, and awards.

Forensic Board.   Responsible for policies and programs in all speech activities.

Publications Board.   Selected staff and established policies for the school paper, annual, and handbook.

Other high schools have reported all-school committees, established for a great variety of projects. They have managed the school store; planned the school camping program, the school farm, or the school coöperatives; set up student loan funds, alumni organizations, follow-up studies, speakers' bureaus, and lost-and-found departments; planned patriotic observances, open houses for parents, rural school visits to orient incoming students, and a host of other special projects which are of interest to the whole school. The council which undertook to keep to itself the management of all projects would doom the program to an extremely limited scope.

The minutes of the council should be duplicated regularly for all home rooms and other constituent groups as a means of keeping all citizens oriented to what is going on. An occasional open-forum discussion of certain important problems can be scheduled as an assembly program. These town-hall assemblies can be successful, even in relatively large schools.

Factors which prevent all student from taking part should be eliminated as far as possible. The schedule should be such that boys and girls who have jobs after school can belong to the council or to an active committee. Scholastic eligibility, still a common council requirement, should be eliminated. The marks received by students in their classes are no valid criterion of their potential service as school citizens. Furthermore, we cannot encourage participation by raising barriers to it.

4. GIVING STATUS TO THE PROGRAM

The prestige of the council must derive in the last analysis from the reality of its achievements. No plan of student participation can achieve any status unless there is genuine responsibility for real tasks. The principal who is chiefly concerned about controlling the council will end by having nothing to control. Faith and confidence in young people are essential for adults who seek to develop a successful program of student participation.

Some principals make the mistake of assuming that problems that are real to them are also real to students, who are likely to be interested in projects for school improvement but not necessarily in the particular projects the principal has in mind. He must expect that some ideas will evolve from the representatives and from other students, and he must treat these ideas with respect.

No good can result from pretending that democracy obtains, if at the same time an attempt is made to manipulate the machinery of popular government from behind the scenes. Great damage to the ideals we seek can be done by this cynical use of the forms without the reality. To repeat, the status of the program will generally rest on the reality of its achievements to the persons involved—especially to the students.

When a project has been successful, the principal should see that proper credit is given to student and faculty leaders involved. He will get his greatest satisfaction from seeing such leadership strengthened and given status in the school and community. Nothing is so damaging to the prestige of a program as the assumption of all credit for its success by the administration. It would be better to err on the side of giving more credit than is due than to give no credit or to retain it for the principal.

The place of meeting may be a factor in the prestige of the council itself. If no proper place can be found for the council meetings, the impression created is that no particular importance is attached to the whole business. Some councils use classrooms that are poorly adapted to the purposes of the meeting. The best room in the school is not too good for the important school council.

In the same way, if meetings are so scheduled that they must adjourn in twenty minutes, everyone is likely to feel that nothing important is expected to happen. An hour each week is not too long a period. Some lively school councils use much more time than this, scheduled in the regular school day so as not to penalize students who work after school. In some high schools the council is scheduled as a regular "leadership" class meeting every day for credit. The council business comprises the curriculum of this "leadership" class.

In one school a cabinet group was established within the council, composed of the four officers elected at large and one representative of each high school class. This group, with the principal and the faculty representative, met for an early breakfast each week on council day to discuss the coming meeting and evaluate recent sessions. Such a group can make a significant contribution to the morale and prestige of the program. Care must be taken, however, to avoid the development of an in-group or political clique which appears to control the council meeting.

Inauguration and nominating assemblies can also make a contribution to the status of student participation in a school. Many junior and senior high schools have developed effective programs in which all students and teachers participate through responses, songs, and pledges. The alumni who are past presidents of the student body are sometimes brought back and featured at the inauguration assemblies. Nominating assemblies can furnish many significant educational opportunities. Here can be focused and emphasized the continuous search by all school citizens for leaders with the right qualifications for the job. Other assemblies can contribute indirectly to the prestige of the program through the use of student chairmen, the featuring of the school officers in leadership roles, the presentation of an actual council meeting on the stage, and by other means that keep the reality and importance of student leadership constantly before all the citizens.

Publicity can be given to projects in other ways than by assemblies. Home-room bulletins and posters, council minutes, and corridor posters serve important functions. A regular column in the school paper can be helpful. Many community papers welcome school news, which can help keep adult citizens continuously informed about plans and achievements. Special publications such as alumni and faculty newsletters should report the latest developments in school government. This will tend to happen automatically in a school where most of the staff and student body are actively at work on real projects for the improvement of their school life.

In an effort to dramatize the achievements of student participation, two kinds of "student days" have been used by secondary schools. In one type the students take over the responsibility for the school for a day, while the teachers visit other schools. In the other, the various student officers assume responsibility for the municipal governmental tasks for one day, usually under the tutelage of the adult officials. Both of these plans can serve the purpose of dramatizing the ability of students to assume supposedly adult responsibilities. On the other hand, neither kind of "student day" has anything to do with the concept of "student participation," which involves the coöperative efforts of both students and adults working in a team relationship. If these dramatic assumptions of adult responsibilities result in play acting or a paternalistic attitude in the community, they may possibly do more harm than good. In the long run, the status of the program will be most enhanced by the quiet sense of achievement and interaction which accompanies the doing of worth-while things by effective teamwork.

ACTIVITIES OF THE COUNCIL

It is hard to name any single project which has not been sometime achieved by some student council somewhere. The record of projects successfully undertaken by school councils is a truly impressive one. The student activities committee of the National Association of Secondary School Principals listed in 1944 the following types of projects reported by various high school councils: [3]

Attitudes

1. Secure students' suggestions for changes
2. Support safe and sane Hallowe'en pledge
3. Conduct an attitude campaign
4. Conduct campaign to improve school spirit
5. Establish a merit system patterned after the Civil-Service plan
6. Develop a fifty-question test for hall officers
7. Make survey of individual abilities and interests in an effort to provide programs for the student body
8. Conduct "Accident Prevention" campaign
9. Issue monthly bulletin on what students can do to develop courtesy, citizenship, discipline
10. Petition for opening of local civic youth building for the recreation of high school students with activities planned and supervised by Student Council members
11. Sponsor Most Courteous Pupil Contest
12. Plan and promote a "better manners" campaign

[3] "The Student Council in the Secondary School," *Bulletin of the National Association of Secondary School Principals, XXVIII,* No. 124, October, 1944.

Awards

13. Determine kinds and recipients of athletic awards
14. Give recognition to outstanding person among former graduates of school
15. Present awards for service to the school in a special awards assembly
16. Give public awards to students who have received very little recognition for hard work
17. Give an Awards Banquet for all those who have participated in the school activities program
18. Award honor monograms
19. Provide badges for cafeteria workers
20. Award prize for best assembly program of year

Co-operation with Other Councils

21. Visit other schools to gain new ideas
22. Invite and entertain a visiting Student Council
23. Maintain an activity program for Student Council meetings
24. Plan student-community activity for each week
25. Serve on student-faculty committees
26. Attend meetings throughout the state as representative of the student body
27. Send representatives to local, district, state, and regional conferences of the Student Council

Financing Projects

28. Furnish homeroom flags
29. Purchase cheer-leaders' outfits
30. Furnish soap and towels for washrooms
31. Maintain a flower fund
32. Provide mirrors for girls' lavatories
33. Provide stage furniture
34. Provide mid-morning lunch
35. Provide scholarships
36. Furnish lounge for faculty

37. Furnish lounge for students
38. Produce a drama to raise money for shades and flags

Long-Term Planning

39. Build a postwar school fund
40. Keep in touch with alumni and keep alumni informed of school work
41. Sponsor Life-Career Conferences
42. Survey school needs and make recommendations to the Board of Education through the Principal
43. Finance and conduct Senior follow-up study
44. Formulate and adopt a school creed
45. Gather information about colleges
46. Study youth delinquency and aids to alleviate it

Public Relations

47. Elect members of Council to adult community Youth Council
48. Give talks about the school before local community organizations
49. Present program over the local radio station
50. Take over city government for a day
51. Have several regular periods of the school day one evening each year so that the public may see and visit the school
52. Carry out a work plan survey with local Chamber of Commerce
53. Conduct "Open House" so public sees the school at work
54. Serve on a war council of parents and faculty
55. Expedite the work of the alumni association
56. Co-operate in community clean-up and paint-up campaigns
57. Provide programs for civic organizations
58. Participate in all community drives for funds, books, et cetera
59. Conduct Hallowe'en parties in co-operation with local Kiwanis, or other business organizations
60. Hold school forums
61. Co-sponsor a faculty night with the Parents' and Teachers' Association.

62. Prepare history of locality
63. Participate in inter-school (city-wide) popularity contest sponsored by local radio station
64. Establish and maintain a school museum
65. Sponsor radio broadcast over local station sometimes as often as once each week
66. Sponsor art and music appreciation program for both the student body and the public
67. Provide local high school talent program for community organizations

School Services

68. Assist in library
69. Be responsible for money from school activities
70. Charter school organizations
71. Assist teachers in grading papers, mimeographing, typing, et cetera
72. Man information desk
73. Conduct lost and found department
74. Send representative to Principal's curriculum adjustment council
75. Serve in the cafeteria
76. Conduct orientation day for incoming ninth graders
77. Plan and conduct sale of season student activity tickets
78. Keep interesting displays on bulletin board
79. Conduct student employment bureau
80. Design school awards and emblems
81. Require annual reports from all school organizations for study by the Council
82. Plan activity type of commencement program
83. Conduct Pep Assemblies
84. Sponsor Homecoming Day
85. Give annual football banquet
86. Supervise student traffic in and about the school building
87. Manage a co-operative store

88. Operate and care for camera
89. Run campaign for new cheers, songs, et cetera, for school
90. Conduct snack bar
91. Conduct book exchange or book store
92. Manage used-book store
93. Conduct student locker inspection every month
94. Keep open house in the school two nights a week for recreational purposes
95. Take over the responsibility of raising and lowering the flag on the pole on the school ground
96. Sponsor selection and coronation of a king and queen (or more commonly, a queen)
97. Sponsor declamation events
98. Exchange speakers and assembly programs with other schools
99. Send sympathy notes to all ill and bereaved students and faculty members
100. Write letters of welcome to new teachers before school opens, or as soon as possible
101. Act as coaches
102. Act as tutors
103. Check eligibility of all club and class officers and Council members every six weeks
104. Compute the scholastic rating of students at the end of each marking period, as well as at the end of each semester and school year
105. Serve as guides and ushers
106. Sell milk and change dollar bills to speed up cafeteria lines
107. Conduct and direct lunchrooms
108. Keep scrapbook of year's school activities
109. Care for the trophy case
110. Assist school nurse
111. Provide posters for special events for use in the school and in public places of the community
112. Decorate for holidays
113. Supply door and ticket committees

114. Landscape and care for school grounds
115. Maintain a record of students' extracurricular activities
116. Keep the Constitution up to date
117. Care for the stage and sound system of the school
118. Have charge of fire drills and air-raid practice
119. Assist the janitor
120. Keep records of graduates in the Service and maintain a Service Flag
121. Adopt a war orphan

Social Activities

122. Conduct noon-hour programs
123. Plan program of social activities
124. Hold teas
125. Hold roller-skating parties
126. Hold get-acquainted party for incoming class and other new students
127. Arrange for all intramural sports
128. Encourage student participation in extracurricular activities
129. Conduct a Senior-Freshman party
130. Provide free movie for school
131. Conduct one all-school party per month
132. Sponsor annual spring outing and painting of large school letter on hillside
133. Operate youth centers

Student Information

134. Maintain a column in the school's weekly newspaper in regard to Student Council activities and projects on which it is working
135. Publish a printed annual report in newspaper or booklet form
136. Publish school paper
137. Publish handbook
138. Get out Freshman handbook (mimeograph) in addition to regular printed handbook

139. Prepare student directory
140. Present a typical Student Council meeting as an assembly program
141. Commemorate holidays
142. Develop and distribute standards of citizenship
143. Plan and give courses in school government and leadership for class and club officers
144. Make movie of school activities to show students in lower grade about to enter high school
145. Sponsor daily school and world news broadcasts over school's public address system
146. Conduct a "Who's Who" contest
147. Keep student body informed of innovations of other Student Councils

Welfare

148. Collect clothes for unfortunates at home and abroad
149. Present baskets of food at Thanksgiving and Christmas to the needy
150. Collect, repair, and distribute toys

The activities of a good school council will tend to flow over into the community. Kelley and Faunce have suggested the following generalizations about the activities of student organizations:

1. Youth is eager to serve the school, the community, and the nation, when aroused by a real challenge.
2. Youth wants, and has earned, a part in the planning for such school and community service.
3. The most appropriate areas for service are those which represent the real interests and problems of youth themselves.
4. Council services need not be confined to limited areas within the school, nor even to the school as a whole.
5. The real limits to youth service should be the limits imposed by youth themselves in accordance with their willingness and ability to assume and perform the services.

6. Faith in the ability of youth will reap dividends in community service, unleashed human power, and skilled leadership.[4]

SOME DO'S AND DON'TS

It may be helpful to include in this chapter a few cautions about student participation in school government:

1. Avoid adult domination, either openly provided by the constitution or covertly engaged in under the forms of democracy. Young people cannot be deceived about the real attitudes of adults. There is no substitute for faith in youth.
2. On the other hand, do not confuse democratic participation with anarchy. If adults abdicate their role in the school's civic affairs, it is an evidence of laissez faire, not democracy.
3. Remember that we learn to govern by governing. Leadership in democracy is not a gift, but a hard lesson to be learned. It can only be learned through actual experience, and adults in the school can help to provide the experience.
4. Take definite steps to gain the wholehearted support of the entire faculty for the goals of student participation. This can best be attained by involving them in satisfying experiences which will build their faith in young people.
5. Remember that all students are citizens and should have an active part. The whole test of government, in school or anywhere, is the extent to which a real sense of civic responsibility can be developed in all citizens.
6. Don't limit participation—extend it! The only purpose served by "safeguards" and eligibility standards is that of excluding the mass of school citizens from the opportunity to learn democracy through its practice.
7. Don't mimic the government patterns of other schools, or those of the city or state. Develop a functional organization geared to your own school's needs.
8. It will be helpful to develop a clearly-written statement of the

[4] Earl C. Kelley and Roland C. Faunce, *Your School and Its Government,* New York, National Self-Government Committee, 1945, p. 21.

goals, scope, and organization of your plan of student participation.

9. Remember that we walk before we run. Young people can be plunged into responsibilities for which they have no readiness and insufficient skills. On the other hand, we must not use the above argument as a rationalization for doing nothing. Go *slowly*, but go forward! [5]

ROLE OF THE PRINCIPAL

It has been suggested throughout this chapter that an all-school council might include in its membership the principal or his representative, an elected representative of the faculty, and perhaps two or three other adults who are citizens of the school. There are excellent reasons for the principal himself to work with the council as one of its sponsors. Much of the fear and suspicion which often prevails with regard to the principal's attitude can be resolved if he is working actively and skillfully with the council. His ability and his attitude toward the students can be crucial factors in the success or failure of student participation.

If he nags, threatens, or bullies the council nothing good can happen in its meetings. If he maintains a benevolently paternal attitude, controlling the council behind the scenes while observing the outward forms of democracy, cynicism and frustration will eventually develop; young people cannot be fooled in such a manner. If he smiles indulgently at their ideas and proposals, he will instantly betray himself as one of little faith. If he uses the council as an instrument for advancing his own status in the school, he will hurt the cause of student participation beyond repair by destroying the total faculty support which it must have.[6]

The principal, of course, has the right of veto over the actions of the council. He will neither need to use the veto nor to wield it

[5] Johnston and Faunce, *op. cit.*, pp. 54–55.
[6] *Ibid.*, p. 53.

as a threat if he is an effective sponsor. He must like young people, and earn their affection and support. He must be the kind of person whom students can trust. He must have faith in boys and girls, and a deep respect for the process of democracy. He must be genuinely dedicated to the important task of group planning and be determined to help it succeed. He must, in short, believe in students and take seriously their participation in school government.

The principal who has, or who can develop, these qualities can help the council immeasurably:

1. He can be a *participant* in their planning.
2. He is often their *interpreter* to the faculty.
3. He is *expediter* of any plans which require immediate outside help.
4. He is their *resource person* in the process of planning and legislating.
5. He can be their *counselor* in civic as well as personal problems.
6. He provides *inspiration* toward council and school improvement.
7. He is a friendly *evaluator* of their effectiveness.[7]

Some principals fear that there will be no authority or status left for them if they share it with student and faculty leaders. The contrary is apt to be true. When authority is shared it multiplies its effectiveness and reflects credit on the leader who shares it. A recent book on administration has pointed out that "Under a dominating leader the goals to be achieved are the leader's goals, and not the people's. . . . The success of a program in a community depends upon how thoroughly people accept, endorse, and support it.[8]

This acceptance and support depend basically upon the program's origin. The principal who succeeds in securing student participation in school government must be sincere in his belief that

[7] Adapted from *ibid.,* pp. 53–54.
[8] Clyde M. Campbell (ed.), *Practical Applications of Democratic Administration,* New York, Harper & Brothers, 1952, p. 46.

students, and teachers too, can develop and carry out good projects for the improvement of the school.

A real challenge and a thrilling reward await the secondary school principal who has sufficient faith in young people to help them participate in the government of their school. Only thus can it become really *their* school; and only thus can it become a better school.

For Further Reading

Douglass, Harl R., *Modern Administration of Secondary Schools,* rev. ed., Boston, Ginn & Company, 1954, chap. 15.

Educational Policies Commission, *Learning the Ways of Democracy,* Washington, The National Education Association, 1940.

Faunce, Roland C., "How Can the Student Council Function More Effectively?", *Bulletin of the National Association of Secondary School Principals,* March, 1950.

Johnston, Edgar G., and Faunce, Roland C., *Student Activities in Secondary Schools,* New York, The Ronald Press Company, 1952, chap. 3.

Kelley, Earl C., *Student Cooperation: A Report of Student Government in the High Schools,* New York, National Self-Government Committee, 1941.

Kelley, Earl C., and Faunce, Roland C., *Your School and Its Government,* New York, National Self-Government Committee, 1945.

McKown, Harry C., *The Student Council,* New York, McGraw-Hill Book Company, 1944.

McKown, Harry C., and Baillard, Virginia, *So You Were Elected!,* New York, McGraw-Hill Book Company, 1946.

Meier, Arnold, Cleary, Florence, and Davis, Alice, *Let's Look at the Student Council,* Detroit, Wayne University Press, 1949.

Michigan Department of Public Instruction, *Democracy in Action,* Bulletin 320, Lansing, Mich., the Department, 1941.

National Association of Student Councils, *The Student Council Handbook,* Washington, The National Association of Secondary School Principals, *Bulletin* No. 89, March 1940; *Bulletin* No. 144, October, 1947.

Smith, Joe, *Student Councils For Our Times,* New York, Bureau of Publications, Teachers College, Columbia University, 1951.

"Student Council at Work, The," *Bulletin of the National Association of Secondary School Principals,* No. 132, October, 1945.

"Student Council in the Secondary School, The," *Bulletin of the National Association of Secondary School Principals, XXVIII,* No. 124, October, 1944 (reprinted, 1946).

....

CHAPTER 11

The Principal and the Building

―――――――――――――――――――――――――――――

IMPORTANCE OF THE BUILDING

School buildings are an important factor in educational programs. The quality of living and learning in a school is significantly affected by the physical environment provided in the building. The health and safety of young citizens are dependent on the kind of building in which they live. Its cleanliness, efficiency, and safety are important in establishing standards and habits for youth to live by. The instructional program can either be facilitated or hampered by the physical facility. It is true that good learning can go forward in an old, inefficient school building if teachers are ingenious and interested in youth. That learning would be greatly facilitated, however, by an up-to-date, efficient school building

The task of creating a good physical environment is not completed when a new school has been built. It is an ongoing task that confronts all those who use the building. Unless administrators, teachers, custodians, students, and the community share in assuming responsibility for maintaining and improving the building, it is likely to deteriorate rapidly. Even a new building can soon become dirty and shabby unless the hundreds of persons who use it coöperate in keeping it clean. The administrator cannot do this alone, nor can the custodians. It is a challenge to all who use the building to share the responsibility for keeping it clean, beautiful, and functional.

TEACHERS

Teachers can wield an important influence in maintaining a building. Indeed, without their active help even the best custodians cannot keep a building clean and orderly. The teacher who checks to make sure that his room is in order, that books are back on the shelf, that movable furniture has been restored to its original position, and that the floor is reasonably free of paper is treating the custodian as he himself would like to be treated if the roles were reversed. More importantly, he is sharing a responsibility as a member of the team. It is both reasonable and rewarding for teachers to assume responsibility for the daily condition of their rooms. Custodians respond warmly to this kind of coöperation. They will usually go out of their way to be of help to teachers who show consideration for them. Being human, they also respond with aggression or withdrawal to the teacher who regards the custodian as a lower class of person, a menial who should get satisfaction from being ordered around. This kind of attitude is both undemocratic and ridiculous in a situation where real teamwork is needed. Fortunately, not many teachers act that way toward custodians. Too many teachers do forget, however, to assume their share of the job of keeping classrooms neat and clean.

As a group, teachers also can share in total building maintenance. They can set up committees to help inspect the building periodically, to study ways of improving traffic flow in the corridors, or to make recommendations about heating and ventilating. They should share in planning changes in the building and in ordering of new equipment and furniture, since all these things affect their lives in direct fashion. Teachers should, of course, have a hand in planning a new school if it is to be as functional as possible. It is to be hoped that the day is past when new schools were planned by architects and administrators without advice or help from teachers. Both as individuals and as a group they have ideas to contribute and can help develop a better school building.

Some administrators fear that the total cost of a new building, or of change in a present building, will be increased beyond practical limits if teachers compete for costly facilities. Experience has shown that this fear is unjustified. When teachers are really "in" on the planning they prove to be as reasonable and as realistic about available funds as administrators. They realize that the budget must make sense to those who own the schools, and that overexpenditure on one part of the budget will make less money available for other necessary items—including teachers' salaries. Competition or jockeying for available funds is more apt to occur in a faculty which does not share openly in planning changes in the building, thus leaving such negotiating to private efforts of individual teachers.

Thus teachers, both as individuals and as a faculty group, should have a significant share in the task of maintaining and improving the building.

STUDENTS

Students are an important part of the team, too. Indeed, the building is theirs in a true sense, since it has been constructed and maintained as their home; they are local citizens for whose use the building was intended in the first place. To the extent that they have a genuine feeling of ownership, they will cherish *their* school and work actively to maintain and improve it. Youth who vandalize a building have not been helped to acquire this important feeling of ownership. One does not deliberately destroy one's most cherished possession. To the vandal, the school appears to be the property of the enemy—of teachers and administrators whom they hate or fear, or perhaps vaguely of adults against whom they must organize an attack. Everything possible must be done to give youth a feeling that they own the school—that it is theirs to maintain, to live together in, and to cherish as their most important group possession. Any policy that prevents this feeling of ownership from developing should be changed. For example, it is a violation of official policies in some schools for students to improve the school grounds or the classroom. Such policies are shortsighted in that they eliminate from the team the very person who can make or break building maintenance. No matter how conscientious the custodians and teachers may be about keeping the building clean, their efforts will come to naught if they do not have the full coöperation of students. The task of keeping a building clean and beautiful is a major challenge to students, and a useful experience in civic education. Both as individuals and as members of student groups, the care and improvement of their school should be high on the list of priorities for students.

In one high school the student council included the chairmen of several commissions whose business it was to check on building maintenance. One group studied the improvement of the school grounds and parking lot. Over a period of years a master plan was developed to which clubs and classes contributed by planting flower borders, shrubs, and trees, laying out walks, erecting a flag pole, and replacing the flag. The commission studied parking problems and proposed new policies on parking designed to improve the use of existing facilities. It also built two new bicycle racks and secured legislation from the council regarding their use.

Another commission made weekly surveys of traffic flow in the halls at various passing periods and suggested changes in the schedule for junior high school classes to reduce congestion. Fire drills were also improved by the removal of impediments at certain exits.

A study-hall commission rated the six daily study halls and made suggestions for changes in seating. They secured an agreement from students in shop classes to refinish all the tables in the study hall during one semester. The same group refinished the corridor patrol chairs at another time.

Student police kept writing off the lavatory walls by constant checking and by educational campaigns in the home rooms. The noon-hour commission secured the purchase of folding tables and supervised the lunchroom hour, with special attention to clean-up. The locker inspectors conducted monthly inspections of the condition of lockers and encouraged better housekeeping by a poster campaign. Each commission consisted of a chairman who was a member of the student council, a teacher adviser, and six to twenty students from various grade levels. The council enlisted the support of the student newspaper in running editorials and slogans designed to keep students aware of their responsibilities. Discussions in the various home rooms helped develop a sense of proprietorship in students with regard to *their* school.

Such a program distributes responsibility to all citizens instead of laying it all in the lap of the custodian. Not only was the school in question a clean one; it was also a laboratory where students learned civic responsibility through practicing it.

It is relatively easy to identify a school where students are actively helping to maintain the building. Not only are their official organizations discussing ways to improve their school, but individuals are picking up paper and checking the condition of rooms at the end of a period. Students can learn to do these things without being told by adults if they are consistently treated as equal citizens with a major interest in a clean, beautiful building. They are unlikely to become interested in doing their part if

Policies forbid them to improve school facilities.

They are always being scolded as a group for the misdoings of a few.

Cleaning up is assigned as a punishment.

Adults do all the work and take all the credit for the condition of the building.

In short, the task of helping youth to assume responsibility for their building is closely linked with the whole philosophy of participation. If participation is on a superficial level or is called for only when adults' goals are involved, it will be hard to convince students that they are not being used as pawns, or as a means of getting free labor for janitorial work. They must be really involved in planning at all levels if the task of improving the building is to acquire reality for them. If they really feel that the building is theirs to make or to mar, almost all students will organize to help develop a better facility instead of to destroy the one they have. Such civic enterprises appeal to the altruism and energy of youth.

Young people are keenly interested in group activities which improve their school and community. Such service appeals to the idealism, enthusiasm, and team spirit which are characteristic of the teens, and richly benefits the school. It gives learning a climate of reality, capitalizes upon real interests and needs, and furnishes a host of genuine stimuli for good group activity.

Boys and girls are citizens too. They can be good ones if they are given a chance. The experience of assuming responsibility for community improvement is an ideal preparation for adult citizenship. Democracy stands in dire need of citizens who can look about them, discover a community need, and then work together to develop a better life for all.[1]

Examples of projects undertaken by student groups for improvement of their own building are numerous and impressive. They range from helping to plan a new building to carrying on campaigns to encourage the picking up of paper. In some schools students have actually constructed such additions to their school as the following:

Greenhouse	Cannery
Shop	Tennis courts
Garden	Henhouse
Toolhouse	Pens for pets
Classroom wing	Pool, skating rink
Deep-freeze locker	Ski run

[1] Edgar G. Johnston and Roland C. Faunce, *Student Activities in Secondary Schools,* New York, The Ronald Press Company, 1952, pp. 310–311.

Projects for improvement of existing facilities include a wide range of activities:

Campaigns on paper pickup, noise, locker neatness, health
Cleaning blackboards
Refinishing furniture, floors
Checking toilets, cafeteria, halls
Building stage scenery, trophy cases, picnic tables, outdoor grills, bike racks, school store, shelving, bird feeders
Raising money for pictures, curtains, statuary, projection equipment, new lighting, showers, sports equipment, flag, scoreboards, TV sets
Rearranging classroom furniture
Painting walls
Cleaning walls, ceilings, windows
Hanging draperies and curtains
Conducting fire and air-raid drills
Decorating windows for special days
Developing diorama exhibits
Maintaining bulletin boards
Furnishing club or council room
Beautifying school grounds
Erecting parking signs
Conducting campaigns
Repairing school buses
Collecting game and toy libraries
Developing school radio station
Developing school museum

All these projects and dozens of similar ones have been carried on by students in one or more schools. Sometimes a single class, such as an agriculture or core class, will undertake a school improvement project. Sometimes a school club will adopt such a project for a year. In other schools the student council spearheads and coördinates a school-wide program through committees such as were described earlier. Included in Olsen's *School and Com-*

munity Programs [2] are descriptions of many projects that relate to school building maintenance and improvement.

CUSTODIANS

The key persons in the program of school building maintenance are, of course, the custodians or engineers. Once regarded as unskilled labor that anyone could do, the job of the custodian has become increasingly a technical and important one. As electrical, heating, ventilating, and sanitary facilities have become more complicated, the modern secondary school building requires a considerable degree of technical competence merely to inspect it and keep it operating. When emergency repairs are needed the custodian becomes a jack-of-all-trades in most schools. He is thrust into such jobs as repairing electrical fixtures, plumbing, furnace parts, doing window glazing, rough carpentry, cabinetmaking, gardening, tree surgery, and a dozen other operations. He is directly responsible for cleaning and heating the building. The lives of hundreds of persons are in his care as he checks the building for fire and health hazards. He must "get along" with administrators, teachers, students, and the general public. In the latter role he is a primary public relations agent because of his numerous contacts with visitors. He must set a good example for students, to whom he is sometimes a more helpful counselor than any of their teachers. He must do a wide variety of jobs reasonably well, be patient with teachers and students, keep himself neat in spite of the nature of his daily work, and be ingenious in planning better ways of maintaining the building.

These are high standards and not all custodians measure up to them. There is a distinct trend, however, toward professionalizing and upgrading school custodians. The National Association of Engineers and Custodians has been active in this effort. Universities and state departments of education have conducted work-

[2] Edward G. Olsen (ed.), *School and Community Programs*, New York, Prentice-Hall, 1949.

shops and institutes for school custodians. Many of them are now under civil service. Wage scales have improved markedly, as have provisions for sick leave, pensions, and vacations. Hours of work, too, have tended to become reduced and extra pay for extra hours has become a general policy.

Boards of education would do well to adopt policies that will attract men and women of high caliber to the job of school custodian, for it is an important position in any school. To the principal, especially, the janitor or custodian is an important person. As Linn, Helm, and Grabarkiewicz have pointed out:

> In a sense, the custodian is the principal's right-hand man. The principal needs his assistance, and he counts on him to a very great degree. He usually realizes the importance of the custodian's position and appreciates the fact that a clean, well-kept, properly heated and ventilated building favorably affects the teachers in their teaching and the children in their learning. He knows that the employee can gain good will for the school through his good work and his friendly attitude toward pupils, teachers, and visitors. He appreciates the employee who is courteous, dependable, and cheerful, who can be counted on to do his work without constant supervision and direction, and who is always willing to do the countless small tasks that must be done.[3]

One of the custodian's problems arises from the fact that these "countless small tasks" keep coming to him, not only from the principal but also from every teacher in the building. Consideration and sensitivity should be shown by those who make requests that take the custodian off his regular schedule. Special technical help should be provided for some tasks that are specialized in nature, such as cabinetwork, electrical repairs, masonry, or furnace repair. The principal should try to protect the custodians from unreasonable demands or overloads.

[3] Henry H. Linn, Leslie C. Helm, and K. P. Grabarkiewicz, *The School Custodian's Housekeeping Handbook,* New York, Bureau of Publications, Teachers College, Columbia University, 1949, p. 8.

Custodians should be more than doers of other people's ideas. They should be evaluators and planners, too. They should be expected to look critically and thoughtfully at every job and process to discover a better way of performing it. As members of the team, their ideas and advice should be sought before any new policy is adopted that will affect building maintenance. It is probable that they should be represented on the school council to ensure that they will have a voice in developing new policies. At any rate, the principal and faculty should consult them with respect and receive their suggestions attentively. Such treatment will pay off in better building maintenance and in better teamwork. Most "custodian problems" that arise stem from feelings of inferior status on the part of custodians. Such problems can be prevented by the recognition of the custodian as a human being who is entitled to respect, and as a technical specialist on the staff team. The custodian, as a member of the team, should deal directly and honestly with the principal and not attempt to carry grievances around him to the board members.

In summary, better buildings will result from a team approach in which administrator, teachers, students, and custodians work together. Such a team will speak of *our* school and *our* problems, not *my* school and *my* problems. There will be no invidious distinctions made regarding those who do their work in overalls and must sometimes get their hands dirty. Everyone will recognize that he shares the responsibility for improving and maintaining "our" building, and will be proud to do his part.

THE COMMUNITY

The citizens of a community have a share in this responsibility that extends beyond their payment of school taxes. As they use the building for community purposes they should feel a sense of ownership and pride. They should treat the building and grounds as their valued possession and seek to keep them in excellent condition. They should also look for ways to improve the facility and work with others to secure such improvements.

In some older buildings this improvement effort has led parents to hold bees for painting schoolrooms, building cupboards, and even constructing additions to the building. They have also bought pianos, record players, moving picture projectors, and dozens of other classroom facilities that they discovered were needed.

It is probable that such improvements should be provided by boards of education out of public tax revenues. Still, this awareness of a need and willingness to make an effort to improve a school speak well of the parents and administration. Through room parents' clubs, parent-teacher associations, and citizens' advisory groups parents have joined with teachers in surveying school building needs and in conducting bond drives to secure needed revenues. Many an improvement has been made in school buildings across the land through the earnest efforts of parents and other lay citizens. As was pointed out in Chapter 6, the coöperation of the community is worth working for as a means of getting better buildings as well as better school programs.

COMMUNITY USE OF THE SCHOOL BUILDING

One way to develop community identification with a school building is to make it available for community use. Secondary schools are substantial civic investments that should serve many community needs. Adult education, club meetings, recreational programs, civic meetings, and youth-serving agencies should be housed in the school if it is the most appropriate facility available. One criterion of a community school is the extent to which it serves the needs of the community. Both during the school year and in summer vacations, community use of a school building is an index of its status as a civic center. Of course there is no need to duplicate facilities, and communities that enjoy a separate civic center may confine their use of the school (after hours) to adult education and parent-teacher meetings.

BUILDING BETTER SECONDARY SCHOOLS

After a long period of inactivity, public school construction picked up in tempo following World War II. The prospects now indicate that a great number of new secondary schools must be built in the near future because of the wave of enrollments now approaching the secondary school and because of the need to replace old buildings. It is of the utmost importance that these new buildings be planned with an eye to the future; a building design can hamper or significantly aid program improvement. It is not usually possible to predict program trends positively in advance; this means that, to permit adaptation to future needs, there must be flexibility in planning.

There are a number of ways to provide flexibility. One is to build the plant on a sufficiently large site and in such a manner that wings can be added. Another way is to provide inner partitions that can be easily moved because they do not support an upper story or carry heating or ventilating ducts in them. Still another way is to equip classrooms with movable furniture and shelving so that conversion to another purpose will be easy.

High schools in urban areas are usually too large for maximum efficiency. It is probable that no school can operate with genuine effectivenesses if it enrolls over 1500 students. It may not be financially feasible to keep schools under this enrollment figure, but boards of education and citizens should at least recognize that they are not buying good secondary education when four and five thousand students are thrust into one school unit. A huge high school loses its human quality and becomes a factory. Split shifts are resorted to. Students come and leave at various hours. Teachers are not all present at any one time. The typical student never gets to know any one teacher really well. Many students drop out of school without anyone's notice. Communities that want good secondary schools should plan to keep enrollments low enough to make interpersonal relationships possible.

Too small a high school is uneconomical, too. Many school

districts should not undertake to build a senior high school but should reorganize to provide an adequate tax base for a good high school.

The school site should be selected with an eye to convenience and space. It should be located near the center of the residential area and provide a minimum of thirty acres (fifty acres would be better for a school enrolling a thousand students or more).[4] These two conditions are not always possible to meet. There may not be space adequate in size and conveniently located in residential areas. If transportation facilities are adequate it is justifiable to locate the senior high school off-center in order to secure a site of sufficient size.

High schools were once gloomy institutional-type buildings that stood out in startling fashion from the environment. Many of today's buildings are one-story affairs with plenty of light and with some degree of harmony with the environment. There should be room on the site for trees, shrubs, and flowers as well as for recreational facilities such as playfields and tennis courts. Parking space is also highly desirable, and makes further demands on the site. A school garden or farm can serve an excellent purpose if it is nearby.

A new school building should reflect the needs of the school program. It is of the utmost importance, therefore, that all persons concerned—teachers, students, and parents—have a share in planning the program which the building is to reflect. While it is not possible to predict future program trends with accuracy, at least the building can be geared to foreseeable needs. In too many cases a building has been designed without reference to changing trends in school programs, and has operated to freeze the program into traditional patterns that are the only kind of instruction the building makes possible. For example, many secondary school faculties now seek to encourage social activities among students.

---

[4] This figure does not, of course, include acreage needed for school forests and farms.

The building can make these social experiences possible or it can be so designed as to discourage all informal contacts among students. Small classrooms with fixed furniture tend to prevent or discourage flexible classroom procedures such as group work or construction of student projects. Teamwork between teachers in the same department is not encouraged when classrooms are not connected. The failure to provide activity space can become a real obstacle to the development of a good activity program.

Koopman describes six kinds of space needed in a modern secondary school:

1. Facilitative space
2. Social living space for all school purposes
3. Reserve or atelier space
4. Specialized learning activity space
5. Self-contained classroom space
6. Extramural space.[5]

He explains that the first category, facilitative space, refers to servicing and maintenance space, administrative offices, and corridors and stairways. Social living space includes adequate foyers, canteens, commons, locker areas, dining space, and committee rooms for informal meetings of small groups of students or adults. Reserve space includes instructional-materials centers, storage displays, collections and libraries. Specialized learning activities include science laboratories, homemaking room, darkroom, etc. The self-contained classroom is proposed to accommodate a group with one teacher on an all-day basis, with individuals and small groups leaving the room at intervals for specialized activities and returning again to the self-contained room as their home base. Such a room would, Koopman suggests, require at least 1200 square feet of space and have an outside door to its own section of the school playground.

Extramural space includes rooms for large-group socializing,

[5] G. Robert Koopman, "A New Theoretical Approach to Secondary School Planning," *The Nation's Schools,* December 1953, p. 50–57.

assemblies, and sports. No mention is made of gymnasiums or auditoriums as such, but "extramural" space most closely approximates these facilities.

Here, then, is one kind of a secondary school plant that serves the needs of one kind of program. This program, centered about all-day home rooms and emphasizing flexibility and social experiences, is the kind of secondary school that some persons visualize in the future. It is interesting to contemplate, whether one accepts all its facets or not. The significant point is that this building reflects a program that has a distinct flavor, and facilitates its operation. Whatever the secondary school program is to be, the building should at least make it possible.

The following judgments as to trends for the future in the secondary school were collected from a jury of twenty curriculum specialists in Michigan. Each of these trends presents some implications for the junior and senior high school building:

CONSOLIDATED LIST OF TRENDS IN SECONDARY EDUCATION

A. *Curriculum*
1. Trend toward integration
   a. By grade level rather than departmental levels
   b. The core curriculum—fused courses, etc.
   c. Integration of physical sciences
   d. Integration of the arts—dramatics, fine árts, music, industrial arts, interior decorating, etc.
   e. Integration of physical education, athletics, health education, recreation, with some type of suitable program for everyone
2. Increased use of problem-solving approach
3. Increased teacher-pupil-parent planning of curriculum experiences—community curriculum study
4. Home and family living emphasis
5. Emphasis on general education—postpone specialization
6. Broader type of vocational education, based on community needs for all age groups

7. Work experience
8. Adult education
9. Guidance, record keeping, individualized instruction
10. Leisure-time education—broad recreation
11. Outdoor education—camping—community service projects
12. Broad reading program
13. Emphasis on international understanding and human relations
14. Functional citizenship education a part of all activities
15. Safety education
16. Extracurricular activities scheduled during the day as part of the regular curriculum

B. *Method*

1. Pupil-teacher planning
2. Increased use of audio-visual education
3. Longer blocks of time—supervised study—increased responsibility of one teacher for a group of pupils
4. Diversified activities in the classroom
5. The self-contained classroom plus small conference rooms
6. Attention to needs of atypical children
7. Decentralized library
8. No study halls

Whether or not these trends represent the shape of things to come in secondary education, they at least suggest some emphases that a new building should not directly prevent by its design. One point appears to have general agreement among students of school building construction—general classrooms should be larger than the 20 by 30 feet allowed for academic classrooms in older buildings. There should be activity space, at least for every two classrooms. There should be space for individual counseling, which might perhaps be provided in combination with the activity room. Thus every two classrooms might share a combined activity room and counseling office between them. The inner partitions may be constructed as soundproof folding doors so that the entire space,

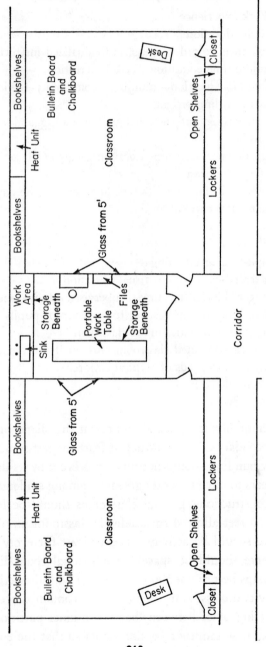

perhaps 30 by 90 feet, could be used by two sections viewing a film or a play. The inner (corridor) wall should carry plumbing to permit each pair of rooms to have running water for washing. It is possible, if a core program of some sort is planned, to include a toilet and built-in lockers to make the entire unit self-contained.

The size of study halls can be reduced materially with the use of these self-contained rooms, since their longer block of time makes possible supervised study. The old study hall with 100 to 500 seats would no longer be necessary, but a series of smaller study rooms could be scheduled as needed.

The auditorium causes much perplexity because of its high cost and only occasional use. Combinations of gymnasium and auditorium have been tried on a wide scale, but have not been generally successful for both purposes. For community use there should probably be a large auditorium in the school if none exists in any other civic building. Educational purposes as such are probably better served by a little theater with an adequate stage. The little theater could be used for assembly purposes by a grade-level group.

Gymnasiums are not always justified on an educational basis, but they appear to be well established as necessary for spectator sports. In schools enrolling 500 or more students there should be a large gymnasium that can be made into two by use of folding partitions. Provision of bright, well-ventilated showers and locker rooms is necessary for an adequate program of group games.

Cafeterias should be light, cheerful, and carefully planned to facilitate food service for large numbers of persons. Furniture should be removable to permit use of the room for informal social activities such as club meetings, class dances, or community group meetings. Tables should be small enough to permit family-type table groups where the social graces are learned through practice. Through rotating the roles of host and hostess, providing some dishes that are passed in family style, and keeping tables small enough for conversational groups, some schools are using the lunch hour as an educational experience. By careful planning, some elements of this approach can be secured in most cafeterias.

The library should be centrally located and large enough for three purposes: a central reading room, adequate book stacks, and workrooms for small groups. If it is to serve also as a community library it should be located on the first floor. Traveling bookracks should be provided to permit transfer of a kit of books or files of materials to any classroom. The provision of flexible classroom libraries is a significant trend in secondary schools. Especially in science, English, social studies, and core classrooms, classroom libraries are now fairly common. In some new schools the classroom bookcases are made of movable units that fit into alcoves in the room and are equipped with castors to make it possible for them to be wheeled back to the school library for the return of materials and reissue of others requested.

PLANNING FOR STUDENT ACTIVITIES

Secondary schools are now generally committed to the support and encouragement of student activities. The building should be so planned as to make activities possible and efficient. Too often the activities program is hampered by the building design. Stages may be inadequate for play production. The school paper may be put out in a room the size of a janitor's closet. Hobby collections may be confined to lockers. Often the only place where students can gather to converse is the halls, and even there such activity may be officially discouraged. Such buildings prevent instead of encouraging the natural social life through which boys and girls learn to get along with others.

One hundred and fifty eleventh- and twelfth-graders in the Royal Oak, Michigan, High School were asked to answer the question: "What would you suggest for a new high school in terms of program and building?" Their suggestions have been briefly summarized in the following list:

(NOTE: These ideas have been listed without regard to order of importance)

1. Big auto shop
2. Small auditorium
3. Student credit union
4. Outside phones in study hall
5. Reference rooms off library
6. Indoor track
7. Recreation room (TV, record player, magazines, etc.)
8. Stadium
9. Recreation room for parties
10. Hockey team
11. Comfortable library chairs
12. Hot-rod club (to promote safe driving)
13. Visitor's locker room
14. Soft floors (asphalt tile, etc.)
15. Air-raid shelter
16. Senate room (student court, etc.)
17. Adequate first-aid room
18. Usable space on roof
19. ROTC (rifle range, parade ground, etc.)
20. Bus-loading platform
21. Glass backboards in gym
22. Expanded athletic program (boxing, wrestling, tumbling, judo, etc.)
23. After-game activities
24. Student planned and participated assemblies
25. More counselor time
26. Custom-car club (hot rod?)
27. More trade subjects (electrical, welding, plumbing, etc.)
28. Student parking lot
29. More and bigger lockers
30. Adequate cafeteria service
31. Indoor-outdoor pool (underwater PA and viewing box, lights)
32. Transportation (a) to and from school daily, (b) school events
33. Air-conditioning, heating

34. Wide stairways and corridors
35. Proper lighting
36. Soundproofing
37. Large windows
38. Voluntary supervised study halls
39. Supervised student lounge
40. More mirrors in girls' lavatories
41. Different-size chairs

Certain categories of need reappear in this list repeatedly. The need for social living appears in requests for a recreation room with television, record player, and magazines, after-game activities, student-planned assemblies, student lounges, vending machines, long lunch hour, and more time between classes. Schools are recognizing this social need by provision of alcoves for conversation, open foyers furnished with comfortable chairs, recreation rooms, and small work-and-play rooms for clubs or committees.

Student organizations have need for meeting space. The Royal Oak students mentioned a small auditorium for plays, student credit union, hockey team, lockers for visiting teams, a hot-rod club, air-raid shelter, Senate room, first-aid room, rifle range, parade ground, expanded athletic program, assemblies, pool, transportation to school events, student-supervised study halls, music practice rooms, field house, double gym, golf-driving range, and an agricultural program. If the school is to lend prestige and support to a program of student activities, the needs of those activities should be met in the building plan. The student council should have a suitable place to meet. Clubs should have appropriate meeting rooms, with adequate storage for their possessions. Speech and dramatics groups should have the use of a little-theater facility. The school-paper staff should be able to spread out materials, use typewriters, and have access to adequate files. The school gymnasium and grounds should be so designed as to make room for twelve to twenty different recreational hobbies to go on simultaneously.

No complete treatment of school building design is possible in this chapter. Many facilities needed in a modern secondary school have not been mentioned at all. There has been limited reference to specialized shops and laboratories appropriate to the senior high school program. Other important features not discussed here are the offices, storage facilities, and corridor space. Technical problems of color, lighting, heating, and ventilating are dealt with in detail in many specialized books. Some of the sources of further information are listed at the end of this chapter.

In summary of this section on building design, the secondary school building should be planned to accommodate a program; this means beginning with an analysis of the trends in curriculum, including school activities, and the probable direction of the program in the predictable future. It means also analysis of community needs over and above the education of its youth. Since program trends can seldom be clearly foreseen, every possible provision for flexibility should be made. One basic principle that is foreseeable is that the school should be an accurate microcosm of the community itself, reflecting in its program and facilities all aspects of the good life that goes on about it. A better program and a better building design will emerge from the coöperative efforts of all concerned—teachers, custodians and other service personnel, students, and adult citizens of the community. In this coöperative planning effort the principal plays a highly important role as leader. This role has been analyzed in Chapter 4.

THE PRINCIPAL

The principal has other kinds of jobs to do in maintaining and improving the present school facility. He will conduct inspections of the building—casual observations every day and more intensive inspections at least once each week. In these weekly inspections he is likely to be joined by a custodian and one or more teachers.

The principal will work closely with custodians, receive their reports and ask their advice, give them suggestions and assignments, and look after their welfare as key employees in building maintenance. He will meet also with committees of teachers who are evaluating any aspect of the building facility. He will make efforts to interest them, as individuals and as a staff group, in the job of maintaining and improving the building. He will be a ready listener to complaints, opinions, and suggestions. He will be ready to make reports to the superintendent or the board of education as to the condition of the building or suggested improvements.

The principal will work with student groups, too. He will continuously involve the student council, and back of it the representative rooms, in the problems of keeping the building clean and improving it as their group home for the years they are in school. He will encourage their suggestions, welcome their active participation, and do his part to carry out group decisions.

He will welcome parents and other citizens of the community into their school building, involve representative citizens in planning ways to use and improve it, and keep the community informed as to how their building is serving their needs and the needs of their youth. Thus the secondary school building constitutes another challenge to coöperative planning of all persons in a community. Effective use of expert leadership and specialized resources can only result from planning that is broadly based.

For Further Reading

American Association of School Administrators, *American School Buildings,* Twenty-seventh Yearbook, Washington, The National Education Association, 1949.

Boicourt, Gerald, "A Classroom Designed for English," *The English Journal,* February, 1951, pp. 94–98.

Caudill, W. W., "Space For Teaching," *Bulletin of the Texas Agricultural and Mechanical Arts College,* College Station, Tex., 1941.

Douglass, Harl R., *Modern Administration of Secondary Schools,* rev. ed., Boston, Ginn and Company, 1954, chap. 23.

Engelhardt, N. L., Engelhardt, N. L., Jr., and Leggett, Stanton, *Planning Secondary School Buildings,* New York, Reinhold Publishing Corporation, 1949.

Fowlkes, John Guy, and Perkins, L. B., "What Are the Trends in Planning and Constructing Junior and Senior High School Buildings and Plants?", *Bulletin of the National Association of Secondary School Principals,* No. 163, May, 1949.

French, Will, Hull, J. Dan, and Dodds, B. L. *American High School Administration,* New York, Rinehart & Company, 1951, chaps. 23, 25.

Herrick, John H., *et al., The School Plant,* New York, Henry Holt and Company, 1955.

Jacobson, Paul B., and Reavis, W. C., *Duties of School Principals,* New York, Prentice-Hall, 1941, chap. 22.

Koopman, G. Robert, "A New Theoretical Approach to Secondary School Planning," *The Nation's Schools,* December, 1953.

Linn, Henry H., Helm, Leslie C., and Grabarkiewicz, K. P., *The School Custodian's Housekeeping Handbook,* New York, Bureau of Publications, Teachers College, Columbia University, 1949, chap. 1.

Michigan Department of Public Instruction, *A Guide for Planning School Buildings,* Bulletin No. 338, Lansing, Mich., Superintendent of Public Instruction, 1945.

Moehlman, Arthur B., *School Administration,* Boston, Houghton Mifflin Company, 1940, chap. 18.

National Council of Chief State School Officers (Frank Cyr and Henry Limm eds.), *Planning Rural Community School Buildings,* New York, Bureau of Publications, Teachers College, Columbia University, 1949.

National Council on Schoolhouse Construction, *Guide For Planning School Plants,* rev. ed., Nashville, Tenn., State Department of Education, 1949.

Olsen, Edward G. (ed.), *School and Community Programs,* New York, Prentice-Hall, 1949.

"Pioneer School," *Architectural Forum,* October, 1949.

Viles, N. E., *The Custodian at Work,* Lincoln, Neb., University Publishing Company, 1941.

Wilson, Russell E., *Flexible Classrooms,* Detroit, The Carter Company, 1953.

CHAPTER 12

....

Administering Funds

IMPORTANCE OF THE BUDGET

One good index of a school's purposes is the budget. We are likely to spend money on the things we really value. The school budget represents, therefore, a mirror that reflects the philosophy and purposes of the school. It is important for the administrator to understand the budget and its implications for the ongoing program.

The accounting for and administering of funds can be a valuable educational experience. As such its benefits should not be confined to the administrator but should be extended also to teachers and students. This extension is unlikely to occur, however, in schools where the principal himself is either ignorant of the sources and disposition of school funds or careless about accounting procedures. The school where students and teachers understand school budgets and participate in administering them is likely to have a principal who is keenly interested in financial administration.

The secondary school principal cannot afford a nonchalant attitude toward school budgets or internal fund accounting. They are much too important in his professional life to be ignored. Our society sets a high premium on integrity of public officials. Not many principals are dishonest in their handling of funds, but some have been careless. A few have found their professional careers abruptly terminated by discovered shortages in internal funds or petty cash. In today's schools a considerable sum of money may be involved in even a single enterprise, such as the school cafeteria or a noon-hour movie. In the state of North Carolina alone it has been estimated that more than $23 million were handled in 1952 in the extracurricular program of the secondary schools.

THE TOTAL SCHOOL BUDGET

In most urban school systems the principal is not directly responsible to the board of education for the preparation of the budget. There are exceptions to this rule—for example, certain secondary school districts in Illinois where the principal reports directly to the board of education as chief administrator. There is a trend toward developing the school system budget by school buildings. There has been an increasing tendency in city school systems for the superintendent or business manager to request a budget annually from each school principal. As this trend continues it will become increasingly important for the secondary school principal and staff to understand the basis for budgets.

Even in schools where there has not yet developed a demand for actual preparation of budgets by the principal, it is necessary for him to understand the whole picture of school finance. The principal is constantly being asked to interpret to teachers the reason why certain requisitions have not been honored or why certain requests are impossible at the time. It can be embarrassing to the administrator to be unable to explain such delay or refusal. Teachers are reasonable about their requests when they know the facts. But if they are unable to find out what funds are available, or if they have reason to suspect that some teachers are more influential than they in getting their requests honored, they can become difficult. The principal should know the situation and should share it with the staff.

Parents and other adult citizens need help also in understanding school budgets. They frequently have only the vaguest of ideas as to the sources of school funds, and the items for which they are expended. The principal is likely to be in the best position to interpret these matters to citizens and to ensure their continued support through better understanding of school financing.

The principal will have frequent opportunities to discuss budgetary matters with the superintendent or with the business officer of the school district. In these contacts with the central office the principal should try to understand and share the problems that result from developing budgets for an entire school system. Neither he nor the teachers should expect always to get everything they request. Realism demands that they accept some reductions in the light of total funds available. On the other hand, business managers should not assume the role of evaluators of the respective merits of various items within a school budget. That function is a professional one that is best assumed by the staff of a school. It is the business of management to assign and account for available moneys, not to evaluate the program. When the money is not sufficient to carry the program, it becomes the task of the staff within a building to set up priorities among the various demands.

In this connection it may be added that the accumulation of large surpluses at the end of a school year may not be an evidence of sound financial management. Such balances are often assumed to be a tribute to the efficiency of the business manager or superintendent. On the contrary, if they are achieved by depriving the pupils of an adequate program of education, year-end balances are a mark of inefficiency. If such balances persist, the suspicion may develop that taxes might as well be reduced, since present funds are in surplus. It is not the job of management merely to save money, but rather to buy the best program possible with the money available. The readiness of a community to invest additional money in its schools will usually depend on its degree of satisfaction with the present program and its degree of sympathy with its unrealized goals.

Campbell listed six criteria of a good school budget in 1935, which still seem useful today, either in analyzing the total budget or any part of it:

1. *Inclusiveness.* The budget presents a complete picture of the financial plan for operating the schools. . . .
2. *Balance* (articulation of ends with means). The budget considers the needs of all legitimate activities in the school system in relation to each other and to the organization as a whole; it contemplates the total expenditures for all purposes from the standpoint of the anticipated income. . . .
3. *Responsibility.* The budgetary procedure definitely places the responsibility for directing the preparation, the presentation and defense, and the execution of the budget on the executive head of the school system and the responsibility for its review and adoption on the board of education.
4. *Fiscal control.* The budget serves as an instrument in controlling income and disbursements.
5. *Flexibility.* In providing for financial control, the budgetary procedure recognizes the possibility of emergencies which necessitate such change from the original financial plan as is compatible with its safeguarding as a whole. . . .
6. *Publicity.* The budgetary procedure includes adequate provisions for informing the public of the proposals contained in the plan for carrying on the school operations; it offers the opportunity of criticism and suggestions to parties interested in the conduct of the schools.[1]

The most commonly used divisions of a school budget are as follows:

General control (superintendent's office: salaries and supplies)
Instructional service (salaries and supplies for teachers)

[1] Raymond Guy Campbell, *State Supervision and Regulation of Budgetary Procedures in Public School Systems,* New York, Bureau of Publications, Teachers College, Columbia University, 1935, pp. 14–18.

Auxiliary agencies (health services, library, cafeteria, etc.)
Operation of plant (fuel, janitors, light)
Maintenance of plant (repairs, redecorating)
Fixed charges (rentals, telephone)
Debt service (interest, bond retirement)
Capital outlay (school sites, buildings, etc.)

Expenditures are largest in the area of instructional service. Indeed, most school budgets allot nearly 80 percent of the funds for this important item, and should do so, since instruction is the function of the school and instruction depends heavily on the quality of teachers.

Revenues are chiefly derived from such sources as local school taxes, state aid, tuition for students from another district, contributions, and fees. In many communities the largest single source of school support is state aid. In some school districts this source contributes over 90 percent of school revenues. As a result of efforts to equalize educational opportunities for all children in a state, the provision of state aid has steadily increased. Federal aid to public schools has been urged because of the differences in the abilities of the respective states to support education.

Pie charts of school income and expenditures should be prepared and discussed widely in a school and community. Some common misunderstandings that tend to prevent support for programs would be removed by such discussions. Eleventh- and twelfth-graders in high school civics or economics classes can profitably spend time on the local school budget.

STAFF PARTICIPATION IN BUDGET MAKING

Teachers should participate in preparing the budget for their school. Their suggestions and (individual) requests involving the budget should be welcomed at all times, but this is a low level of participation. Many of the perplexing problems of competition for existing funds, duplication of requests for expensive equipment, and attempts to develop one's own facility at the expense of others are not relieved by this individual participation in budget making.

Departmental budget making involves more teachers and can be helpful in avoiding some duplication of requests. If no total faculty planning accompanies it, however, departmental budget making can degenerate into a campaign to build one department at the expense of others. At some point the whole staff should review and evaluate the entire budget, and set up some system of priorities to assist their principal in his discussions with the central office. Boards of education should also make systematic provision for a review of the budget by each building staff before its final adoption. Much disaffection and rebellion could be avoided by securing teachers' suggestions all through the process of budget development. An even more significant point is that such shared planning will tend to produce a better budget.

The principal has some important roles in this process. He can be influential in stimulating teachers to take an active interest in the budget. His own example is likely to be contagious in this regard. He can help restore balance to the planning by lending support to areas that need it. Sometimes the more dramatic or aggressive demands tend to overshadow the more important ones. An example of this may be the library, which may be overlooked because there is only one spokesman for it. The principal can help the staff to establish some defensible standards for the total program, to see it as a whole, and to take pride in being objective. He can help provide for flexibility by securing an allotment for a petty-cash fund. He can remind the staff of the need for in-service education funds and support for the student activities budget. He should keep an eye on the condition of the building and make allowance for repairs, painting, and needed construction to ensure the maintenance of the school plant.

In considering the item of supplies for instruction some issues arise in every school. Some junior and senior high schools supply all textbooks to students; some schools rent them to the students, some sell them on a cost-plus basis, and some leave the sale of supplies to local stationery stores. Whatever system is used, careful attention should be paid by the staff to the actual cost to students of going to school. One of the interesting findings of the Illinois Study of Hidden Tuition Costs [2] was that teachers rarely estimated this item as high as it really was. The "Subject Inventory" used in this study revealed a disturbing level of costs, consisting of materials and fees, for all the secondary school subjects. In schools where no careful study of the matter has been made, teachers have no idea of the financial burden they are collectively imposing on students. A cost of $2 or $3 in one subject may result in a total cost of $15 to $20 per student per semester. When the cost of student activities is added to this, it may cost students as much as $150 to $300 per year to attend their "free" public school. This is especially significant in light of the fact that dropouts tend to come from lower socioeconomic groups. In the Illinois study it was discovered that 72 percent of the students who left high school came from lower-income families.[3]

A faculty group that made a serious analysis of this problem would be likely to arrive at some helpful recommendations. At least, it would probably agree that individual teachers should not make collections or financial demands that were unauthorized by school policies. The school council should collaborate in establishing these policies regarding classroom collections, cost of materials, and activities fees.

The principal should help teachers to know how much remains in a given part of the budget. This calls for an accounting system against which all requisitions are checked and balances tallied at regular intervals. A statement which will provide a further check on budget balances should be received from the central accounting office at least once each month. One copy of each requisition

---

[2] Reported in H. C. Hand, *Principal Findings of the 1947–48 Basic Studies of the Illinois Secondary School Curriculum Program,* Bulletin No. 2, Springfield, Ill., State Superintendent of Public Instruction, 1949.

[3] *Ibid.,* p. 15.

should be retained in the principal's office for use in conducting these periodic checks of budget balances.

The petty cash account should be kept small and accurately posted. Access to it should be limited to a bonded treasurer who has the accounting task for the building. This person can be a clerk in the principal's office. In small schools it may be the commercial teacher. It is wise to appoint someone other than the principal himself, since he will have the job of approving such requisitions.

INVENTORY OF SUPPLIES

A further responsibility of the principal is the inventory of supplies used in the building. Most inventory forms have a place for each item and a description of it, including its cost and the requisitioner, date purchased, quantity distributed, and quantity remaining. At least once a semester most inventories must be checked with the supply room and the teachers. A separate order memorandum form is often used to record short supplies of items that should be ordered. In large schools this responsibility may be delegated to such persons as the managers of the bookstore and cafeteria, but the principal is usually still responsible for checking over the inventory and the supply orders. These call for accuracy because of the large amounts of public property that are often involved.

ADMINISTERING ACTIVITY FUNDS

In Chapter 9 some discussion was included of the problems connected with student activities funds. It was pointed out that costs to individual students are frequently so high that they operate to reduce participation of students from poor families. Attention was given to three other sources of revenue: sales or drives, public (tax) funds, and student activity tickets. Some advantages of the activity ticket plan were set forth. These advantages included, among others, the opportunity for students to have actual experiences in budgeting and accounting for funds.

There appears to be a trend toward the use of tax funds for support of student activities. This practice surely operates to equalize opportunities among various economic levels represented in the student body. It should help, therefore, to encourage increased participation in activities among those who could not otherwise afford to take part. A further advantage of board-of-education support is that it permits the launching of an activity that has no prospect of becoming self-supporting. Speech activities in many schools could not raise enough funds to be self-supporting. The same thing is true of most student clubs. Yet these activities may be as valuable for their participants as the more remunerative athletic program is for the athletes.

Some administrators are opposed to any plan involving complete tax support of activities on the ground that such support deprives participants of many valuable experiences in raising money, and in preparing organization budgets. A combination of the two plans of tax support and a school-wide activity ticket can secure the advantages of both, if care is observed to keep the price of the activity ticket low. There will probably still remain some activities for which adult admission charges are legitimate. This is likely to be true of athletic events and school plays, for example. A few projects of the sale or drive type may also be defended if they meet sound educational criteria such as were set forth in Chapter 9.[4]

Budget-making experiences can be provided for an entire school by involvement of all the home rooms or representative groups in preparation and discussion of the activities budget. The first step might be the appointment of a budget committee representing administration, teachers, and students. (The selection of key persons in athletic management and the senior class can help this strategic committee!) The budget committee may ask every student organization that ever raises or spends money to prepare an estimate of the

[4] See p. 213.

amount needed for the coming school year. These organizations would perhaps include

  Athletics
  Debating, oratory, declamation
  Band
  Orchestra
  Choir
  Dramatics groups
  Senior class
  Junior class
  Other classes
  School paper
  School annual
  School handbook
  Clubs that raise or spend money

Members of the budget committee might add to the budget requests some all-school functions that no group sponsors but all students want. These might include regular school parties, appropriations for a social room, assembly programs, student council needs such as printing of ballots and posters, Christmas decorations, new equipment needed for all-school activities—in short, any needs that were overlooked by various organizations requesting funds.

An estimate would then be made by representatives of various groups of the amounts that will probably be raised through such means as

  Sale of individual admissions to
    athletic events
    music events
    speech events
    plays, operettas
    carnivals
  Sale of adult season tickets
  Sale of school paper, annual

Proceeds from bookstore sales

Other student sales revenues

If a student-activity ticket plan is in use the cost of the ticket can then be computed by dividing the expected number of ticket sales into the amount left to raise after all expected revenues are deducted from estimated expenditures. At this point, however, the committee must face the problem of keeping the price of the student ticket low enough to make it possible for every student to buy it. The deficit resulting from such reduction in price can be made up by an appropriation by the board of education.

The completed (tentative) budget may then be distributed in graph form to all student organizations and to all home rooms for discussion and amendment. After a week or two of thorough discussion the budget committee can amend the budget, and report it to the student council for adoption. Copies should then be distributed to all student organizations. If the budget committee is sufficiently representative of the whole school, and if there has been a full and free discussion of the tentative budget, agreement can usually be reached on an activities budget that is fair to all and that encourages students to participate. In many schools the budget requests and fund estimates are collected in the spring of the year in order to establish the budget before the opening of the new school year. This is especially helpful when a deficit appropriation is needed from the board of education, since the board budget is likely to run from July 1 of each year.

In many schools, students are permitted to purchase the activity ticket on a weekly or monthly installment basis. A punch or stamp may be used to record the payment on the ticket. Home-room treasurers collect the money and stamp the ticket on a day regularly set aside for collection. They then deposit their home-room collections at the office and are issued a receipt.

Not all secondary schools employ the activity ticket plan. Many schools do not have a budget system of any kind. Reavis reported in 1940 one study of 72 high schools in which only 22 used a general activity ticket and 45 used a budget plan.[5] Incidentally, only 11 of the schools in this study reported that the board of education directly subsidized any part of the activities budget. Most boards of education aid the activities program by provision of personnel and facilities. A considerable number also stand ready to make up deficits by special appropriation at the end of a fiscal year. It would be equally logical and more businesslike to make this deficit appropriation at the beginning of a new year as a direct means of equalizing participation in activities.

Although many schools operate their student activities on a budget plan, not all of these give the entire student body and faculty a voice in determining the budget as has been proposed in this chapter. Sometimes the principal draws up an operating budget. Sometimes a small group of advisers assists in the drafting of the budget or at least reacts to it before it is adopted. There is more likely to be general support for the budget if all students and teachers share in planning it. The educational experiences offered by such planning are too valuable for them to be confined to a few persons.

ACCOUNTING METHODS

The principal is responsible for the accounting of activities funds. This is true whether the board of education controls the funds or not. It is especially true in situations where local school policy regarding accounting is not predetermined by state laws.

There are many states in which procedures for accounting are definitely established, either by state law or by regulations of the state departments of education. In 1953 a study by Ivins and Anderson of policies in forty-five states revealed that eleven of them regulated extracurricular accounting by specific legislation and ten more states regulated it by policies of the state. All these

[5] L. V. Koos, J. M. Hughes, P. W. Hutson, and W. C. Reavis, *Administering the Secondary School*, New York, American Book Company, 1940, p. 620.

twenty-one states required that a central treasurer be selected for activities accounting, and all but one required that this official be bonded. These states also required that an approved depository (usually a bank) be used for safeguarding funds, that uniform procedures be used in withdrawing and spending, that uniform records be established, and that periodic reports and audits be made for every school activities fund. The remaining twenty-four ' states reporting in this study left the accounting policies for activities funds to local boards of education.[6]

There is some evidence indicating that schools in states where accounting policies are locally controlled do follow some of the practices mentioned above. They usually have an internal account for student activities funds, with a designated treasurer who receives deposits and writes checks upon presentation of requisitions. If the principal does not serve as treasurer, he usually approves requisitions and countersigns checks. There are excellent reasons for the appointment of some person other than the principal as treasurer of the activities account. It provides a double check on funds, gives the responsibility for actually handling funds to someone other than the person who must approve requests, and protects the principal from allegations of financial irregularity. It also helps to distribute responsibility and free the principal for more professional tasks. Johnston and Faunce have suggested the following precautions in the handling of activity funds:

1. The person designated to handle moneys and issue checks should be bonded.
2. A central accounting plan, with a ledger sheet for each organization and activity, should be maintained.
3. A duplicate copy of the ledger should be furnished each organization treasurer, together with a supply of deposit slips and voucher forms for authorized expenditures.

[6] Wilson H. Ivins and Helen I. Anderson, "Extracurricular Funds Accounting in the Various States: A Preliminary Report," *Bulletin of the National Association of Secondary School Principals*, 38:201, March, 1954, pp. 124–135.

FORM 11.

Receipt For Deposit

Received From *Thespian Club*
Organization

$ 73 ⁵⁰ *Harry Ransom*
Treasurer

Proceeds from " *Junior Shows the Way* "

No. *18* Date *10-7-51* *Rex Vincent*
Accountant

FORM 12.

Pay Order

Universal High School
Detroit, Michigan *October 10,* 195*1*

To the School Accountant:

Pay to the Order of *Samuel French, Inc.* $ 25 ⁰⁰
Twenty-five and ⁿᵒ⁄₁₀₀ Dollars
For *Royalties on " Junior Shows the Way " one performance*

Harry Ransom
Treasurer

Charge to Account of

Thespians *Doris Gregg*
Organization Adviser

FORM 13.

Extracurricular Activities Ledger								
Thespian Club					Budget Allowance _____			
Organization					Remarks _____			
Doris Gregg					_____			
Adviser's signature								
Harry Ransom								
Treasurer's signature								

Date	No.	Receipts	Amount	Date	No.	Disbursem't	Amount	Balance
10-7-51	18	Receipt: Play	$73.50	10-10-51		Royalties French	$25.00	$48.50

From John M. Trytten, "Extracurriculum Activity Funds," Bulletin of the National Association of Secondary School Principals, XXV, No. 102, December, 1941.

4. Careful training should be given each organization treasurer in the procedures to be used and the keeping of their books.
5. Periodic reports should be made to the various organizations on the transactions since their last reports.
6. Preparation of tickets for admissions must be made in advance and in such a manner that their number can be accurately accounted for tax purposes.
7. Funds may be centrally deposited in a "school activities account," but ledgers, checks, and vouchers should reveal which organization or activity is involved in the transaction.[7]

A simple set of accounting forms for use with activities funds

[7] Edgar G. Johnston and Roland C. Faunce, *Student Activities in Secondary Schools,* New York, The Ronald Press Company, 1952, p. 333.

has been suggested by Trytten. He explains the use of the three forms, reproduced here as Forms 11, 12, and 13, as follows:

At the time the deposit is made the organization treasurer receives a receipt [Form 11], which he can file with his records, and the school accountant retains a copy of the receipt. A receipt book, three receipts to the page, with carbon copies permanently bound into the book, leaves with the accountant a complete original entry of all deposits made with him.

When the organization wishes to withdraw money from the account, the organization treasurer makes out a pay order [Form 12] with the necessary information filled in. He has the pay order signed by the organization sponsor and delivers it to the school accountant. The accountant then issues a check in payment of the item, and files the pay order as his authorization. The accountant has his record of checks issued which serves him as the original entry of all disbursements.

A ledger card or sheet [Form 13] for each organization completes the system. To this card is posted from the receipt book all income which has been received for an organization, and from the check book are posted all disbursements. A third column gives the balance available.[8]

The monthly report issued by the school accountant or central treasurer to each school organization should show the following items: the balance on hand, an itemized list of receipts and disbursements during the current month, and the balance carried forward. These reports, when summarized, should reconcile with the current bank statement and should be filed in the principal's office and in the accountant's records. There should be audits made at least annually of all internal fund accounts.

OPPORTUNITY FOR STUDENTS TO GAIN EXPERIENCE

The basic reason for involving students in developing the activities budget, collecting and depositing funds, and disbursing them

[8] John M. Trytten, "Extracurriculum Activity Funds," *Bulletin of the National Association of Secondary School Principals*, XXV, No. 102, December, 1941, p. 139.

is that these activities represent a valuable experience in practical economics. One of the commonly recognized obstacles to motivation for arithmetic is that the problems are often drawn from the adult business world. There are challenges to many mathematics skills in the handling of organization funds. There are also experiences in planning together, in orderly budgeting and reporting, and in honest, responsible accounting of these funds. These experiences can have reality to young people. They are actual economic needs and everyday financial processes that contrast favorably with the synthetic problems presented in so many mathematics classrooms. The experience of serving as treasurer of a class or club can be as educative as a whole semester of formal instruction.

Some schools have realized these advantages of financial experiences and have capitalized them by extending their scope. Besides the involvement of school clubs, classes, and organizations in fund accounting and budget making, other real experiences have been devised. Many schools operate student stores that sell books, paper, pencils, and other equipment needed in the classrooms, as well as candy, ice cream, and notions. Some of these stores are operated as projects in arithmetic classes. Others are student council projects. Still others are a part of the commercial department and offer guided experiences in purchasing stock, arranging it, and other aspects of merchandising and salesmanship. The school store is frequently set up on a cost-plus basis as a device for student convenience, and as an experience in cooperative merchandising.

The school cafeteria offers another business opportunity through which students can learn the realities of economic life. Some schools have set out to involve students in the cafeteria, not only as busboys, counter help, and dishwashers, but also as cashiers and members of the various committees that help run this important business. Inventories must be conducted, menus developed, groceries, dairy products, and equipment items ordered, menus printed, prices computed, reports of receipts and expenditure compiled. These are valuable educational opportunities for students. The alert school staff will capitalize on such genuine situations for learning and involve students in them as much as possible.

Some schools have developed ambitious programs of coöperative business enterprise. Student business organizations have developed to conduct a wide range of production and services. Such coöperative groups are raising and selling Christmas trees, raising fruits and vegetables, canning and marketing them, selling honey from their own beehives, producing and selling simple cosmetic items. Much more widespread is the practice of conducting subscription drives for popular magazines. In some schools students are running credit unions and banks that receive student deposits, make loans, and pay interest to their investors.

These economic adventures should be encouraged and extended. The school accounting system can readily be adapted to permit orderly deposit and withdrawal by voucher for all these student enterprises. It would be wise to include them in the central accounting plan for the school. Neither administrators, teachers, nor students should be responsible for funds left around in boxes or drawers without accurate records or depositing facilities.

SUMMARY

In this chapter the job of the principal as administrator of funds has been analyzed. Not only the principal but the whole school staff under his leadership should understand the school budget. This result can best be achieved by involving teachers in developing the budget. As leader in this enterprise, and as interpreter of the school budget to the public, the principal must be thoroughly informed about sources of revenue and purposes for which they are expended. He is responsible for inventory and ordering of supplies for the building. He is chiefly responsible for the activities funds—obtaining them, developing a budget, and accounting for funds. In this area it is of special importance that students share in the handling of money. They are concerned because the activities program should be their own program and one that is available to all, regardless of economic circumstances. They should be involved also for the benefit of the educational experiences presented. The secondary school principal who is concerned to offer young people a lifelike experience should make every effort to share his responsibility for handling and accounting for funds.

FOR FURTHER READING

Campbell, Raymond Guy, *State Supervision and Regulation of Budgetary Procedures in Public School Systems,* New York, Bureau of Publications, Teachers College, Columbia University, 1935, chap. I.

Cleland, George L., "A Centralized System of Accounting for Student Activity Funds," *Bulletin of the National Association of Secondary School Principals,* No. 119, January, 1944.

Douglass, Harl R., *Modern Administration of Secondary Schools,* (rev. ed.), Boston, Ginn & Company, 1954, chap. 19.

Edmonson, J. B., Roemer, Joseph, and Bacon, Francis L., *The Administration of the Modern Secondary School,* New York, The Macmillan Company, 1948, chap. IX.

French, Will, Hull, J. Dan, and Dodds, B. L., *American High School Administration,* New York, Rinehart & Company, 1951, chap. 24.

Ivins, Wilson H., and Anderson, Helen I., "Extracurricular Funds Accounting in the Various States: A Preliminary Report," *Bulletin of the National Association of Secondary School Principals,* No. 201, March, 1954.

Jacobson, Paul B., and Reavis, W. C., *Duties of School Principals,* New York, Prentice-Hall, 1941, chap. 21.

Johnston, Edgar G., and Faunce, Roland C., *Student Activities in Secondary Schools,* New York, The Ronald Press Company, 1952, chap. 14.

Koos, L. V., Hughes, J. M., Hutson, P. W., and Reavis, W. C., *Administering the Secondary School,* New York, American Book Company, 1940.

Moehlman, Arthur B., *School Administration,* Boston: Houghton Mifflin Company, 1940, chaps. 20, 24.

Newsom, N. W., *et al., Administrative Practices in Large High Schools,* New York, American Book Company, 1940, chap. VI.

Russell, John D., and Judd, Charles H., *The American Educational System,* Boston, Houghton Mifflin Company, 1940, chap. IX.

Trytten, John M., "Extracurriculum Activity Funds," *Bulletin of the National Association of Secondary School Principals, XXV,* No. 12, December, 1941.

CHAPTER 13

Developing the Schedule

THE SECONDARY SCHOOL SCHEDULE: A PROBLEM

A unique responsibility of secondary school principals is the development of the schedule of classes. This task has caused a considerable amount of anxiety and many hours of extra work for high school principals, partly because it is an inescapable prelude to the orderly beginning of each school year. The class schedule is important because it is a mirror that reflects with some accuracy the planned curriculum of the school.

[The schedule] is . . . a sort of mirror in which are reflected many interesting images. For example, we see in this mirror that our high school has had a series of aggressive, able music directors. We note that Miss Jones can command a certain room because of her long tenure and status. We observe that the agriculture classes must meet seven clock hours weekly because of federal regulations relating to vocational aid. If we look closely we may see other things in the mirror, the six huge, undesirable classrooms in the old annex, the lack of a sound-proof band room, the long-standing proprietorship which a certain English teacher has had in a class in commercial law, the influence which the college preparatory tradition has had upon our school for many years. These, and many other interesting pictures emerge from an examination of the mirror which we call the high school schedule.[1]

The schedule can facilitate a good instructional program or it can inhibit or even prevent improvement. It serves not only as a timetable but also as the tracks on which the engine runs.

The elementary school schedule offers no such problem to administrators. There are no electives and therefore there are no conflicts to resolve in the programs of elementary pupils. The schedule of classes is a creature of departmentalization. Even the junior high school offers no serious problem of schedule arrangement, if most classes are required of all pupils. It is in the senior high school, with its varied elective program, that the scheduling of classes becomes difficult.

The checkerboard pattern of the typical high school schedule reflects an earlier, now outmoded concept of education. The short periods, ranging from 40 to 60 minutes in length, were designed to accommodate an instructional program that largely consisted of assignment, recitation, and testing for mastery of small, daily segments of a textbook. For such purposes as these the need was for a series of short periods of equal length, through which the pupil moved daily to demonstrate his temporary command (or lack of it) of a series of unrelated facts and skills. Over the years these segmented schedules became fixed by tradition and by attempts to measure instruction in Carnegie units of credit. Regional and state accrediting agencies may have been instrumental in crystallizing the standard schedule of classes during the period when improvement of schools was thought to be dependent on creation of objective criteria, such as the length of class periods. This offered an arithmetical base for objectifying high school instruction. It gave us a convenient, though superficial, means of

---

[1] Michigan Department of Public Instruction, *Planning and Working Together,* Bulletin No. 337, Lansing, Mich., Superintendent of Public Instruction, 1945, p. 147.

equalizing pupil-and-teacher loads and of recording progress of each student for his high school career.

FAULTS OF THE SEGMENTED SCHEDULE

The standard schedule of classes has been modified in many respects over the years, but it is still common in senior high schools. It has persisted down to the present in spite of its numerous faults. It reflects an outmoded standard curriculum that is only gradually and reluctantly giving way in the light of known facts about growth and development. The very inflexibility of the standard schedule of classes prevents it from adaptation to individual needs of the learner. The schedule, with its fixed provisions of time and place, tends to fix the nature of learning experiences in a relatively tight strait jacket. It forces teachers and students into a kind of lock step. It thus becomes an end in itself, to which instruction must be geared, instead of serving its proper function of facilitating instruction.

One serious drawback of the conventional high school schedule lies in the short time span it allots to various learning experiences. The 45-minute period was long enough—perhaps too long, some students thought—for the assign-recitation-test kind of instruction. It is all too short for most real experiences. Teachers who have tried to use group activities have discovered the handicaps of the short period. It is significant that even those limited modifications which have been made in the conventional schedule were the result of attempts to give students a chance to *do,* to *try,* or to *make* things as a means of experience learning. Thus the double periods for science laboratory, shop, homemaking, and agriculture classes resulted from the realization that students simply could not "learn by doing" in a 45-minute period.

Teachers in other subject fields have also discovered a need for longer blocks of time as they have tried to introduce their students to real experiences. Such activities as building, drawing, painting, or dramatizing require time—not only for the activity itself but for the preparation of materials and the cleaning up of the room afterward. Physical education teachers complain that the time consumed by changing to gym suits, showering, and dressing leaves little time for any play activity. Teachers in science and social studies who are convinced of the value of class excursions to places of interest in the community have nevertheless refrained from these valuable experiences because the length of their class periods prevents it. Moving picture films or recordings must be chosen carefully to insure that the class period will accommodate these learning aids. Even then, there is often no time for adequate preparation for, or follow-up of, the audio-visual aid. School camping, which has proved so dynamic an experience for elementary school pupils, has not been generally extended into the high school because the students "would miss too many classes."

Teacher-pupil planning takes time, too. Teachers who have been successful with this technique have discovered that their achievement was the result of patient efforts over a long time span. The initial difficulties will often cause students to become discouraged with the planning procedure. Only by persistent efforts and patient guidance can this initial discouragement be overcome and success achieved. The short periods provided for classes by a conventional schedule do not provide any consecutive span for the time-consuming process of coöperative planning. This applies also to participation of students in evaluating their own growth, either as individuals or as members of groups. In short, the experience curriculum requires time, which is lacking in the conventional 40- to 60-minute period. The net result of the time limitation is to prevent the extension into the high school of the best learning procedures discovered in recent years. The junior high school shares this handicap to the introduction of real learning experiences to the degree that it limits the length of class periods. Even in the elementary school the separation of subjects may prevent the teacher from using modern learning activities; it is at least possible, however, for an elementary teacher to vary classroom procedures without infringing on the time assigned to other teachers.

Perhaps the most serious handicap of the short class period and of the separate subject curriculum which it reflects is the effect it has of fractionating the student's learning experience. Any adult who followed a high school student around for one entire school day would have trouble finding any relatedness in the activities of various classes. Every 45 minutes he would see materials hastily gathered up, and hundreds of youngsters dashing off to new subjects, quite unrelated to those they have just quitted. Some wit has observed that each group must first be unmotivated from its previous class and then remotivated to the new one. (This process can be observed every period in most high schools, and is particularly evident just after an activity that has aroused the interest of students, such as a gym period or a school assembly.)

We have known for many years that the learner operates as a total organism, attacking each new experience with mind, muscle, and glands. He is not an English learner at 10 A.M., a history learner at 10:45. He is a total person whose make-up as a whole conditions his readiness for each new experience. Life and real problems are not divided into subjects, either. It is only in school that these artificial divisions into subjects occur; and in most school systems, it is only the senior high school that is so fractionated into separate periods that a related approach to learning is impossible.

The unit method has been accepted for at least three decades as the logical approach to learning. While not all elementary schools have adopted the unit approach, it is much more common at the elementary level. In high school textbooks the word "unit" has been corrupted to mean "chapter"—sometimes related to a larger topic or "unit" in the same subject, but seldom to one that is included in some other subject. The subject-matter curriculum does not encourage the unit approach. The fractionated high school schedule does not permit the development of any relationships among separate subjects.

Another effect of the short high school period has been discussed in Chapter 7. This is the limitation placed on effective guidance by the lack of continuity of pupil-teacher relationships. Teachers who daily face five or six sections totaling perhaps 150 different students cannot initiate many guidance procedures. The home-room plan has only added one more (unrelated) adjustment for both students and teachers. It has also added another section, frequently composed of students different from those in his "regular" classes, to the teacher's daily load.

Thus the basic faults of the conventional high school schedule, with its segmentation into a series of short, separate periods, are that it tends to be inflexible, that it discourages continuity of experiences because of its time limitations, that it prevents related or total learning, and that it limits the effectiveness of the guidance program. Efforts have been made to adapt it to emerging needs. The shorter activity period and home-room period have been added, extended, diminished, and frequently abolished. Double periods have been provided for some classes. The length of periods has varied over the years and from one school to another—generally from 40 to 60 minutes. The number of periods per day has shifted from six to seven to eight, and back again. Large urban schools have inaugurated eleven- or twelve-period schedules, with students arriving and departing every period in order to accommodate an overflow enrollment to limited building facilities.

Yet all these changes have not really affected the basic design of the high school schedule. With some superficial differences, it is the same old separate-period schedule designed for a separate-subject curriculum. The time has undoubtedly come for basic changes in the schedule of the secondary school. The direction which these changes may take will be discussed in a later section of this chapter. Perhaps some attention should first be paid to the methods commonly used for developing the standard class schedule.

DEVELOPING THE STANDARD SCHEDULE

Most newly appointed secondary school principals develop the schedule by a combination of tradition, pressure, and hunches. They begin with the present schedule, make some allowances for various demands by teachers, and then "cut and try" to reduce students' conflicts. There are various hidden factors operating in this process. The nature and extent of the school plant are known factors that affect the schedule. So also are state or local requirements that fix the curriculum, policies of accrediting agencies, and various school traditions that affect the program. Teachers' preferences—for certain subjects or grade levels or periods in the day or rooms—have become known over the years and are often influential without even being discussed. The present schedule is the most powerful influence of all because it is usually easier to keep what one has than to change it. This tends to fix such matters as the number and length of periods, including home-room or activity periods and lunch hours. One factor that is seldom mentioned is the need of the students!

CHOICE OF SUBJECTS

The principal usually sets out in the spring to get registrations for the fall semester. These may be based on a three- or four-year plan earlier signed by students and their parents. They may be obtained in advance for incoming ninth- or tenth-graders by a series of registration visits to the elementary or junior high schools that these students are presently attending. Any changes in requirements or offerings must of course be relayed to students as they make their selections for the coming year. The home-room teacher or counselor will be helpful in advising students in this process. Choice-of-subject blanks should provide for the signatures of the student, his parent, and the teacher or counselor responsible. (The latter provision is usually omitted in the numerous high schools enrolling one hundred or less students.)

TABULATING CHOICES AND CONFLICTS

The total registration in each subject can then be tabulated, usually in the office, to indicate the number of classes and teachers needed. School policies regarding minimum numbers of elections required to make up a section will apply at this point. Some intelligent guessing about additional student elections from transfers or failing students may help, too.

A conflict tally may be helpful in high schools of any size. This is done by cross listing all subjects for which there are likely to be only one or two sections (the others won't conflict) and tallying the numbers of students in each. For example, if a total of twenty-one students elect advanced algebra and fifteen of these students elect French 3, it is clear that a single-section class in each of these two subjects should not be scheduled at the same hour. The conflict-tally sheet is simply a cross-ruled sheet of paper with half the subjects concerned listed across the top of the sheet and half the subjects down the left side.

DRAFTING THE SCHEDULE

The tentative draft of the schedule can then be prepared, beginning with the placement of the above-mentioned one- and two-section electives for which conflicts are probable. The known data may at this point include a number of items that will influence placement of subjects:

1. The preferences of teachers for certain subjects, periods, or classrooms
2. The training of teachers in certain subject areas
3. Special assignments, such as coaching activities, study-hall supervision, work-experience supervision, guidance and counseling, bookstore, library, or office responsibilities
4. Provision of "free" periods for planning
5. Traditions regarding early or late hours for various grade levels (in "swing-shift" schools the seniors are often awarded early class periods)

6. Needs for connecting double periods for science laboratories, vocational classes, etc.
7. Availability of older students who hold part-time jobs
8. Bus schedules, in schools where all students do not arrive and depart at the same time.

The classes that enroll three or more sections can be spread across this tentative schedule last of all, and in such a way as to avoid or minimize conflicts. This avoidance of conflicts will be easier in a school enrolling 500 or more students than in smaller schools. It may be impossible to eliminate every conflict, particularly in schools with only one, two, or three sections for each grade level. One further conflict occurs in a small high school where not enough students can elect a given subject to make an adequate single section each semester, but some students need the subject for rather definite reasons. Thus advanced mathematics or science classes may be alternated by years (chemistry this year, physics next) to ensure an adequate section in these classes. Some forethought about the probable future demands is therefore required. Even then a few conflicts will develop as a result of students' transferring from another school or needing to repeat a required subject.

It is rather common for principals to start the schedule with the seniors because conflicts during the last year of school can be most difficult for students. Other grades are then added one at a time, with one eye on the conflict-tally sheet.

Some writers claim that conflicts can be practically eliminated through use of such methods as have been described above. Jacobson, Reavis, and Logsdon estimate that there should not be more than twelve or fifteen conflicts in a schedule for a high school of 1,000 students.[2] There are so many factors that create conflicts, however, that it appears hazardous to assure oneself of any particular minimum number. Double-period classes are likely to multiply

[2] P. Jacobson, W. C. Reavis, and J. D. Logsdon, *Duties of School Principals,* New York, Prentice-Hall, 1950, p. 103.

conflicts. There are only about half as many conflicts in schools using the 60-minute period as in schools with periods of 40 or 45 minutes. Small schools have more conflicts than large schools. Schools with numerous elective courses and less than 500 students will be likely to have conflicts. In general, of course, conflicts are the result of elective variety in the curriculum. Requirements create conflicts, too. If hard-and-fast rules are made that certain courses are required for college recommendation, conflicts are likely to be created for some students in small and medium-sized schools.

Most small high schools should explore the possibility of supervised correspondence study to permit the formation of an entire section of students, possibly with each individual at work on a different course. A competent teacher can supervise all these contract-type units, with occasional advice from his colleagues. Some state universities sponsor high school courses by correspondence. Many conflicts can be resolved by such a plan.

SCHEDULING BY GROUPS

The method described above is usually called the "mosaic" plan of developing a schedule because of the piece-by-piece manner of its construction. Large schools often use some variation of the block or group plan of scheduling classes. This plan involves setting up a conflict-free schedule for an entire group of students, usually selected by grade levels, who must all take certain subjects. It is easiest to use this plan at lower grade levels, where there are fewer elections than requirements. The elective subjects are fitted in for each block or group after the multiple sections are established. Sometimes certain morning and afternoon periods are previously held free for electives, and the group schedule established in the remaining periods. If there are several sections of an elective desired for the group involved, they can be spread out through the day, or even included in the blocked schedule. For example, if 120 students in a school must take English, history, and mathematics and all of them also elect occupations, this one elective can be made a part of the block for the group of four sections of thirty students each, thus:

Periods

Groups	1	2	3	4	5	6
1	English	Free	History	Free	Math.	Occup.
2	History	for	English	for	Occup.	Math.
3	Math.	other	Occup.	other	History	English
4	Occup.	electives	Math.	electives	English	History

It will be immediately observed that the group method is most useful in the junior high school and in very small or very large senior high schools. Junior high schools and small senior high schools can use it because of the relative absence of elective courses. High schools of 2000 or over can use an adaptation of the group plan because of the number of sections possible for many electives.

STAFF ASSISTANCE

In practice, experienced administrators usually work out some variation of the block and mosaic plans that seems to work most effectively in a particular school. Common sense and good judgment are more useful than any set of gadgets in developing a schedule. A sense of justice demands that the needs and problems of individual students be considered. It is possible to make a detailed study of the seriousness of conflicts that are still unresolved by the tentative schedule. The home-room teachers can help again at this point by identifying the students who present the remaining conflict problems and counseling with each one individually. They can usually make some adaptation of the students' plan of study if there is freedom for substitution of courses. The teachers can also make suggestions for further change in the tentative schedule at this point. Some faculty groups put the schedule on the blackboard and study it together to try to eliminate conflicts and to improve it in other ways. In schools where the faculty is too large to make this procedure feasible, class advisors or representative teachers from each grade level can work on the schedule with the principal. The goal should be the best possible schedule, in terms of criteria accepted as valid by the staff. It is hoped that the needs and interests of individual students will be particularly considered among these criteria.

MAKING OUT PROGRAM CARDS

After the revision of the tentative schedule, the periods now established for each subject can be marked on the students' choice-of-subject cards. It is important at this point to distribute registrations about evenly in those subjects that are offered in more than one section. This can be done in the principal's office by use of a tally sheet, or it can be done in the home rooms and then balanced and consolidated in the office. Program cards for each student can then be made out in the home rooms, following the choice-of-subject forms with the periods indicated for next semester's election. The program cards may be taken home for parental inspection or students may simply be encouraged to copy the program on a sheet of paper to take home. A few changes may be made before the start of a new semester because of failures or other emergencies, but not enough to affect the schedule.

INTERPRETING THE SCHEDULE TO PARENTS

When the schedule has been approved by the staff, some principals present it at a parent-teacher meeting to the parents for interpretation and explanation. This might be particularly important if changes have been made in the previous schedule. If changes have been made that will affect the opening or closing hour for school, or the time of the lunch recess, this consideration by parents should come much earlier. They should be consulted for suggestions *before* a solution in the form of a new schedule has been prepared. In some schools there are parent representatives on the grade-level planning groups who may take active part in discussion of the new schedule from the start.

THE GOOD SCHEDULE

The schedule will be improved by the involvement of the staff (and indirectly students) in its development. This means that it should always be regarded as a tentative schedule during the period of discussion and resolution of conflicts. It does not follow that a conflict-free schedule is a perfect schedule. There are principals who pride themselves on their speedy development of a conflict-free schedule of classes, when the truth is that important human values have been sacrificed to achieve this result. There are many factors to consider besides the complete elimination of individual conflicts. DeVilbiss has suggested four criteria for a good schedule:

1. To make it possible to provide and to administer the kind of learning experiences needed to implement the purposes of the school; this includes a flexible schedule to provide for common learnings and to provide for free activities.
2. To provide maximum utilization of all the human resources within the school for the benefit of the students. This includes allowing the principal time for supervision as well as for management, and assignment of teachers consistent with their training.
3. To provide the maximum utilization of all the physical resources of the school.
4. To facilitate an effective program of guidance.[3]

THE TREND TOWARD A DIFFERENT TYPE OF SCHEDULE

Early in this chapter some faults of the conventional schedule were presented. Since many secondary school principals must begin

[3] Wilbur DeVilbiss, "Criteria of a Good Master Schedule," *Bulletin of the National Association of Secondary School Principals,* No. 31, November, 1947, pp. 31–38.

their work with a conventional schedule, some methods of developing it have also been presented. In spite of careful planning by all those concerned with the matter, a good schedule cannot be developed on a basis of a uniform time allotment for each period and each class. This condition violates the first criterion of a good schedule, which is flexibility to serve any constructive purpose or need. It may be well to examine some alternatives to the standard schedule with uniform periods.

Manley has listed the shortcomings of the conventional schedule as follows:

1. The conventional daily schedule lacks flexibility that will:
    a. Permit students frequently to work continuously for two or more consecutive periods.
    b. Provide time for field trips, excursions, etc., without undue interference with other school activities.
    c. Permit students to have access to teachers and teachers to students at periods other than those in which they are regularly scheduled together.
    d. Permit students to be readily shifted from one class group to another.
    e. Allow frequent re-arrangements of time and variation in the use of school facilities in order to meet the needs of teachers and students.
2. The conventional daily schedule does not permit adequate co-ordination of the efforts of teachers.
    a. No time is planned for conferences and cooperative planning.
    b. Lack of such a planning period makes inadequate provision for the in-service training of teachers in the new techniques and procedures involved in a program of education that promotes integration.
3. The conventional daily schedule greatly hampers attempts to make guidance and instruction integral parts of the total learning activity.
    a. In it teachers are, as a rule, primarily concerned with instruction in subject matter.

   b. Teachers have little opportunity for conferences with other teachers relative to pupil interests and needs, and ways and means of meeting them.

   c. As a rule, teachers are not charged with responsibility for meeting the interests and needs of students if these do not lie within the compass of the subject taught.

4. The conventional daily schedule does not reflect the aims or philosophy of the school attempting to develop a program of evaluation that promotes integration. It divides the school day and the educational offerings into the piecemeal bits which are the outgrowth of the philosophy on which the subject curriculum is built.[4]

In brief summary of Manley's critieria, a good secondary school schedule should be characterized by (1) flexibility, (2) provision for teacher planning, (3) provision for guidance as a part of instruction, and (4) provision for integrated learning. Not many senior high schools have provided for core or common-learnings classes at the present writing. Still, hundreds of high schools have such programs on an experimental basis and thousands of teachers are either presently involved or would be willing to try such assignments if the schedule made it possible. At the junior high school level it appears that block programs of one kind or another are rapidly becoming the norm. This development is more clearly evident in some parts of the country than in others. The trend would be sharply accelerated if it were understood, in every secondary school, that the schedule could be so developed as to make it possible for any interested teachers to experiment with what Manley referred to as "integrating learning."

BLOCKING FOR LONGER PERIODS

A simple beginning can be made without any threat to anyone by creating a double-section block consisting of two teachers and

---

[4] C. B. Manley, "Secondary School Organization and Schedule Making for the Integrating Curriculum," Type B Project, Teachers College, Columbia University, 1941, pp. 141–144.

two sections of students. The block could be made up by a combination of two required courses, such as American literature and American history. It would obviously represent but one part of the schedules of the two teachers involved. The two sections would remain intact as in the case of the group method described in this chapter:

PLAN 1

Sections	Teachers A	B	
1	American literature	American history	Period free for both teachers
2	American literature	American history	and students

As a beginning, the two classes would not need to be combined in any way, but could be taught by a team consisting of an English and a history teacher who plan some units together, consult with each other about individual students, and occasionally combine the two sections for a film or a special program. The third period is kept free for such planning, and for counseling the students, who are scheduled in a study hall for that period.[5]

As the two teachers gain in skill and self-confidence, they may try out a number of different team projects. The units they plan together may "catch fire" and grow into other units that combine the two subject fields. One teacher may take both sections for some kinds of experiences, the other teacher for others. Division of the entire block may be variously made for small-group research and presentations, or for one large group engaged in some common activity guided by one teacher while the other works with individuals who have other needs. The free period may be drawn into the block on occasion when a trip or other extended project is

---

[5] Each teacher could also have his section in home room, if there is a home-room plan in the school.

planned. A joint planning committee representing both sections may help the teachers plan the schedule. Eventually the two periods may flow together into a real block composed of two teachers and two sections:

PLAN 2

Two periods, two sections, two teachers	Third period used for counseling, planning, and supervised study.
Fused course in American history and literature	On occasion combined for field trips, etc.

As this fused course proves successful and more time is needed, the "supervised study" period can be actually incorporated into the block, since the weekly plan can provide time for reading and writing anywhere in the three-period block. Once or twice a week the two teachers could have a free period for planning by use of student leaders, cadet teachers, substitutes, or community help. As this trend continued, the divisions between periods and subjects would tend to disappear:

PLAN 3

Three-period block, two sections, two teachers. Used either to fuse two subjects plus a study hall or to develop a core class of three periods.

This plan assumes that a room can be found to accommodate a double section. Some new high schools have soundproof folding partitions separating two classrooms. (See the room design for general-education classes presented in Chapter 11.) Lacking such a room facility, there is usually a possibility of either making shift with the cafeteria, little theater, or a study hall, or removing a partition to create a larger room.

The team approach has been suggested only as one simple way to make a beginning toward block schedules. It has the advantages of simplicity and of not departing too rapidly from conventional scheduling. It will work rather well when the two teachers involved are able to form a compatible team. There is a hazard, however, that the correlated or fused course may never become anything else, as has been pointed out in Chapter 3 in the discussion of the core curriculum. There are some distinct advantages in the single-teacher core class, with one teacher responsible for a single section for two or more periods. This can be an outcome of the team approach diagramed as Plan 1. Instead of working toward a permanent team arrangement, the two teachers may instead tend increasingly to keep one section both periods:

PLAN 4

Periods	1	2	3
Teacher A	Section 1: English and social studies (core?)		Study period
B	Section 2: English and social studies (core?)		counseling, planning

This single-teacher plan is more likely to develop out of Plan 1 if the emphasis of both teachers is on the students instead of on the separate subjects. It is not uncommon, of course, for English teachers to have a history minor or for social science teachers to have an English minor.

Again, the third period provided for study and counseling can be gradually drawn into the block as more time is needed:

PLAN 5

Periods

Teacher	1	2	3
A	Section 1: three-period core class		
B	Section 2: three-period core class		

This development of a core class from a simple block of two classes placed in juxtaposition depends on many other factors besides the schedule. These have been discussed in an earlier chapter. The teachers and students must want this kind of a development, and their parents must understand and value it. The point of these five little diagrams is simply that the schedule can provide the opportunity for "integrating learning" without any radical or threatening change at the outset. Out of Plan 1 can emerge either a teacher team or a single-teacher approach to the core curriculum; or, if neither of these is desired, Plan 1 can simply continue to provide for a pair of teachers with frequently related subjects operating as a team for good teaching and for effective guidance of two sections of students.

The extension of the block program throughout a grade level is shown in Plan 6. The schedule is, of course, a fragment of the total schedule. It provides only for the ninth grade, numbering about one hundred students. The plan could be expanded or contracted for grade groups of different size. Passing time would have to be provided between periods, in terms of the size of the building.

Plan 6 gives each of the ninth-grade sections a three-period core class, two electives and a study period. Physical education could either be elected as a subject or added in place of the study period. The core class lasts three hours and includes supervised study time. The other classes are one hour each, including passing time.

The period of time from 11:30 A.M. to 1 P.M. is divided into three "activity-lunch" periods of 30 minutes each. Two of these can be used for clubs, class meetings, intramural sports, and assemblies; the other period can be used for lunch, scheduled in such a way as to ensure quick service by not overburdening the line. (Other grade schedules would be geared to the ninth grade to provide three possible times for lunch.)

Time for planning could be provided core teachers either during elective (one-hour) periods or during the three noon periods. This is demonstrated in Plan 7, which is set up by teachers rather than by sections. Plan 7, like its predecessor, is only a fragment of the total schedule. In this case it includes students in grades 9 and 10. Some of the electives indicated would enroll eleventh and twelfth grades also.

Teacher G in Plan 7 is included as an example of a special-subject teacher who would have five classes of one period each and no particular responsibility for guidance of any one group of students. Eleventh- and twelfth-grade students might have a two-period block with their core teacher and two or three single-period electives. It will be noted that the total schedule implied by Plan 7 includes periods of three different lengths—30, 60, 180 minutes. The flexibility and continuity provided by such an arrangement not only can facilitate the core curriculum but also provide for a variety of interest classes and for clubs and activities as well.

USES OF SHORTER PERIODS

The three brackets of 30-minute periods can be useful in many ways. Not only is this method a solution for the problem of including clubs and sports in the regular school day, but it can become a vehicle for short courses or remedial work to serve the needs of certain students. Those who are going to college may want a quick overview of grammar, for example, during their last semester in high school. The 30-minute period can provide for such a short course without this rather special (and temporary) need becoming the main concern of core or English classes. Occupational explorations can be scheduled for eleventh- and twelfth-graders in one of these 30-minute periods. Corrective work in physical education, remedial-reading help, spelling drill, speech correction, or number work could be provided for by these brief daily periods. Class meetings and assemblies could be easily scheduled on certain days. Counseling opportunities would also be much enhanced by these three noon periods. The core room could serve as a home room for students not scheduled elsewhere.

PLAN 6 Ninth-Grade Schedule, 100 Students

Periods

Section	1 8:30–9:30	2 9:30–10:30	3 10:30–11:30	11:30–12:00	12:00–12:30	12:30–1:00	4 1:00–2:00	5 2:00–3:00	6 3:00–4:00
1	Core class	Core class	Core class	Activity and Lunch Period	Activity and Lunch Period	Activity and Lunch Period	Elective	Elective	Study
2	Core class	Core class	Core class	Activity and Lunch Period	Activity and Lunch Period	Activity and Lunch Period	Elective	Study	Elective
3	Core class	Core class	Core class	Activity and Lunch Period	Activity and Lunch Period	Activity and Lunch Period	Study	Elective	Elective

PLAN 7   Ninth- and Tenth-Grade Schedule

Teacher	1 8:30–9:30	2 9:30–10:30	3 10:30–11:30	11:30–12:00	12:00–12:30	12:30–1:00	4 1:00–2:00	5 2:00–3:00	6 3:00–4:00
A	Ninth-grade core	Ninth-grade core	Ninth-grade core	Activities	Activities	Lunch	Elective	Elective	Planning
B	Ninth-grade core	Ninth-grade core	Ninth-grade core	Activities	Activities	Lunch	Elective	Elective	Ninth
C	Ninth-grade core	Ninth-grade core	Elective	Activities	Activities	Lunch	Elective	Elective	grade
D		Elective	Elective	Lunch	Activities	Activities	Tenth-grade core	Tenth-grade core	Elective
E	Planning	Elective	Elective	Lunch	Activities	Activities	Tenth-grade core	Tenth-grade core	Elective
F		Elective	Elective	Activities	Lunch	Activities	Tenth-grade core	Tenth-grade core	Elective
G	Elective	Elective	Elective	Activities	Activities	Lunch	Elective	Elective	Elective

French, Hull, and Dodds propose a ~~somewhat similar~~ schedule with three or four different length-time blocks in it. They suggest the following needed changes if schedules are to reflect modern curricular trends:

1. There is need for shorter as well as longer class periods than are customarily provided. . . .
2. Each teacher who is made responsible for given groups of pupils (not over two groups) should retain these groups for from a quarter or a third up to a half of the day. . . .
3. There is need for cooperative teaching in the integrated program if and when teachers want it. . . .
4. There should be more opportunity for pupil-teacher conferences. . . .
5. There needs to be time for teachers' conferences for joint planning. . . .
6. Greater flexibility in the schedule is needed . . . what is desired is freedom for a group of teachers with a group of classes within a group of periods and a group of rooms, and outside of these rooms, too, if this does not constitute interference with the work of other teachers with their classes.[6]

In support of the more flexible type of schedule, these writers go on to assert:

This type of schedule making is being evolved to cope with the situation produced in modern high schools by present-day social conditions and their demands upon the high schools, by the newer concepts of the function of secondary education in America, and by newer methods and materials of teaching. In time it promises to be as appropriate for these changed conditions as the conventional daily schedule pattern was for the concepts prevailing when it was developed.[7]

GRADE-LEVEL PLANNING

It will be noted that the three blocks provided in Plan 7 for the

[6] Will French, J. D. Hull, and B. L. Dodds, *American High School Administration,* New York, Rinehart & Company, 1951, pp. 325–327.
[7] *Ibid.,* p. 332.

ninth grade are scheduled in such a way that teachers A, B, and C can use the entire morning in any way that seems reasonable and educationally productive, either as three separate sections or as a grade-level group operating as a unit. The same thing is true of the tenth-grade afternoon blocks assigned to teachers D, E, and F. They can either work as three separate sections or come together as one grade-level unit for class meetings, reports, open-forum discussion, panels, or films. They can use the whole time block for excursions without affecting any other elective class. With a minimum of further arranging they can go to camp for an entire week as a grade with their three core teachers accompanying them. In short, each grade can operate, if desired, as a small separate unit within the total school.

This grade-level plan is useful in any school where teachers and administrators are concerned about effective guidance and a continuity of the learning experience. It is especially crucial in large urban schools, where students tend to get lost in the crowds and form no "home base." High schools enrolling 1500 or more students have a tendency to become huge factories where people are handled in large groups and the individual is seldom given help in personal adjustment. Some administrators and teachers are planning school buildings that really consist of four more or less separate grade-level schools, or "schools-within-the-school." The central portion of such a building would include those specialized facilities—laboratories, shops, gymnasium, pool, and cafeteria—that serve all four grade-level units at various times during the day.

Whether or not provided for by a special building design, large schools can be broken up into more manageable units by skillful planning of the schedule. The achievement of good guidance and good instruction depends on pupil-teacher contacts. Such contacts cannot be assured in a large school without some plan of decentralization. The grade-level schedule which frees the students and teachers to plan their own program for at least part of the school day appears to be a promising device.

The connection between period length and the Carnegie unit of credit has been referred to earlier in this chapter. At one period in their history, secondary schools were standardized by efforts to translate the program into credits. It is no longer common to find school leaders bound by this rigid concept of the Carnegie unit. The activities program has made important inroads on the old concept of academic credit. Colleges, accrediting agencies, and state departments of education have become more liberal in their attitudes toward local experimentation. It is generally true today that a school staff could develop any kind of a schedule, and provide any length of periods within the schedule, that could be logically defended on such grounds as this chapter has presented. Further analysis of the problems of credit and promotion will be included in the ensuing chapter.

NEED FOR COÖPERATIVE PLANNING

At the beginning of this chapter the schedule was referred to as the mirror in which the curriculum is reflected. Neither the mirror nor the program that it reflects can be magically altered overnight by the principal as he sits at his desk. It is a complex reflection of many recognized and some hidden factors. Before the schedule can be markedly changed, the school program must be changed. This in turn must hinge on changes in values that people hold, as was emphasized in Chapter 5. Schedule development must, in the last analysis, be a result of changed attitudes and behavior on the part of the persons most concerned. Students and parents must feel that changes will better meet their needs. Most important of all, the staff of a school must want a given program change, and the schedule change that will make it possible.

The alert administrator will not wait in his office for such desires to develop, but will challenge the faculty to think together about the present program and how it might better serve the needs of youth. He will invite its ideas and suggestions about the schedule at all times. Above all, he will make it clear to all teachers that the schedule of classes is not a fixed thing nor an end in itself, but rather a means of facilitating a better program, which they are involved in developing as a professional group.

FOR FURTHER READING

Educational Policies Commission, *Education for All American Youth,* Washington, The National Education Association, 1944.

DeVilbiss, Wilbur, "Criteria of a Good Master Schedule," *Bulletin of the National Association of Secondary School Principals,* No. 31, November, 1947, pp. 31–38.

Douglass, Harl R., *Organization and Administration of Secondary Schools,* rev. ed., Boston, Ginn & Company, 1945, chap. 6.

Edmondson, J. B., Roemer, Joseph, and Bacon, Francis L., *The Administration of the Modern Secondary School,* rev. ed., New York, The Macmillan Company, 1948, chap. 6.

Faunce, Roland C., and Bossing, Nelson L., *Developing the Core Curriculum,* New York, Prentice-Hall, 1951, chap. 12.

French, Will, Hull, J. D., and Dodds, B. L., *American High School Administration,* New York, Rinehart & Company, 1951, chaps. 15, 16.

Ivok, Leo, *How to Prepare the Schedule for a Secondary School,* Harvard Workshop Series No. 5, Cambridge, Mass., Graduate School of Business Education, Harvard University, 1944.

Jacobson, P., Reavis, W. C., and Logsdon, J. D., *Duties of School Principals,* New York, Prentice-Hall, 1950, chaps. 3, 4.

Langfitt, R. E., *The Daily Schedule and High School Reorganization,* New York, The Macmillan Company, 1938.

MacConnell, Charles; Melby, Ernest; and Arndt, C. O., *New Schools for a New Culture,* New York, Harper & Brothers, 1943, chap. II.

Manley, C. B., "Secondary School Organization and Schedule Making for the Integrating Curriculum," Type B Project, New York, Teachers College, Columbia University, 1941.

Michigan Department of Public Instruction, *Planning and Working*

Together, Bulletin 337, Lansing, Mich., Superintendent of Public Instruction, 1945, pp. 145–153.

Mudd, Dorothy, *A Core Program Grows,* Bel Air, Md., Harford County Board of Education, 1949, chap. II.

National Association of Secondary School Principals, *Planning for American Youth,* Washington, The National Education Association, 1944.

Noar, Gertrude, *Freedom to Live and Learn,* Philadelphia, The Franklin Publishing Company, 1948.

Stratemeyer, Florence B., and Associates, *Developing a Curriculum for Modern Living,* New York, Bureau of Publications, Teachers College, Columbia University, 1947.

CHAPTER 14

....

Promoting and Grouping Students

SECONDARY SCHOOLS FOR ALL AMERICAN YOUTH?

Throughout this volume there has been a recurring emphasis on the trend toward making the secondary school an institution that serves the needs of all our youth. The high school's phenomenal growth in enrollment during the first three decades of this century has been described; it has been pointed out that in spite of some fluctuations, the high schools have generally tended to enroll a higher percentage of youth of appropriate age until over four out of five now enter. Evidence indicates that this trend may continue until the high school approaches 100 percent enrollment of boys and girls up to 18 years of age.

School administrators and teachers have been concerned over the fact that many of these young people drop out of school after a trial. Investigations have been made of the cost of high school, and some efforts have been made to reduce this factor in order to ensure that a high school education does not remain the prerogative of the well-to-do. Most educators are also concerned about giving this educational opportunity to youth of every race and creed. Efforts have been made to provide enriched and functional programs in the secondary school in order to interest potential dropouts in remaining in school. In short we are committed to the concept that secondary education is for all our youth.

Teachers generally tend to accept this principle. They are inclined to agree that the high school is for all—with one significant exception. We are still not agreed that youth of low ability in the verbal and academic skills should graduate from high school. We admit all boys and girls, frequently with misgivings, but we are perplexed as to what to do about those who do not measure up to our standards. We speak of students who "are not ready for high school work" (as though there were some other way to define this phrase than as work that our high school students can and do perform). We fear that the elementary and junior high schools are not "preparing the students adequately for high school." We still encourage people to believe that the high school diploma should mean some standard level of mastery of knowledges and skills for all who "earn" it. We fear that standards will be lowered if a student can graduate from high school on a basis of effort rather than scholarship.

The fact is that many secondary school teachers are torn between this desire to maintain academic group standards for all and the desire to accept all youth who wish to enter high school. The elementary schools have largely begun to live up to their legal role as common schools. The concept that all children should be accepted and should progress through the elementary school with a minimum of failure has received rather general acceptance among elementary school teachers and principals. Continuous progress is becoming the rule, repetition of a grade the exception. Although this policy is not yet universal, it has been accepted so generally that failures have been sharply reduced. It is no longer a common thing to see 16-year-olds in the sixth and seventh grades.

The high school has progressed, too, from its early role as a selective institution. The state laws have reflected the growing conviction that the high school is for all youth. Four states require full-time attendance until age 18, six states until age 17, and thirty-eight states until age 16. The right to enroll in school is legally assured to youth up to age 20 or 21 in most states. There are a few places left in this country where eighth grade graduates are required to pass a written examination for admission to high school, but these are exceptions. Most high schools now accept all elementary school graduates upon the recommendation of the elementary school principal, without regard to subjects completed or level of mastery. It is becoming a general practice also to give a diploma to all those who persist in high school and appear to make an effort for the required number of years.

Yet we are often ashamed of our own best practices in this regard. We still hold a degree of the former selective idea in our thinking. We graduate boys and girls of low ability but we fear we should not. We have reduced subject and grade failure but we feel guilty about it. The old concept of the high school diploma as a measure of scholarship still lingers, and carries with it ethical overtones. We fear that we are not being fair to those students who "really earn" the diploma when we pass those who do not measure up to the norms. In many high schools those teachers who continue to fail a considerable number of their students are regarded as defenders of standards. They are sometimes thought of as the sturdy souls who have the courage of their convictions, and who are maintaining the prestige of the school in the face of many difficulties. On the other hand, teachers who accept all students, give them all the help they can, and then pass them along on a basis of their growth and effort are sometimes ashamed and fearful. They dread becoming known as easy markers or as teachers with no standards.

SHOULD MORE STUDENTS "FAIL"?

Various arguments are advanced for failing students. One of the most common of these is that standards will be lowered if students of low ability can pass. In a psychological sense the only standards that matter are those which an individual learner sets for himself. This kind of standard is not actually lowered by continuous-progress policies. What is really meant is that the average ability of all high school graduates may tend to be reduced if the range of academic ability among graduates is widened. This is likely to be true if the definition of ability is limited to the skills of reading, writing, and computing that were held in such regard by the old school. No one doubts their value, but many people think there are other kinds of abilities that are valuable too. Our graduates need such abilities as those involved in successful social adjustment, group planning, leadership, and critical thinking. Regardless of their command of the academic skills, all people have value and uniqueness—and they need to succeed at something. The time is long past due for high school teachers and administrators to accept and glory in the fact that all kinds of people can finish high school. Because we are graduating more students than ever before, we are graduating more people of high mental ability with a good grasp of the academic areas. We are also graduating more people than ever who have less verbal or number ability, although they have other fine qualities necessary for success.

Another argument for failure that is still heard is that life is bitterly competitive, and characterized by frequent failure. The school, some say, should reflect this lifelike quality and include opportunities for failure too. This argument is based on two fallacies that should be more generally examined. The first fallacy is the assumption that failure of a high school subject is analogous to failure on a job, which may result in loss of pay or even in loss of the job itself. The differences between these two situations are often overlooked. The industrial worker in a large plant is seldom penalized by factors that are not under his own control, as is the student in school. If the worker cannot perform one operation he is shifted to another. It is the business of personnel workers and foremen to discover his aptitudes and to find a place where he can succeed. The school student has only limited opportunities to shift about in this manner—especially if he is "failing" a required subject. The worker can even change jobs without loss of prestige or self-respect. The school student, on the other hand, faces social disgrace and loss of a whole semester's or year's work if he fails. The worker is free to make a choice of the basis on which he will compete. The school student has no choice but competes on conditions established by other people.

The second assumption in the argument for failure is that one is best prepared for success by failure. The specific argument goes like this: "Life is bound to include some failures; it is best to prepare young people for this experience by confronting them with the possibility or even the reality of failure in high school." By this reasoning the best-prepared products of the schools would be those who have failed so repeatedly that they have quit school in search of success elsewhere. Failure actually prepares one for nothing except more failure. If the goal is to prepare young people to *withstand and survive failure*, it follows that they must have courage, self-confidence, and faith in themselves. These qualities are not the product of academic failure, but rather of success. The most urgent need of every person is for the quiet conviction that he or she can meet life and its problems with reasonable success. The neuroses that spell failure are often bred in people by their school experiences.

THE VALUE OF SUCCESS

Again, the word "failure" has been given more than one meaning in this connection. School experience should provide plenty of opportunities for mistakes and even for failure in the sense of not managing to achieve one's own goals. There should be guidance in analyzing this kind of failure in order to avoid it on the next attempt. Projects in the classroom or in student organizations may not always be successful. Both individuals and groups need a chance to experience this kind of failure, which is vastly different from receiving no credit for a year of living. The school has a responsibility for helping students to arrive at a realistic self-appraisal of their own strengths and weaknesses. It is possible to meet and survive temporary failure of an enterprise if one has chosen the enterprise realistically and if he really believes he can ultimately find a way. Indeed, the greatest personality need of all is the feeling referred to as "can-ness" by Rasey and Menge: ". . . it is first essential that an individual see himself as a simple doer—as one who can. So long as he sees himself as one who cannot, he is lamed and blind to his own enhancement. He cannot try. This we believe is the right word. When it is said that he won't try it is probably then most of all that he cannot try." [1]

Every human being needs to succeed at something. Through success he builds the qualities that make for more success—he becomes more courageous, more secure, more self-respecting, more confident. Failure, on the other hand, paves the way for further failure by developing in the individual timidity, suspicion, fear, and self-doubt. That is the real reason why subject failure must be eliminated in the secondary school. It simply does not help build better people, and it thus defeats the very purpose of the school.

Some teachers are convinced that without fear of failing marks or rewards of good marks high school students would not do any work in school. This, of course, hinges on whether the students see any sense in the particular learning experience involved. If it is sufficiently divorced from their real interests and needs, they will have to be coerced or extrinsically motivated to go through the motions of learning. As Kelley and Rasey have pointed out, however, this is a losing game for teachers:

> While competition for grades is held by many to stimulate learning, it actually has the opposite effect. When the learner has done all he needs to do in order to get the grade he wants, he naturally quits. Some students who are adept at the tricks of the trade find it possible to get good grades with scarcely any learning at all. So the effect of the grading system is to delimit and stultify learning, to hold learning activities below the creative level, to confine what is learned to what will pay off.
>
> The grading system also delimits learning by shifting the objective

[1] Marie I. Rasey and J. Wilmer Menge, *What We Learn from Children,* New York, Harper & Brothers, 1955.

away from learning. It changes the object of the enterprise. When one is concentrating on the vagaries of the teacher and what he is likely to include in his examination, he is diverted from that which might have been learned and is perverting his energies in the direction of ephemeral and spurious value.[2]

If the value alleged for failure is a spurious one for the able learner, it is a hopeless one for the failing student. He seldom sets out to fail; he finds himself trapped into a competition he did not seek based on rules he did not make and involving qualities he cannot command. Under these circumstances he is likely to give up and quit. If he does persist, it is on a basis not of learning but of getting a passing grade by any possible means.

FAILING STUDENTS DROP OUT

Many well-meaning teachers rationalize the persistence of failure policies by the statement that school just is not for some boys and girls. They might better quit, it is argued, and achieve some success on a job. One difficulty is that there are no permanent jobs for adolescents. Industry, business, and agriculture do not want full-time workers 16 or 17 years of age. The armed services do not generally welcome their enlistment before high school graduation. If they take a job it is likely to be at unskilled work of a temporary nature. Both management and labor prefer to hold permanent jobs with possibilities of advancement for young men and women who have finished school. In today's industrialized world there is no market for the permanent labor of adolescents. This means that boys and girls who quit school will be recurrently unemployed as well as being deprived of constructive social relationships and leisure-time activities with their age peers.

There are other reasons for retaining students in school at least until high school graduation. These reasons have been elaborated in earlier chapters of this volume. They may be summed up by

[2] Earl C. Kelley and Marie I. Rasey, *Education and the Nature of Man,* New York, Harper & Brothers, 1952, p. 99.

saying that citizens in our difficult world need all the education possible, and that every boy and girl deserves the chance to receive a high school education. This is an article of faith to which teachers would subscribe, too. What is often overlooked is the fact that this chance deserved by all youth must not be restricted to those with a particular IQ or spelling score.

In summary of this discussion of the need to serve all secondary school youth regardless of their ability, the trend today is toward the unconditional admission to high school of all youth, and the provision of experiences for them that will make it possible for them to progress continuously and receive a high school diploma at the end of an appropriate number of years. This trend is both educationally valid and ethically sound. It is time for both educators and the public to stop being critical or ashamed of its application in the modern secondary school. French, Hull, and Dodds have pointed out that this policy of continuous progress need not require that standards be abolished, but only that they be adapted to the individual:

Such a program does not mean merely the abolition of fixed promotion standards and the establishment of a policy of universal promotions; it means developing standards for each student based upon an adequate assessment of the progress he is making toward goals that are appropriate for him. Helping the student set his goals and then helping him to evaluate his progress toward them is time consuming, but it should not be considered an extra or additional task for the teacher; it is an important part of the teaching.[3]

These writers go on to warn that a few failures may occur, even when the programs are appropriate to the students' interests and ability, because of refusal to make a reasonable effort. The trouble with this criterion is, as Rasey and Menge pointed out in a quotation earlier in this chapter, that some students are so conditioned to failure that even "a reasonable effort" is beyond their powers.

[3] W. French, J. D. Hull, and B. L. Dodds, *American High School Administration*, New York, Rinehart & Company, 1951, p. 382.

Such cases may be salvaged by special programs and skillful counseling. The effort to provide continuous progress for all students hinges on success in revision of teaching methods and curriculum. Most of all it hinges on the willingness of teachers to accept a different standard for every individual student and to individualize the evaluation process.

REQUIRED COURSES

Students should not fail required courses. As in the elementary school, instruction in such courses should be adapted to the interests, needs, and abilities of every individual. It should be expected that all students progress regularly through any course that is required of all. It follows that the experiences provided in required courses should be within the power of all students to achieve. A few individuals may need more time than the rest to mature, as a result of illness, overprotection, or other causes. Such persons may logically be asked to spend an extra year in junior high school if it appears that they will be helped to succeed by working and living with a younger group. This decision should be made after thorough study of the child and his total adjustment, not merely on a basis of his failure to pass a course. In general, the experiences that any student confronts in a course required of all students should be geared to his ability and interests. Under such circumstances, failure should be practically eliminated in required courses.

ELECTIVE COURSES

Elective courses need not suffer a high failure rate, as many of them do. Such failure in an elective course is usually evidence that the student should not have elected the course in the first place. It is possible and feasible to collect such evidence early in a semester. When all the available evidence indicates that a student has no aptitude for certain specialized experiences, he should not be held in the course for an entire semester but transferred to some other, more appropriate course. It should be possible to begin a new course in certain (elective) fields at any week in a semester without the penalty of failure for withdrawal from the first course elected. In many schools this is possible in the case of typing, shop, or other project- or individual-contract classes. Some schools provide one or more sections of "occupations" or "individual problems" classes in which a contract plan is used to permit individualization. A student can enter such a class at any time, complete a semester's or a year's work, and drop it when a satisfactory record of completed projects has been achieved. A few sections of classes of this type provide flexible programs that enable schools to reduce subject failure in elective courses. It should be possible virtually to eliminate semester failures that are due to lack of ability to perform certain skills or to master certain concepts that are considered basic in elective courses. For example, shorthand demands a certain kind of aptitude that not all students have. It should not be necessary to hold a student in a shorthand course for an entire semester after it has been amply demonstrated that he cannot master the skills required. There should be other courses in which he can succeed, and it should be possible for him to shift to those other courses at any time in the semester.

Many schools have provided such alternative courses. One difficulty lies in persuading the parents of a boy or girl that a change of election is indicated. They may be blinded to the facts by their own ambitions for their child. Skillful interpretation may be needed to convince parents that certain experiences are simply not appropriate or even possible for their boy or girl. It may not be enough to have all the facts and to share these with parents. They may need to share also the basic planning that will obviate failure in a secondary school. Specifically, they need to understand that no lowering of standards is involved, but rather an adaptation to individual needs and abilities. Such adaptation may actually result in a raising of standards for the individual who now discovers goals that are possible for him to achieve. This concept of individual standards should be shared with parents. The actual decision to change a student's elective program should be agreed to by the parent, as well as by the student, the teacher, and the counselor or administrator.

The preceding discussion of elective courses should not be construed to imply that absolute standards of mastery are necessary or valid in all such courses. Many of these are so individualized as to permit, within a given class, a wide range of varying abilities and levels of achievement. In classes such as art, crafts, typing, and shop it is perfectly possible for an individual to proceed at his own rate and be evaluated in terms of his ability level. Other elective courses, such as speech and journalism, can be so taught that there is a respected role for students of various aptitudes. As teachers of elective courses become better acquainted with their students and more acceptive of differences between various students, they will tend increasingly to evaluate achievement on a basis of interest and effort. This more flexible, more human approach to teaching method will tend further to reduce subject failure. It will also help to inspire the student of superior ability by confronting him with unique challenges as an individual learner.

REMEDIAL HELP

Another means of reducing failure has been proposed in the chapter devoted to scheduling. Every high school could make effective use of short courses and tutoring for remedial help in such areas as reading, speech, spelling, and arithmetic. Two approaches to this problem have proved successful. The first involves provision of a special teacher to whom various individuals can go for special help during other classes. This clinical type of help might not last a whole semester or require daily visits. It would need to be held to small groups composed of those who are really in need of a different approach than that used with large, heterogeneous classes. No special credit or similar incentive is needed to motivate students in these special classes. They go to them for as long a time as needed to get at least a promising beginning toward overcoming a handicap. They can then return to their regular class with some degree of confidence that they can succeed with the group.

In the second type of remedial work a special schedule of short courses is set up to accommodate a wide variety of needs. Among these short courses might be remedial reading classes, refresher courses in grammar or arithmetic, drill classes in spelling or penmanship, and a number of prevocational courses that give a few interested students some exploratory experiences in various specialized occupations. These short courses might run a month or six weeks and students might be permitted to reëlect them or to elect another course at the end of that period. They might be set up during 30-minute periods at noon, as suggested in Chapter 13, or they might occupy the student's entire day for six weeks at the end of a school year. The latter plan has been found successful for seniors who desire refresher courses in certain areas just before beginning their college career or taking permanent jobs.

These clinical or remedial experiences are just as important in the area of corrective health and should be available to those who need special help (and counsel) in overcoming physical deficiencies. It is not a complicated matter to plan a schedule for these special-help courses. A good secondary school will include such help in further reducing academic failure.

In summary, it is both desirable and possible to eliminate subject failure in the junior and senior high schools if staff, students, and community understand the purpose of such efforts. Through adaptation of instruction to individual needs and abilities, through flexibility for changes in election, and through provision of special remedial help, a staff can insure every student a chance to succeed. When we once realize the dynamic contribution of success, as contrasted with the stultifying effect of subject failure, it is probable that this unique kind of failure will tend to disappear from our schools.

GROUPING STUDENTS

There has been much controversy in recent years about "homogeneous versus heterogeneous" grouping. Those who advocate homogeneous grouping should probably use the term "ability" grouping instead. Complete homogeneity could only be secured by having "every pupil in the group equal to every other pupil in ability, age, industry, previous experience, and *all* other factors which affect learning." [4] Even with all factors theoretically even, the interests and attitudes that directly condition learning would vary significantly from one student to another. Thus a really homogeneous class group exists only in theory.

On the other hand, heterogeneous grouping is a fiction, too. The general practice of promotion by grade levels denies the heterogeneous principle, as does the provision of elective courses in which students are grouped by interest or vocational goals. This provision of electives has a tendency to group students by ability. For example, students in an advanced mathematics or foreign language class are roughly an ability group in terms of the particular skills or concepts involved in that class. Most educators would not object to this application of ability grouping. The objection arises when students are grouped by ability in the various sections of required courses or general-education classes. The basis for the objection here seems to be that students have no choice of subjects in the case of required courses, and accordingly the decision to place them in a "better" or in a "poorer" or "slower" group is made without reference to their desires. The social implications of superiority or inferiority that accompany such grouping practices seem to be more objectionable when there is no individual choice.

Opponents of ability grouping point also to the frequently invalid basis used for such classification. As a matter of fact, the research in this area does not make clear what the basis of classification by ability should be. As many as twenty-three different

---

[4] *Encyclopedia of Educational Research,* rev. ed., Walter S. Monroe (ed.), New York, The Macmillan Company, 1950, pp. 376–377.

criteria, applied singly or in combinations, have been used. The basic problem in establishing criteria is the selection of that factor, or those factors, that will predict school achievement accurately. This problem is complicated by both developmental factors and by the variety of curricular goals and teaching methods. For example, let us assume that the criterion selected for classification is previous school achievement (often selected as one criterion). The well-known factors of learning spurts and plateaus may completely invalidate this criterion. Every teacher has known boys and girls who suddenly contradict all assumptions about their ability based on their previous achievement. Or let us assume that the criterion selected for grouping is the score on one or more reading tests. The student who ranks low on such tests may then encounter a teacher who does not penalize the slow reader or even particularly emphasize the reading skill in comparison to some other ability, creative art, for example.

In light of such variations in child development, curriculum, and teaching methods, it is small wonder that research has so far failed to point clearly to some predictive factors that can be effectively used in grouping students. Some studies seem to support certain kinds of bases for grouping—but it is grouping for a particular kind of educational purpose. Other studies appear just as clearly to invalidate these bases for grouping—but the goals of education may be different in these studies. It seems clear, therefore, that the basis for grouping must be selected in terms of the educational purposes to be served. In general, ability grouping based on students' marks, reading scores, or achievement test scores is most appropriate in schools where verbal skills and information are valued highly as the ends of instruction. In schools where teachers generally use the same assignments for an entire class and expect all students to compete for marks on a basis of uniform mastery of these assignments, ability grouping may provide a better break for students at both ends of the scale of verbal ability. Likewise, for classes whose prime purpose is the sharpening or perfection of certain specific skills, ability grouping based on the particular skills involved can be defended. An example of this drill-and-skill function might be a class in grammar for those seniors about to enter college. Another example might be an advanced course in machine shop. It is worth noting that both of these examples are chosen from elective courses, where some approximation of ability grouping is a common and accepted practice.

Required courses involve a different kind of educational goal. By definition, general-education classes are required of all students on the ground that they are concerned with the educational goals needed by all citizens. Thus required courses face one basic challenge not confronted by the elective program—they must be geared to those purposes that are common to all persons in our culture. If they are common to all persons it follows that they must be within the range of comprehension of all students, and that they must be concerned equally with the growth and development of all. In grouping students in required courses, the criteria used should be such as to facilitate coöperative efforts toward the good life for all members of the group. To the extent that such coöperation of all members is the goal in a required course, ability grouping appears to be a poor basis for selection of a class section. This is true because it does not furnish a sound base for sharing among students of various kinds (and levels) of ability. Kelley and Rasey have pointed out the value of uniqueness in coöperative endeavor:

The opportunity to specialize, to perform separate functions better than any one cell could do them all and to perform these functions for others while others were doing different tasks for them, is the basis for all living tissue or organism above the level of the single cell. And so it is when people do things together. Their uniqueness is what gives individuals value in social organization. If people were all alike, had the same abilities, there would be little value in association. None could learn from others; none could perform tasks which others could not do for themselves.[5]

[5] Kelley and Rasey, *op. cit.*, pp. 90–91.

These authors go on to analyze the effects of ability grouping on the coöperative (learning) process:

> The customary method of teaching, where what is to be learned is decided in advance by the teacher, fails to cherish uniqueness. This quality, which gives the individual his place and points his possibilities for service, is discouraged and diminished. Rather than cultivating uniqueness, we try to get everyone to be as much alike as possible. We even group together people who are similar so that we can make their similarities more complete. Then we give them all the same lesson and strive for the same learning. The X groups are quite proud of their Xness, but they are deprived of the special and necessary talents of the Y and Z groups. Such a practice is a denial of the basic need for cooperation, where each has a unique contribution for all. Uniqueness, communication, cooperation form the basis for human development; any practice which limits these is encouraging growth in abnormal and unhuman ways.[6]

Thus instruction in general education is concerned with social-civic goals. Among these goals is that of coöperation with others, of working together on common tasks and using the resources of others in the solution of problems. Leadership and followership are important in such group enterprises. Group cohesiveness and democracy in human relations are goals that set high value on human differences, not on similarity. Students of high verbal ability have needs that require association with students with other kinds of abilities. Learning to help each other and to be helped, to lead and to follow, to seek and find different kinds of resources in one's fellows—all these and similar kinds of coöperative learning call for diversity of class groups, not uniformity.

The best criterion for grouping in required courses is probably social maturity. This will most often be achieved by grouping students by their chronological age. This procedure will not violate the principle of needed differences stated above, since a range of at least five years in most of the academic skills will be found in

[6] *Ibid.*, p. 99.

a single class composed of students of the same chronological age. A special kind of difference results from the more rapid maturation of girls than of boys at junior high school years. Even though this factor may temporarily create marked differences in social maturity between the sexes, chronological age still appears to be the best single index. Any other known basis will introduce less promising elements into the grouping plan that will often interfere with instead of furthering the process of coöperative learning. French, Hull, and Dodds have pointed out the purpose of such grouping: "The sole aim of grouping according to social maturity should be to provide a learning situation in which students of different abilities and interests can work together with other students on content and at a rate adapted to them, thus making it possible for students to succeed with what was expected of them and therefore be eligible for promotion." [7]

Within a class other kinds of subgroups will be formed for various purposes. These small groups will for some purposes be based on interests, for others on specific responsibilities that have been assumed, and for still others on abilities that will further some goal of the class. Subgroups may be formed for social activities, too. Thus the individual learner will have many opportunities within the class to work with others both like him and unlike him in different ways.

The school as a whole will provide other kinds of grouping. The gifted musician will be playing in ensembles with older students; the athletic and speech programs will mix students of various ages; the student who is keenly interested in photography will join a camera club that brings together enthusiasts from all high school grades; the elective program of the senior high school will permit grouping by interest and special ability. The assemblies and parties will provide opportunities for social grouping. There is no lack of chances for joining various kinds of groups in the typical secondary school.

[7] French, Hull, and Dodds, *op. cit.*, p. 386.

The home base of the student should be the general-education classes where students of approximately similar social maturity work together on mutual problems and learn to get along with others. These groups should not be affected by semester promotion. They should remain together at least a year, and perhaps for two or three years. With such continuity a teacher can have a chance to collect real information about each individual and to use that information intelligently in furthering his development as a person. Semester promotion has already been replaced by annual promotion in most high schools. It is possible in such schools to hold sections of general-education classes together for two years or more, while at the same time resectioning many elective courses every semester.

SUMMARY

In this chapter a dilemma which confronts the secondary school has been presented. That dilemma arises from our acceptance of the ideal that the public school is for all youth, and our persistent clinging to the tradition of rewarding and promoting some kinds of ability in preference to others. As long as entrance examinations and subject failure are retained, the high school will tend to be selective rather than comprehensive. If we really mean to provide education for all American youth, we must stop thinking of the diploma as a reward for special abilities possessed in marked degree by only a few students. We must stop being ashamed of our own efforts to adapt instruction to the needs, interests, and abilities of all youth.

The secondary school is a tax-supported social enterprise with an important contribution to make in American democracy. It has been, and can become even more truly the means by which all men may hope for a better life. As the basic vehicle for social mobility in our complex culture, the secondary school must seek constantly to serve all youth more effectively. It should accept all, regardless of ability, and do everything possible to enrich their lives during the period of their schooling. Policies that operate in such a way as to penalize those of lesser ability or to classify them as inferior persons must be changed. Not only the college-bound are entitled to success in high school but those also who will go from school to jobs. Not only the fast reader but also the slow reader will (and should) receive a diploma. Not only the mathematician and the linguist but also the woodsman, the homemaker, and the athlete should find success in the secondary school. Policies must be developed that provide full acceptance and continuous progress for all youth.

For Further Reading

Alberty, Harold, *Reorganizing the High School Curriculum*, rev. ed., New York, The Macmillan Company, 1953, chap. II.

Billett, R. O., *Provisions for Individual Differences, Marking and Promotion*, U.S. Office of Education, Bulletin No. 17, Monograph No. 13, Washington, Government Printing Office, 1932.

Douglass, Harl R., *Secondary Education for Life Adjustment of American Youth*, New York, The Ronald Press Company, 1952, chap. 5.

Federal Security Agency, *Requirements and High School Programs*, U.S. Office of Education, Circular No. 300, Washington, Government Printing Office, February, 1949.

French, Will, "What Should Graduation from the Secondary School Mean?", *Bulletin of the National Association of Secondary School Principals*, No. 94, December, 1940.

French, Will, Hull, J. Dan, and Dodds, B. L., *American High School Administration*, New York, Rinehart & Company, 1951, chap. 19.

Kelley, Earl C., and Rasey, Marie I., *Education and the Nature of Man*, New York, Harper & Brothers, 1952.

Leonard, J. Paul, *Developing the Secondary School Curriculum*, rev. ed., New York, Rinehart & Company, 1953, pp. 200–208.

Monroe, Walter S. (ed.), *Encyclopedia of Educational Research*, rev. ed., New York, The Macmillan Company, 1950, pp. 1122–1123.

Rasey, Marie I., and Menge, J. Wilmer, *What We Learn from Children*, New York, Harper & Brothers, 1955.

Segel, David, *Intellectual Abilities in the Adolescent Period,* Federal Security Agency, Office of Education, Bulletin No. 6, Washington, Government Printing Office, November 6, 1948.

Smith, E. R., and Tyler, R. W., *Appraising and Recording Student Progress,* New York, Harper & Brothers, 1942.

Spaulding, Francis T., "Graduation Without Equivocation," *Harvard Teachers Record,* Vol. 5, No. 3, June, 1935.

Trout, David, *The Measurement of Student Adjustment and Achievement,* Ann Arbor, Mich., University of Michigan Press, 1949.

Yeager, William A., *Administration and the Pupil,* New York, Harper & Brothers, 1949, chaps. 20, 21.

CHAPTER 15

....

The Board of Education,
the Superintendent, and the Principal

Preceding chapters have been largely devoted to discussion of ways to improve secondary schools. The focal agent in such improvement is the principal. He has great power and responsibility in most American communities. This power and responsibility are delegated to him by the board of education through the superintendent of schools. At this point it may be appropriate to analyze these sources of the principal's authority and to discuss the relationships that should obtain between professional administrators and the board of education.

THE BOARD OF EDUCATION

LEGAL POWERS

The American school board has great power. In our form of government it is the agency responsible to the people for the establishment and operation of their schools. Constitutionally the separate states have control of education, but this control is generally delegated to local boards of education. The federal government exercises practically no control over local school systems. Even the state governments maintain only minimum controls, chiefly relating to conditions under which state aid will be supplied, and the enforcement of certain (general) state laws. The powers left to local boards of education are far-reaching. Not only are school boards generally free from control by the state and national governments, but they are also largely autonomous at the local level. City, township, and county governments have very little control over the boards of education, which are separately elected and directly responsible to the people for the operation of the schools.

This phenomenon of local school board autonomy puzzles foreign visitors. In many other countries a national school system prevails, with the policy function lodged in a department of the national government. The supervision of schools in these countries is also likely to be a national rather than a local function.

The American plan originated in the New England colonies and grew up with our country. The belief that education should be locally controlled is rather firmly established in the United States. Any trend toward state or federal control is vigorously opposed as a move toward making the schools an instrument for political indoctrination. Thus local control of education is closely linked in our thinking with the preservation of freedom and democracy. This tradition has enormously enhanced the importance of the board of education.

ADMINISTRATIVE ROLE

The early school boards, or "trustees," actually administered the school program in the long period prior to the evolution, about 1840, of the professional school administrator. A recent yearbook of the American Association of School Administrators quoted an example from board minutes during the nineteenth century: "The following rule, taken from an early record, shows how far these boards would sometimes go in regulating school affairs: 'Every class or scholar must be placed upon the floor by or near the teachers, that they may have the better opportunity to hear them read or spell with distinctness.' " [1]

Spears has quoted a regulation from the Committee of Trustees of the Cincinnati schools in 1838: "In the absence of the trustee of the district and his special instructions, or the instructions of the board of trustees, the principal-teacher is expected to give the necessary instruction to his assistants, and to classify the pupils and regulate the school under his charge." [2]

It is evident from this rule that trustees were expected actually to visit the school daily and issue instructions. This administrative function of school boards was not unique to the Cincinnati schools of 1838 but common throughout the country. In the absence of a central administrator the school boards "ran" the schools. They became, on occasion, superintendent, principal, supervisor, and janitor. They even became teachers when the need arose.

As schools became bigger, professional administrators developed and the boards of education gradually withdrew from the field of school operation and administration. In our large urban school systems it would be quite impossible for the lay board members to exercise control of the numerous, complex procedures by which schools are operated. In smaller school systems, even today, there are some boards of education that still cling to the administrative role. They have been known to perform such functions as the actual purchasing of supplies, interviewing of prospective teachers, or visiting classes in a supervisory capacity.

POLICY ROLE

Fortunately, such interference with the administrative function is the exception rather than the rule. Most boards of education

---

[1] American Association of School Administrators, *School Boards in Action,* Twenty-fourth Yearbook, Washington, The National Education Association, 1946, pp. 10–11.

[2] *Tenth Annual Report of the Trustees and Visitors of Common Schools* [of Cincinnati], 1839. Quoted in Harold Spears, *The High School for Today,* New York, American Book Company, 1950, p. 332.

today see themselves as the legally elected representatives of the people, their task to deal with goals and principles for the school system, rather than with routines and details of operating it. They expect to employ a competent superintendent to whom they can delegate the actual administration of the schools. The task of the board of education is threefold: (1) to analyze educational needs for the whole community, (2) to develop basic policies in harmony with the facts at hand regarding needs, and (3) to appraise results of school administration based on these group-adopted policies.

The power and responsibility of the board arise from their operation as a group. No individual board member has any legal authority when the board is not in session. He becomes exactly as responsible and as powerful as any other citizen of the community when he is not in a board meeting. Some board members forget this fact and interfere with the administration of the schools on their own. Or they may permit themselves to enter into deals or bargains that will affect their voting on certain issues when the board meets. No individual member has any right to commit the board in advance of its meeting, or to assume responsibility for actual administrative problems. The superintendent who leans on one or two particular individuals on the board, seeks their personal advice, and reports privately to them as individuals is encouraging bad school-board policies. He may also be making himself a puppet in the hands of a lay administrator of the schools.

Since the board of education is elected by, and responsible to the community as a whole, the members should avoid making promises to, or bargains with any particular pressure group. As citizens, the board members are entitled to work actively with others interested in similar goals. As board members, however, they must avoid making promises that will commit the board.

THE PEOPLE AND THE BOARD

This total-community responsibility of the board need not preclude the organization of citizens committees and other groups of persons interested in better schools. The citizens' commissions, which have been widely organized in recent years under the stimulus of the National Citizens Commission for the Public Schools, have been objected to by some school administrators as an invasion of the legal authority of the board of education. They need not represent any invasion of the board's powers. They may, on the contrary, strengthen and reaffirm the powers of the board of education by helping to furnish a wider base for decisions:

It is clear, of course, that extralegal groups of citizens cannot make decisions for the board of education. That is the legal duty of the board. But every policy, every decision must be adopted on the basis of ideas—good or bad. If the source of all ideas has to be the superintendent of schools, the policies thus based will be limited to the ideas and insights of one person. If the board of education contributes ideas too, the base is widened a bit—perhaps to seven persons. If techniques can be found for getting the ideas of thousands of people in the community, the base for policies will be immeasurably enriched and strengthened. If finally, procedures can be developed for enabling these thousands of potential idea-presenters to discuss their ideas with others, to seek and secure data, and to reach agreements by groups, the board of education will have a really sound basis for enacting school policies. Policies thus developed by wide consensus will enjoy solid support throughout the community—support that is well deserved because they are likely to be better policies than any one group could have developed.[3]

Thus the board of education, which is responsible to all the people of a community, should seek constantly to develop means whereby the voice of the people can be articulate. Without such a broad base of consensus, the board is always operating in a vacuum. The members seldom see their constituents or hear their ideas unless there are broadly representative groups concerned with school policies. There is a constant danger of response to

[3] J. W. Menge and R. C. Faunce, *Working Together for Better Schools,* New York, American Book Company, 1953, pp. 121–122.

small pressure groups in the absence of really representative or-ganizations.

THE SUPERINTENDENT

DUTIES

It is the job of the school board to develop policies. The super-intendent of schools has the job of administering the schools in accordance with these policies. He has the further responsibility of assembling the facts needed for decisions by the board of educa-tion, and of making recommendations to the board on specific problems. He must also report to the board regularly regarding developments and progress toward results sought by the board of education.

WHAT THE SUPERINTENDENT SHOULD NOT DO

The superintendent should not determine policies himself, or create situations in which the board has no choice of alternatives. He should resist the temptation to manipulate the board, to get his way by indirection and maneuvering, or to pit one group of board members against another in order to secure action he desires. He should not select nominees for the board or campaign for cer-tain members. The superintendent, like other school employees, is responsible to the board of education and should not seek to "pack" it with presumably favorable or sympathetic members. He should avoid personal links with selected members—any superin-tendent's clique or kitchen cabinet will tend to divide the board instead of uniting it in working for the welfare of the entire com-munity. The superintendent should also avoid taking orders from certain individuals on the board who wish to be the power behind the throne. He should share information equally with all mem-bers, not have secrets with one or two members. His responsibility and authority are derived from the whole board, meeting as a group, not from any individuals on the board. This does not imply that superintendents should not spend any time with individual board members. Many superintendents find it most useful to supply information to board members through direct conversations. It does mean, however, that he will not press for commitments or try to persuade individual members to take a position on an issue not yet before the board as a whole. Even when the board has met and is considering an issue, the wise superintendent will supply all the data at his command, make his own recommendation if it is requested, and then wait for a real consensus on the issue. Premature voting may create a split board, which can in turn affect the board's ability to reach a decision on other issues.

A special task of the superintendent is the orientation of board members to the school program and to the duties of board membership. New members especially will need such help. Older members of the board may be helpful in this orientation process.

In acquainting the board with the various aspects of the school program the superintendent may often invite principals, supervisors, and teachers to attend board meetings and make informal reports. Such staff participation in board meetings should be on invitation of the superintendent, who is responsible to the whole community through the board of education.

SHARING RESPONSIBILITY

The superintendent is not responsible to the teachers but, through their elected board, to the people who own the schools. This responsibility is not diminished or relocated when it is shared with others. Many superintendents believe that their responsibility to the board cannot be shared at all, but only delegated to selected subordinates. They argue that a bad decision by a group penalizes the responsible administrator, not the group. They would prefer to keep to themselves, or to delegate, under carefully controlled conditions, the responsibility for making decisions. Since authority and responsibility cannot be efficiently separated, these advocates of line-and-staff administration withhold all authority from the teaching staff. Certain legal principles have fortified this point of view and helped it to remain the dominant philosophy of school administration. The trouble with this concept is that it reduces the effective base of administration to a few persons—in fact, to one man if it is followed logically. It is unsound and wishful to expect teachers to make suggestions or to devote any effort to problems for which they can have no responsibility. The result of failure to share responsibility is the lodging of faith in the ability of the superintendent as one who knows all that is necessary for anyone to know. He must plan directions and goals; he must have ready answers to all questions, he must supply all the ideas that are supplied for the improvement of the schools.

Of course, few superintendents are as authoritarian as the above paragraph describes. Yet the logic of the line of authority that pervades many school systems leads inevitably in the direction of one-man control. The superintendent may ask advice of many persons. He may be a friendly, communicative individual whom teachers like and respect. But the whole situation will push him gradually toward an autocratic regime unless he develops the courage to share his authority and responsibility with others who are concerned. It is perfectly true that the superintendent cannot rid himself of his responsibility by sharing it. It is still his responsibility legally, but it can be functionally shared with other members of the team. He is likely to obtain better decisions by such a sharing process. He will also find in it a tremendous stimulation and challenge that are never found in an authoritarian regime. The sharing process is based on faith in people and respect for their contributions. This faith and respect will eventually pay off in better policies, which are the product of better human relationships. Many superintendents have discovered that their responsibilities and powers can be fully shared with the staff without violating any laws or losing any face with the board of education.

THE PRINCIPAL

DUTIES

This process of sharing administrative responsibility places the building principal in an entirely different role from that which he plays in a conventional line-and-staff system. In his traditional role, the principal is responsible to the superintendent, or to an assistant superintendent in large school systems. He is informed of policies by memos from the central office. As a member of a hierarchy, he administers "his" school in accordance with the policies laid down by someone else. He may wish he could share his leadership role, but he is unlikely to have the courage to do so in school systems where the emphasis is on responsibility to someone higher up the ladder. The watchword in such schools is likely to be loyalty, which is interpreted to mean unquestioning acquiescence. Of course, there are many areas in which the principal has considerable scope. Not all the policies needed have been thought of as yet. It would require unusual courage to share these broad areas of undeveloped policy with the staff, if such sharing appears to be a violation of the superintendent's philosophy. There is always a possibility that the staff may develop through such experiences to the point where it may ask embarrassing questions about school policies already in force.

The philosophy of delegated powers will not always lead to such a dark picture of autocratic administration. People who like each other and who get really well acquainted are unlikely to precipitate an issue which could reveal how authoritarian the system may really be. Teachers are apt to accept such a regime as natural and even welcome. It leaves them to the job of teaching and it furnishes a convenient scapegoat on whom to blame whatever is wrong. Schools may go along pretty well without shared administration—that is, if no one catches a glimpse of the far greater potential that lies in group planning. Finally, there are usually some areas in which shared planning is possible, even in those school systems where official powers are carefully designated for most situations. It is not usually a case of no shared planning, but rather one of extending the areas in which sharing is successfully attempted.

RESPONSIBILITY AND AUTHORITY REQUIRED

The principal plays a most important role in the effort to extend the sharing process. If he is regarded by the superintendent as a competent, responsible, professional administrator, he will be granted rather full authority and responsibility for the educational program of the school which he heads. Without that degree of responsibility for the program within the building, the principal cannot very well develop a sharing process with the staff. If he is in an insecure position, uncertain of the extent of his own powers, he will be unlikely to invite teachers to participate in the planning of the program.

Many superintendents have been secondary school principals before assuming their present positions. Some of them have rather definite ideas about how to run a good high school. In fact, if not in title, a few superintendents continue to be secondary school principals as well as superintendents.

In the numerous small high schools it may be more efficient for the superintendent to serve also as high school principal. If this plan is used, the title of principal should not be bestowed on some other person who has no real authority. If the superintendent is also principal of a building, that fact should be openly acknowledged. If a teaching principal is also needed because of frequent absence of the superintendent on other business, his title should be assistant principal. Under no circumstances should a principal be appointed without any power or responsibility. There should never be a pretense that a principal has such power when he really has not.

Even in much larger schools there have been instances when a principal has been given the title without the authority or responsibility which must accompany it. This error may be due to any of a number of factors or to a combination of them. The superintendent of schools may wish to retain control of the secondary school because of his own enjoyment of that role, or because he wishes to try out the new principal for a while before giving him any real responsibility. There may be some areas of the secondary school that local tradition has assigned to others. For example, the athletic director or the music director may have enjoyed a direct control of their respective activities, with authority assigned by the board of education. The improvement of instruction may have been under the control of a separate supervisory staff. Public relations, budget development, or financial accounting may have been the prerogatives of special school officials directly responsible to the board or to the superintendent. The activities program may have been assigned to a separate activities director.

RESPONSIBILITY MUST BE REAL

All these partitions of responsibility are administrative errors, for they operate to separate the responsible head of a school from the real authority to plan, to improve, or to seek ideas from others on how the school program can become a better one. Even if the motive is to try out a new appointee temporarily, such failure to assign any real responsibility to the principal makes for bad administration. The way to learn how to administer a school is to have the power and duty to try things, to make some mistakes, and to learn from them. Teamwork in a school staff depends on sharing real responsibilities. Even if such sharing is not contemplated, a new principal will have little or no chance to grow in service or to prove his worth if he enters upon the position without any genuine authority.

A previous chapter has included some discussion of the division of responsibilities, sometimes seen in urban school systems, between a principal and a central supervisory staff.[4] No real progress

4 See Chapter 5.

toward improving instruction can be made under a system of dual responsibility. The supervisors must be responsible to the principal (and through him to the staff) in their efforts to upgrade the program in a secondary school. This is entirely possible to achieve if these officials are not on the line of authority stemming from the superintendent of schools. Neither the supervisors nor the director of curriculum or instruction should be "line officials," but rather staff members without authority over teachers. In short, they must earn their way in order to be effective.

The status of secondary school principals has improved significantly since the early period when they were known as the "principal teachers" and had a full teaching load. In medium and larger schools, at least, the principal has tended to become a professional administrator who has powers commensurate with his responsibilities. There are still areas that need attention, however, even in large high schools. French, Hull, and Dodds quote the Reavis survey of 1937 in this connection:

In his investigation of the principalship in large cities Reavis found many evidences of strength in the professional status of the position, but in at least three areas there were weaknesses as well. "Generally, the principal was held responsible for his building and its condition, but he was given no authority over the custodial service. The principal was held responsible for the quality of instruction in his school but often he had to accept any teacher sent him by the central office. The principal was expected to interpret the educational program to the teachers in the school, but his influence at the time it was drawn up was insignificant in most of the cities studied. Evidently there are large schools as well as small ones in which a redefining of the authority and responsibility of the high school principal is needed." [5]

There is some evidence that the junior high school principal enjoys a somewhat lower status in most school systems than does

[5] Will French, J. Dan Hull, and B. L. Dodds, *American High School Administration,* New York, Rinehart & Company, 1951, pp. 129–130.

the senior high school principal. If the latter position needs some redefinition of authority, it is likely that the junior high school position also would benefit by such analysis.

OFFICIAL STATEMENT OF DUTIES OF PRINCIPALS

Many school systems have an official statement of the duties of principals and of their relationship to the superintendent of schools. Such a statement can help to improve school administration if it is sufficiently broad to permit new relationships and new assignments to evolve. On the other hand, a hard-and-fast list of duties of principals can operate to discourage creative administration. The relationships that develop between a superintendent and a secondary school principal will condition the assignment of specific duties in many significant ways. Such a relationship should have room to grow and a permissive base from which to start. It can be stultified by arbitrary board regulations about who does what.

RELATIONSHIP WITH SUPERINTENDENT

The relationship of the superintendent and the secondary school principal can be the key factor in all efforts to improve the school. It is likely to have a chain effect on all relationships in the school, which in turn can significantly influence the quality of living there. These two officials are likely to have much in common—both in their backgrounds and in their current interests and problems. If each feels a sincere respect for the other, they can develop a fine fraternal relationship that can enrich their work in the schools and community. The superintendent has perhaps a little greater responsibility for setting the tone of this relationship. He is usually older and more experienced. French, Hull, and Dodds have pointed out the importance of his guidance of the building principal:

The superintendent is a busy man, but if he is interested in the execution of his policies he has no more important work than that of providing the motivating force for the professional development of the principal. Fortunate is the beginning principal whose superintendent is available for professional guidance but at the same time careful never to make himself indispensable. There is no fairer way of estimating the effectiveness of a superintendent than by the success of the principals and teachers whom he has appointed and to whom he has given in-service training.[6]

It might be added that the building up of the secondary school principal by the superintendent is a fair test of the latter's security feelings. In many communities the tradition has become confirmed for the high school principal to succeed the superintendent. For various reasons this tradition often produces pressures that interfere with good school administration. Mature persons can, however, overcome this handicap and achieve a warm personal and professional relationship. There is so much to be gained on both sides by good teamwork and mutual respect that no administrator can afford to permit the relationship to deteriorate. The secondary school principal should be the major adviser to the superintendent in all matters affecting secondary education. His advice should be sought and welcomed. He should feel that he can disagree completely with the superintendent's proposal without disturbing the warmth of their relationship. If steps are finally taken with which he cannot agree, he should support the superintendent publicly in the interest of teamwork. Of course, if he cannot conscientiously support decisions, he should resign and seek another position in a more congenial situation. In most cases this outcome can be avoided if sincere efforts are made to exchange and clarify views and to find a basis for consensus.

ADMINISTRATIVE COUNCILS

In many larger school systems the principals, as a group, comprise the major professional advisory body to the superintendent. Such a council of principals, meeting regularly, can become an

[6] *Ibid.*, p. 132.

invaluable sounding board for evaluating ideas before they have become crystallized as board policies. A superintendent of schools may find such an administrative council his greatest professional asset.

In summary of this discussion regarding the relationship between the superintendent and the secondary school principal, the following lists of cautions may be helpful:

The Superintendent Should:

1. Consult principals on all issues affecting their schools.
2. Treat their suggestions with respect.
3. Deal openly and honestly with the principal.
4. Give the principals public credit when due.
5. Communicate with teachers of a school through the principal.
6. Invite principals to school board meetings periodically to present reports and advice.
7. Refer to the principal all requests and complaints from patrons.
8. Have the principal present when an issue is to be settled.
9. Be always available for counsel.
10. Encourage the principal to have confidence in his own ability to form good opinions.
11. Maintain warm personal friendships with principals.
12. Encourage principals to express disagreement with the superintendent when they do not agree.
13. Build up the principals as important professional leaders by any legitimate means.
14. Seek professional advancement and success for the principals by being warmly interested in their welfare.
15. Insist that principals have both authority and responsibility for the educational programs of their schools.

The Principal Should

1. Deal honestly and directly with the superintendent.
2. Contact the board of education through the superintendent.
3. Keep the superintendent advised of developments in the school.
4. Maintain warm personal friendship with the superintendent.

5. Give him credit when credit is due.
6. Offer advice when it is requested or appropriate.
7. Disagree when necessary, without loss of temper.
8. Support the superintendent publicly.
9. Resign when such support cannot be continued.
10. Administer the school within limits of present board policies until such policies are changed.
11. Accept the fact that an appeal (from the principal's decision) to the superintendent is always in order.
12. Help keep the superintendent informed of trends and developments in secondary education.
13. Seek to clarify confusion regarding overlapping of functions of various administrators.
14. Assume responsibility commensurate with the authority the principal should have for the educational program of a school.
15. Seek constantly to share this responsibility with the professional staff, the students, and the patrons of the school.

IS PRINCIPALSHIP NEEDED?

It has been noted earlier in this chapter that responsibility can be shared without its being dislocated or dissolved. There are those who argue that the position of principal is not needed in a modern school—that the staff can run the school through elected chairmen. This plan has worked successfully in small schools. It should be noted, however, that the authority thus assumed by the staff must come from somewhere—in this case from the superintendent of schools, who is thus the real titular head of the school. As schools grow larger and more numerous in a community, it becomes increasingly difficult for a superintendent to serve this dual role. The position of the principal is both legally and logically a sound solution. Before power and responsibility can be shared they must be present. The building principal is the leader who accepts this authority and responsibility on behalf of the persons who will help to exercise it. He is still responsible, but this need not prevent his sharing that responsibility with the staff. On other levels, and for some purposes, he will share it also with the student body and with the parent group that the school serves.

Thus the status role of the secondary school principal is highly important in a democratic school, for it forms a crucial link between the authority legally derived from the board of education and the people who need that authority in order to improve a school. As has been pointed out in previous chapters, the principal's authority role is not an unmixed blessing. It frequently gets in the way of his efforts to work with his colleagues, with students, and with lay citizens. Sometimes it appears to principals that their greatest need is to escape from their own status for a while—and many administrators are learning how to achieve this difficult feat. Yet it must be recognized that the status leader is an essential part of the modern secondary school, through whom are funneled the authority and responsibility needed for operating and improving the school.

IMPROVING THE PRINCIPAL'S ROLE

This conception of the function of the principal has not yet been generally realized. Spears points out that the position of the principalship was originally "conceived and developed as a position to assure the operation of a fixed curriculum [and] has had little occasion to date to shift this emphasis." [7]

It is certainly true that the authoritarian role of the principal was stressed in earlier school practice, as revealed in board of education regulations in communities across the country. The principalship was considered a means of delegating authority for the enforcement of standardization and rigidity within a school system. This is indeed a far cry from the function of leadership for adaptation, change, and improvement.

Even today, the concept of the principal as leader in curriculum reorganization has not been universally accepted. Many obstacles remain to block the principal from assuming the role he must play

[7] Spears, *op. cit.*, p. 340.

if secondary schools are to be improved. These obstacles have been discussed at various points in this volume. One of the most important is the principal's own image of himself, together with his own dreams of what he may become. The final chapter will include some analysis of ways in which a secondary school principal can evaluate his own effectiveness.

For Further Reading

American Association of School Administrators, *School Boards in Action,* Twenty-fourth Yearbook, Washington, The National Education Association, 1946.

Douglass, Harl R., *Modern Administration of Secondary Schools,* Boston, Ginn & Company, 1954, chap. 2.

French, Will, Hull, J. Dan, and Dodds, B. L., *American High School Administration,* New York, Rinehart & Company, 1951, chap. 7.

Jacobson, Paul B., Reavis, W. C., and Logsdon, J. D., *Duties of School Principals,* New York, Prentice-Hall, 1950.

Menge, J. W., and Faunce, Roland C., *Working Together for Better Schools,* New York, American Book Company, 1953, chap. 8.

National Society for the Study of Education, *Changing Conceptions in Educational Administration,* Forty-fifth Yearbook, Chicago, University of Chicago Press, 1946, Part II, chap. 4.

Reavis, W. C., "Relations of School Principals to the Central Administrative Office in Large Cities," *Bulletin of the National Association of Secondary School Principals,* No. 66, April, 1937.

Spears, Harold, *The High School for Today,* New York, American Book Company, 1950, chap. 20.

Thomas, Maurice J., *et al., The School Board and Public Education,* Pittsburgh, University of Pittsburgh Press, 1951, pp. 1–41.

Washburne, Carlton, *A Living Philosophy of Education,* New York, John Day Company, 1940, Part 5.

"Ways to Better High Schools in Illinois," *University of Illinois Bulletin, XXXVIII,* April, 1941.

Yauch, Wilbur A., *Improving Human Relations in School Administration,* New York, Harper & Brothers, 1949.

CHAPTER 16

Appraising the Principal's Growth

WHY EVALUATE?

The first chapter of this volume began with a description of the
secondary school principal, attacking his problems in a state of
loneliness created by his own inability to bridge the gap between
himself and his colleagues. In no other area is that gap as apparent
as in the area of evaluation. It is human for people to wonder how
they are doing. Most principals are handicapped in finding a de-
pendable answer to this vital question. They know, of course,
that they are being evaluated. Every day, in countless relationships,
they are being assessed by teachers, pupils, parents, and other
citizens. Other administrators and members of the board of education are forming or confirming opinions about the secondary
school principal. In many, perhaps most, communities, he is one
of the few public personages who is most widely discussed.

No other single person is as influential in determining the
quality of living for our youth as the secondary school principal.
More than any other individual, he sets the tone and establishes
the kind of education that will go on in our junior and senior high
schools. The principal symbolizes the school in the eyes of many
people. In our culture, the secondary school is an institution that
is held in high esteem. In a sense, the administrator of this important basic institution is the most influential person in our

society. It is small wonder that he and his work are a matter of such general interest in the community.

The principal who wishes to fulfill his role successfully must be concerned with ways to evaluate his own work. The whole direction of his future growth is affected by such appraisal. In a dynamic, ever-changing institution a leader who fails to grow will not merely stand still but actually retrogress in reference to his environment. Administrators need to know their areas of greatest weakness in order to correct them. They should also learn their strengths in order to capitalize them.

EVALUATION RELATED TO PURPOSES

Any evaluation is made within a frame of reference. That frame consists of the goals or purposes that people accept as sound. We appraise the effectiveness of an administrator in terms of what we conceive to be the function or purpose served by administrators. This, in turn, is affected by our whole philosophy about schools. We tend to accept one criterion or another that defines a good school and go on from that point to measure its leader.

For example, there are those whose major criterion of a school is its cleanliness or good order. If we are measuring a school in terms of any of the following questions, we shall praise or indict the principal by applying these simple criteria: Is the school clean? Is the school orderly? Is the school quiet? Is the school systematic?

Or perhaps we are not content with such superficial criteria. Perhaps it has dawned on us that the cleanest, quietest, and most orderly place in most communities is the cemetery rather than the school. In that case we may seek the answer to other kinds of questions: Is the school lifelike? Is the school dynamic? Does the school provide satisfying experiences? Is the school social, communicative? Is the school lively?

As answers are sought to such questions as these, an entirely different set of criteria emerges for appraising the principal's effectiveness. Thus purposes—both of administration and of schools in general—will affect the approach to evaluation. Since the principal tends to symbolize the school in the minds of citizens of the community, their appraisal of his work will be influenced by their appraisal of the school's effectiveness.

This kind of appraisal goes on every day, with or without any effort on the part of the principal. It is a basic phase of the public relations program to help people develop values by which the school can be judged, and techniques for intelligent evaluation. This evaluative process ought to be systematic and continuous, not sporadic. It should be based on sound purposes that are accepted as desirable by both lay citizens and staff of the school. Teachers and other citizens can be helped to distinguish between immediate goals which can be realized in a short period by intelligent effort and long-range goals which will never be completely achieved but which constantly beckon people toward the better life for boys and girls.

In all these efforts to appraise the school's effectiveness, the role of leadership must be singled out for special analysis. Teachers and community groups should study the nature of leadership and its contribution to group planning. They can engage in the evaluation of leadership as a part of their own coöperative efforts to improve the school. It should become possible for persons and groups experienced in the planning process to identify the strengths and weaknesses of leadership without causing embarrassment or trauma to anyone. This will be most likely to take place in groups in which leadership emerges from the staff or community group itself, and changes as various needs appear. It will be possible in such groups to analyze the goals and techniques of leadership without casting reflections on any particular person.

This developing of the habit of evaluating leadership, and of the techniques involved, is of great significance to the secondary school principal. His need for appraisal of his own effectiveness can only partially be met by self-appraisal. He needs help also from the people with whom he works. But they will usually be reluctant to evaluate his work in a personal, direct way. Particularly in schools where the status of the administrator has been built up as a value in itself, it is usually impossible to get any appraisal of the principal's work while he is present. He can get invaluable clues about his own work from the group's analysis of the leadership role in general.

People generally set high standards for the personal and professional qualities of the secondary school principal. This is perhaps a tribute to the importance of the job in the eyes of most observers. The principal is expected to have all the qualities of any good teacher, plus some other assets. He is expected to be intelligent and literate, to have reasonably sound scholarship and a special command of at least one subject area. He should be a good speaker and chairman; should be pleasant, personable, neat, honest, and conscientious. He should furnish a good example to youth and adults in his personal life. In dealing with others we expect him to be patient, fair, and sympathetic. We look for a special kind of energy or drive in him, a set of ideals that leads him to look for the best in other people.

All these qualities and others that have been mentioned elsewhere seem to add up to a kind of superman whom no one alive could hope to emulate. One might well despair of attaining such perfection and cast about for a few minimum standards on which to settle as personal goals. Perhaps analysis of some studies that have been made of the effective administrator and his traits will help us to arrive at certain common elements sought in good administrators.

THE CRITICAL-INCIDENT TECHNIQUE

One such approach was made by Sternloff through use of the "critical-incident" technique. A critical incident was defined as a "situation involving behavior of the school administrator which was crucial enough to result in marked success or failure in a given situation." One hundred and seventy-nine administrators reported a total of 184 "effective incidents" and 164 ineffective incidents. Two hundred and sixty school board members described a total of 314 effective and 149 ineffective incidents. A total of 1076 behaviors were identified from the 811 incidents reported, from which the following list of 27 "basic general behaviors of the effective administrator" was compiled. These are arranged in rank order with the behavior reported most frequently heading the list:

An Effective Administrator

1. Interprets adequately the status, needs, problems, policies, and plans of the school.
2. Provides pertinent information concerning school problems, and suspends judgment until the pertinent facts have been examined.
3. Conducts all school affairs in an honest, ethical, and tactful manner.
4. Utilizes consultants and specialists outside the school and cooperates with them in solving educational problems.
5. Encourages all persons who will be affected to participate in policy development, and stimulates cooperative planning.
6. Administers discipline effectively.
7. Deals impartially and equitably with all individuals and groups.
8. Shows a sincere interest in the welfare of school personnel.
9. Organizes citizen or parent advisory groups, and cooperates with them in study and solution of school problems.
10. Willingly devotes extra time to important school affairs.
11. Thoroughly understands the important requirements of jobs under his supervision, selects and assigns persons according to the requirements, and promotes growth of personnel.
12. Courageously demands that recommendations he considers necessary for the welfare of the school be accepted and holds to these recommendations in the face of unjust pressures and influences, in spite of jeopardy to his personal position.
13. Accepts criticism gracefully.
14. Conducts meetings and conferences effectively.
15. Organizes the schools to offer community services and provides for community use of school facilities.

16. Accepts full responsibility for achieving the educational objectives of the school system.
17. Ably defends the school, school personnel, and himself from unwarranted criticism and unjust action.
18. Safeguards the health of school personnel and provides for their personal safety.
19. Sets a good example by his own personal behavior.
20. Encourages interested persons to visit the schools and board meetings.
21. Provides counseling and other guidance services for school personnel.
22. Administers the budget prudently and keeps accurate financial records.
23. Speaks effectively.
24. Initiates action promptly in cases of emergency.
25. Familiarizes himself with school board policy before making public statements or taking action.
26. Identifies himself with the policies of the school system, and supports those policies.
27. Utilizes parents, and cooperates with them, to solve pupil problems satisfactorily.[1]

This list furnishes some interesting clues to the judgments of administrators and school board members about the qualities desired in school administrators. Examination of the longer list of specific behaviors, from which Sternloff compiled the 27 categories of behavior, reveals the following traits of the successful administrator: exercise of good judgment, knowledge of human behavior, skill in interpersonal relationships, ethical standards, emotional stability, and courage.

TEACHER JUDGMENTS

Another approach to the listing of behavior traits is exemplified by an article by Mack Horsman, a teacher in the Battle Creek,

[1] Robert Elmer Sternloff, "The Critical Requirements for School Administrators Based Upon an Analysis of Critical Incidents," unpublished doctoral dissertation, School of Education, University of Wisconsin, Madison, Wis., 1953.

Michigan, schools. Mr. Horsman directs the following alternative questions to the school administrator:

1. Do you create or perpetuate a barrier of any kind between yourself and your faculty?

   or

   Do you strive for an atmosphere that encourages free, frank, and respectful communication among all personnel?

2. Do you encourage artificial, stultifying formality?

   or

   Do you encourage that informality which is the germ of meaningful communication?

3. Do you, as an administrator, display an attitude of superiority?

   or

   Are you humble in your position and in what you know, realizing that you, too, may still learn?

4. Do you, when supervising, give the impression that you are "checking up"?

   or

   Do you supervise in such a way that it is recognized as sincere and interested help, not spying?

5. Do you pose as the overburdened and harassed administrator, thus warding off possible communication with your staff?

   or

   Do you present an appearance of efficiency, competence, and satisfaction in your job, open at all times for consideration of new problems?

6. Do you put on a "show" for visitors or superiors, just for the sake of impression?

   or

   Do you and your school proceed in its natural way, thus displaying its everyday appearance?

7. Do you fail to back up your teachers in any matter?

   or

   Do you show your confidence in them by standing behind them at all times?

8. Are you the secret or evasive type, dwelling in ambiguities and subtleties?

   or

   Are you frank, giving honest and direct answers when they are sought?

9. Do you dictate policy, values, or anything?

   or

   Do you create an atmosphere of sharing, out of which common decisions will be accepted and growth for all may take place?

10. Do you make a faculty member's decisions for him, trying to keep him from making mistakes?

    or

    Do you encourage him to formulate his own plan of action, to test it, and thereby grow through experimentation and possible error?

11. Do you burden your faculty with useless meetings, and then dominate these meetings?

    or

    Do you call meetings only when there is a clear need; and then do you allow the meetings to center around problems common to all, not just your own?

12. Do you veto group decisions when they are contrary to your own thinking?

    or

    Do you regard yourself as one of the group and abide by its findings?

13. Do you treat a faculty member's problems, comments, or questions as trivialities?

    or

    Do you share a concern for the personal welfare of your entire faculty?

14. Do you neglect your responsibility for personal and professional growth of your staff?

    or

    Are you constantly utilizing opportunities to help your staff in these matters?

15. Do you expect your teachers to be "red-hot" zealots every day they're in school?

or

Do you realize that they are human beings, subject to the same ups and downs as other people? [2]

Many aspects of administrative "behaviors" appear in this teacher's list of searching questions. The first four questions are directed at the deliberate attempts of some principals to create a special kind of status for themselves, as opposed to the ability of other principals to derive satisfaction from being a real member of a team. Questions 5, 6, and 8 deal with sincerity, question 7 with loyalty. Questions 9, 10, 11, and 12 relate to democratic practices in staff planning. The remaining three questions seem to bear on the quality of human relationships that prevail between the principal and teachers. Thus this teacher's basis for evaluating the principal seems to consist of the following areas of behavior:

1. The "we" feeling or unity in the staff
2. The integrity or sincerity of the administrator
3. His loyalty to his colleagues
4. Respect for personality
5. Skill in democratic planning
6. Acceptance of teachers as persons

SELF-ANALYSIS

Perhaps the crucial test of the principal is that of his ability to spearhead democratic planning. If the administrator has one indispensable role in our culture, it appears to be that of providing leadership in coöperative planning activities. Through no other means will secondary schools be improved. The principal who wishes to test the quality of his own leadership in this area of shared planning might well ask himself certain questions.

These questions acquire increased significance when the major

[2] Mack Horsman, "A Teacher Looks at Administrative Techniques," *Michigan Educational Journal*, XXXI:13, March, 1954, p. 327.

function of school administration is realized. That function is the strengthening and confirming of the democratic way of life. The principal is uniquely challenged to this task by his position as titular head of the major social institution responsible for the future of American democracy. Evaluation of the principal's effectiveness should adhere closely to this basic administrative task.

A specific series of questions about democratic administration may be found in the volume *Learning the Ways of Democracy,* by the Educational Policies Commission. A section of this helpful book divides school administration into three levels: the routine, the imitative, and the constructive. The following questions for self-appraisal are suggested for each of these three levels:

Routine level: Do teachers in your school always wait for instructions before varying one iota from the standard procedure? Do they feel that the making of educational policy is a job for someone else— anybody else except themselves? Do the administrative officers doubt the good judgment of their own staffs? Do they take the public into account but never into confidence? Would they be shocked at the idea of consulting the students themselves on any important question relating to student life? Is the program of professional study and growth legislated in the superintendent's or principal's office? Are teacher's organizations discouraged and their activities limited? . . .

Imitative level: Has your school built elaborate machinery for democratic policy-making, but little enthusiasm for making that machinery work? Is there confusion and wasted effort because of failure to distinguish between policy-making and executive functions? Do you have endless and innumerable committee meetings on unimportant details while really important matters are settled by small groups meeting behind closed doors? Are the teachers organized in so many different groups that effective and united action is difficult? Have your attempts to achieve democracy resulted in uncertain responsibilities, bungling administration, or other symptoms of inefficiency? . . .

Constructive level: Does your school morale improve with every expansion of the base of participation in policy-making? Do teachers feel that their opinions really count on important questions? Do the teaching and administrative staffs work in harmony because they have a common vision of the job to be done, a generous sharing in deciding the best way to do it, and mutual respect for each person's contributions? Does the lay public participate in the discussion of citizenship education and cooperate in carrying it forward? Is there a two-way street for the flow of ideas between the public and the teaching profession? Are teacher organizations themselves examples of efficient democracy? Do students also share generously in the processes of discussing and deciding educational policy? [3]

PERSONAL TRAITS

These questions under the third heading, "constructive level," provide a fair summary of the administrative provisions for democratic planning. As they are seriously applied to a given school, they should be helpful in discovering *the extent and nature of machinery* for coöperative policy making. In the last analysis, however, it is not the machinery but the quality of the person in the leadership position that will determine the extent of true democracy. As a principal evaluates his own personality and measures it in terms of his impact on teachers, pupils, and parents, he may find it helpful to ask himself some rather personal questions. Kelley has suggested some such questions as a beginning:

Do I consider my own self-preservation on the job as the most important objective, or do I feel that there are more important considerations than my own tenure of office? Am I so bent on my own tenure that I cannot take my counsel from courage, but always have to act from fear, and play it safe? Do I operate a safe little schedule which will never do much for the children, but with which no one will be able to find much fault? Do I have faith in the general rightness of others, or do I feel that I have to see to it that everyone does what I think is right? Do I have enough faith in teachers so that I can take them into my confidence, and encourage them to do some of

[3] Educational Policies Commission, *Learning the Ways of Democracy*, Washington, The National Education Association, 1940, pp. 474–475.

the planning? Do I have faith enough in children so that I can abandon fear, coercion, and repression as a way of life, and encourage them to assume responsibility? Do I have faith enough in parents and citizens so that I can involve them in the mutual task of the education of the young? Can I keep in mind that everything going on in the school is supposed to contribute to the good life of children, that they are the object of the game? Do I realize that even my own success and well-being, in the long run, depend on the success and well-being of students and teachers?

Do I feel the unique worth and dignity of even the most unpromising student in the school? Do I seek ways of making him feel that he can share in the project? Do I look for and encourage teachers to assume a share in leadership?

Am I vigilant that I do not value routine for itself, because it appears to make life easier? Am I wary of the machine that runs too smoothly? Can I remember that providing the life fit to be lived for children and teachers cannot be routinized and set up for all time? Can I remember that noise may be the product of happy people living fruitfully together? Can I continuously realize that what people learn is probably less important than how and why it is learned? Am I faithful to the ideals of democracy in that I always put human values above institutional custom and routine? [4]

TARGETS FOR GROWTH

These are hard, penetrating questions. Only a mature, courageous person would feel comfortable applying them to himself. The reader may conclude at this point that being a good principal is the task of a superman. Of course, no one fully exemplifies all the traits desired in a good administrator. If one is to grow, however, he will need a target toward which to grow. Without some ideals established as to what traits, what behaviors, characterize a really effective principal, no growth toward the ideals is likely to occur. No matter how uncomfortable it is to evaluate one's own capacities and achievements, we all need to set some directions for

[4] Earl C. Kelley, "The Function of the Principal in a Modern School," *American School Board Journal*, June, 1947.

our efforts at self-improvement. The alert administrator is always concerned about this matter of self-improvement. He does not worry about it constantly, for he knows that his own mental health demands that he think well of himself; but he reflects upon the various roles he plays in the school and community, and tries to analyze ways in which he might do better. For this business of growing in service, ideals are all-important.

Thus it is unrealistic for us to ask ourselves whether we have already achieved all the ideal traits set forth in the various lists of questions posed in the preceding section. The useful question is, How much have I grown, and in what directions? Is my way of working with people a bit more effective than it was last month, last year? What does "more effective" mean in this case? Just what ideals do I accept as my targets for growth?

Everyone can grow in service. Some people assume that this is only possible for young or inexperienced administrators, and support the assumption by a variation of the bromide about not being able to teach an old dog new tricks. Yet all of us have known men and women, grown gray in service and approaching retirement age, who are still eagerly searching for ways to improve, for new ideas and new techniques. Some of our "youngest" administrators are old in years. This is not universally the case, because we are built into whatever we are by our past experiences. If those experiences have been in stultifying, routinized regimes, we tend to become creatures of routine. If our experiences have produced in us the habits of fear, deference, or obsequiousness in our dealings with our superiors, it may have become increasingly hard for us to display courage. Even these dubious habits and attitudes have been shaken off, however, by principals who have acquired a new superintendent with insight and wisdom. Other kinds of experience, too, can occur "on the road to Damascus." It may have been a summer workshop experience or a period in a camp situation with a staff group or a graduate seminar in administration. It could have been the involvement of the school in an intensive study program of some kind, and the invasion of its doors by visitors with larger vistas of education. It is often the inspiration or the pressure of a group of citizens in the community who are interested in studying some phase of the school program.

Whatever the stimulus, administrators do change their values and their resulting behavior, as many examples can attest. It is a matter of great significance to examine what factors may operate to prevent or block changes in administrative behavior, and what factors, on the other hand, operate to stimulate such change. Since the school cannot change very much without changed behavior on the part of the principal, this phenomenon of change in administrative behavior is basic.

FACTORS THAT BLOCK GROWTH

Perhaps the greatest single barrier to change is the authoritarian tradition. The autocratic school administrator has eliminated all ideas and suggestions except his own. Thus the field of ideas for constructive change has been significantly narrowed. Since the existing program is regarded as the property of the leader, any real evaluation of it becomes impossible. Any suggestion for change is interpreted as an attack on the status leader, and thus it cannot be tolerated. By one means or another the autocratic administrator manages to throttle all critical thinking, to surround himself with yes men, and to label all criticism as an unwarranted or irrational attack on the administration.

The secondary school principal who has worked with a superintendent of this type has become progressively disabled from creative evaluation of the school program, or of his own work. He has played the yes-man role so long that he has lost most of his original capacity and courage. He may rationalize his acceptance of the situation as an evidence of loyalty to his superior. This is particularly easy to accomplish if the superintendent is personally likable, one who looks after "his" subordinates and has a fatherly interest in their personal welfare. Perhaps the most difficult autocrat to escape or dislodge is the benevolent despot whom most people like and accept. The halo image which comes to surround such a person over the years makes it difficult to evaluate his program (for it is really his), or to offer any suggestions for change.

If the principal has himself acquired some of these same autocratic traits, he will have cut himself off from his only source of real help. It is difficult indeed to develop ideals of democratic leadership when one is convinced that he has already arrived at them. Any genuine evaluation becomes impossible without personal attack on the leader.

Such an administrator has no base for communicating with his colleagues. His efforts to maintain his hold on the entire situation make it imperative that he avoid discussion of certain matters with the staff, with parents, or with students. The issues that cannot be freely discussed somehow keep growing until they eventually include everything that really matters. The principal may, as chairman of a meeting, simply rule certain discussions out of order. He is more likely, however, to plan meetings in such a way as to avoid opportunities for any discussion. If this device fails, he may discontinue faculty meetings entirely on the ground that they are a waste of time. He is likely to pursue the same plan with parents and other citizens. He can, over a period of years, build up certain traditions that become so strong that it will not even occur to anyone to challenge them. Not all autocratic leaders are as successful as this in stifling communication and discussion. Still, the natural result of autocratic leadership is reduction of communication, which in turn makes any change less probable.

Thus the autocratic tradition, which translates all criticism into personal attack and reduces communication to a minimum, is the major barrier to growth of the principal in service. There are other barriers also. The common dependence on routines for their own sake, or for the comfort they furnish, prevents growth. The suspicion that other persons on the staff are "after" his job may prevent a principal from growing into a more competent leader. The assumption that no one else in the school can be trusted to do certain jobs will result in the principal's wasting his time doing clerical work or issuing supplies in person. His own shyness or fear of new contacts may discourage him from establishing a friendly interchange of ideas that could help him. His fear of the unknown may prevent his exploration of what local citizens think of their schools. His yearning for security may cause him to get in a rut. Ruts sometimes get so deep that one cannot even see the promising vistas that lie outside them.

FACTORS THAT AID GROWTH

It is fortunate that there are factors that can aid a principal to escape the handicaps that have been mentioned above and to grow into a more effective leader. Perhaps the most potent of these constructive factors is the free interchange of ideas with others. Since growth depends significantly on ideas for improvement, no barrier to the free presentation of ideas should be tolerated. Every possible channel should be provided for the expression of criticism and suggestions by teachers, by parents and other citizens, and by students. Many of these media of evaluation have been discussed in earlier chapters. They include advisory councils of teachers and parents; school councils that are broadly representative of all persons concerned; informal staff meetings, department meetings, and grade-level planning groups; parent-teacher organizations and room-parent clubs. They include also the innumerable individual conversations that a principal will have as he moves freely about the school or maintains an open office door.

Not only will the alert principal permit and encourage free discussion of any aspect of the program; he will actively seek evaluation of the school program and of its leadership by all legitimate means. These may include opinionaires or questionnaires, rating scales, a suggestion box, surveys of public opinion, written suggestions by students, and recorded panels or interviews that are evaluative in nature. In short, a basic factor in growth toward better administrative leadership is the free flow of ideas for improvement. The principal who seeks to do a better job will neglect no opportunity to secure ideas from all persons concerned.

The modern principal has other sources for new ideas besides the local school and community. He is likely to belong to his state association of administrators, and to the National Association of Secondary School Principals. Through the *Bulletin* of the National Association and through state and national conferences of administrators he will be exposed to many ideas of other secondary school administrators. He may also belong to a county or regional group of principals that meets regularly for the exchange of ideas.

In contrast to the high school principal of twenty-five years ago, today's administrator of a secondary school is likely to have at least a year of professional graduate training. Farmer's study in 1947 revealed that the secondary school principal in that year had, on the average, twenty-eight graduate hours of education. About half of the principals included in the study had earned graduate credit in the five years preceding 1947.[5] Thousands of principals have launched programs of doctoral study in the various professional schools. It is becoming increasingly difficult to secure a good position as secondary school principal without having had recent graduate work. In the near future a doctor's degree will become the normal expectation in urban school systems, at least for the senior high school principalship. This increasing trend toward professional study has exposed more and more secondary school principals to new ideas, lifted their horizons, and stimulated them to evaluate their own growth as school leaders.

Other kinds of stimuli to growth have developed. The workshop movement is one of these. Translated into local curriculum-study projects, the workshop has stepped up the evaluation of school and leadership in hundreds of communities. This process has

[5] Floyd M. Farmer, unpublished doctoral dissertation project, New York, Teachers College, Columbia University, 1947.

provided the occasion for bringing visitors into the school to provide consultant help of one kind or another. Professional visitors are a major source of stimulation and new ideas. Accrediting agencies have utilized this tool through formation of visiting teams which have helped local school faculties to evaluate their own program.[6] Aside from the useful materials devised for such evaluations, the visit itself by other school administrators and university professors has paid off in growth for the local principal and staff. The principal may also have an opportunity at some time to join a similar team for an evaluation visit to some other school. This can be a rewarding experience.

Thus the free sharing of problems and ideas in the local community, in conferences and workshops, and in graduate courses is a factor that increasingly encourages the growth of secondary school administrators. In all these situations the influence of the group-dynamics movement is more and more evident. There is a wide and increasing interest in the nature of leadership and the ways in which it can be effective. We not only know much more about leadership than we did a decade ago; we are also much more interested in learning the things we still do not know about it. This emphasis on the role of group leadership has permeated graduate courses and professional conference programs. It has been a recurring theme in professional journals which are read by principals. It appears probable that this kind of concern has already aided the growth of administrators to a significant degree.

A FINAL WORD

There are many ways to improve one's own effectiveness as a secondary school administrator. There is no one too old or too inflexible to change. There is no one so perfect as to need no change. It is not expected that anyone will be able to exemplify all the attributes of a good administrator. Communities do have a

---

[6] Materials used for such appraisals include the *Evaluative Criteria of the* Cooperative Study of Secondary School Standards, Washington, American Council on Education, 1950.

right to expect constant, if gradual, growth toward greater effectiveness. Without such growth the administrator will become a hampering influence on the school, which must be ever changing to meet new challenges and needs.

Changing programs is a matter of changing people and their relationships. The most crucial figure in this process is the secondary school principal. No significant adaptation of the secondary school can take place without his constructive leadership. In a real sense he is the most important person in today's world.

The principal is beginning to realize the significance of the position he occupies. He sees, vaguely or clearly, that he can be a factor either for constructive change or for holding the fort. He is often perplexed by the conflicts of values represented in the school system and in the community. He is aware of some forces that operate to keep him a cog in a machine, without much control of its direction. He may be aware, on the other hand, that he can build an exciting and rewarding career as leader of a coöperative project for improving school programs. Most principals would sincerely like to know how to go ahead with such a project. They would like to play a major role in helping to build a better education and a better life for boys and girls.

There is hope for the future of secondary schools. That hope rests, more than on anything else, on the growth, inspiration, and courage of the principals. It is possible for administrators to help build a better life for all our citizens. The satisfactions that result from such efforts are great indeed. Those who have once felt the thrill that comes to the leader of a successful group enterprise will never again be content to spend their days in office isolation. They will be more self-confident, more self-respecting, and more courageous to tackle the next problem.

And there will be other problems. They will never cease as long as important things are being attempted. Administrators who stoutly face the ever-changing future, reinforced by a steady faith in the people with whom they work and fortified by skill in group planning, are the greatest need of our culture.

For Further Reading

Bossing, Nelson L., "Wanted: A New Leadership for the Secondary Schools," *Bulletin of the National Association of Secondary School Principals,* No. 138, April, 1946.

Cooperative Study of Secondary School Standards, *Evaluative Criteria,* Washington, The American Council on Education, 1950.

"Democratic School Administration," *Progressive Education,* November, 1952 (entire issue).

Educational Policies Commission, *Learning the Ways of Democracy,* Washington, The National Education Association, 1940.

Eikenberry, D. G., "Standards for the Secondary School Principalship," *Bulletin of the National Association of Secondary School Principals,* March, 1948.

Eikenberry, D. G., "Training and Experience Standards For Principals of Secondary Schools." *Bulletin of the National Association of Secondary School Principals,* November, 1951.

Farmer, F. M., "The High School Principalship," *Bulletin of the National Association of Secondary School Principals,* April, 1948.

Gorman, Burton W., "Some Characteristics of a Successful High School Principal," *American School Board Journal,* June, 1949.

Horsman, Mack, "A Teacher Looks at Administrative Techniques," *Michigan Education Journal, XXXI:13,* March, 1954.

Jensen, Lisbeth J., "I Remember Eight Principals," *Clearing House,* September, 1948.

Kelley, Earl C., "The Function of the Principal in a Modern School," *American School Board Journal,* June, 1947.

Roe, William S., "Criteria of a Well Administered High School." *Bulletin of the National Association of Secondary School Principals,* January, 1945.

Sternloff, Robert Elmer, "The Critical Requirements for School Administrators Based on Analysis of Critical Incidents," unpublished doctoral dissertation, Madison, Wis., University of Wisconsin, 1953.

Wiles, Kimball, *Supervision for Better Schools,* New York, Prentice-Hall, 1950, chap. 13.

INDEX OF NAMES

....

Aikin, Wilford M., 32, 38, 199
Alberty, Harold, 40, 60, 137, 145, 147, 159, 341
Alexander, William, 40, 60
American Association of School Administrators, 130, 274, 345, 360
American Council on Education, 159, 166, 200
American Youth Commission, 34
Anderson, Helen I., 288, 294
Arbuckle, Dugald, 159
Arndt, C. O., 321
Association for Supervision and Curriculum Development, 13, 15, 73, 81, 111, 131, 159, 165, 199
Ayer, Fred C., 111

Bacon, Francis L., 88, 111, 294
Barr, A. S., 93
Baxter, Edna D., 159
Bell, Howard M., 34
Benerd, Gladys, 219, 221
Bieker, Helen, 165
Billett, R. O., 341
Boardman, Charles W., 93, 111
Boicourt, Gerald, 274
Bossard, James H. S., 7, 15
Bossing, Nelson L., 6, 15, 19, 38, 55, 60, 81, 159, 185, 190, 191, 321, 380
Brady, Elizabeth Hall, 143
Briggs, Thomas H., 15, 111
Buros, Oscar K., 150

Campbell, Clyde M., 131, 249
Campbell, Raymond Guy, 279, 294
Caswell, H. L., 81
Caudill, W. W., 274
Chamberlin, Dean, 32, 38
Chamberlin, Leo, 15
Chisholm, Leslie L., 147, 159
Cleary, Florence, 250
Cleland, George L., 294
Cook, Elaine, 131
Cook, Lloyd A., 131
Corey, Stephen M., 102

Cox, Philip W. L., 111
Cubberley, Elwood P., 38
Cunningham, Ruth, 159
Cushman, C. Leslie, 112
Cyr, Frank, 275

Davis, Alice, 250
Davis, C. O., 89
De Vilbiss, Wilbur, 308, 321
Dewey, John, 64, 203
Dewhurst, J. Frederic, 20, 38
Dodds, B. L., 15, 81, 94, 111, 200, 221, 275, 294, 318, 321, 330, 339, 341, 354, 356, 360
Dolan, Francis H., 210, 221
Dorsey, Mattie, 136, 160
Douglass, Harl R., 15, 60, 81, 93, 111, 200, 250, 274, 294, 321, 341, 360
Dugan, Willis E., 200

Edmonson, J. B., 88, 111, 294
Educational Policies Commission, 30, 35, 38, 58, 60, 79, 81, 217, 221, 250, 321, 371, 380
Eells, Walter C., 38
Eikenberry, D. G., 380
Engelhardt, N. J., Jr., 274
Engelhardt, N. L., 274
Erickson, Clifford E., 134, 159

Farmer, Floyd M., 377, 380
Fedder, Ruth, 159, 221
Foster, Herbert H., 111
Fowlkes, John Guy, 275
French, Will, 15, 81, 94, 111, 200, 221, 275, 294, 318, 321, 330, 339, 341, 354, 356, 360
Fretwell, Elbert K., 219, 221

Galbraith, Adria, 166
Gaumnitz, Walter H., 25, 39
Giles, H. H., 32, 39, 58
Gorman, Burton W., 380
Grabarkiewicz, K. P., 260, 275
Gwynn, J. Minor, 131

Hamrin, Shirley A., 134, 159
Hand, Harold C., 36, 39, 131, 210, 221, 282
Hanna, Lavone A., 123
Hanna, Paul R., 41, 60, 131
Havighurst, Robert J., 202, 221
Helm, Leslie C., 260, 275
Herrick, John H., 275
Hill, Clyde M., 131
Hollingshead, A. B., 131
Hopkins, Ellsworth, 221
Horsman, Mack, 369, 380
Hughes, J. M., 287, 294
Hulburd, David, 131
Hull, J. Dan, 15, 25, 39, 81, 94, 111, 200, 221, 275, 294, 318, 321, 330, 339, 341, 354, 356, 360
Hutson, P. W., 287, 294
Hymes, James, 131

Ivins, Wilson H., 288, 294
Ivok, Leo, 321

Jacobson, Paul B., 16, 275, 294, 321, 360
Jensen, Lisbeth, J., 380
Jenson, T. J., 128
Johnson, Paul, 111
Johnston, Edgar G., 95, 139, 159, 200, 212, 221, 224, 248, 250, 257, 290, 294
Jones, Galen, 166, 221
Judd, Charles H., 295

Kelley, Earl C., 7, 13, 16, 60, 66, 81, 97, 98, 111, 158, 247, 250, 329, 337, 338, 341, 372, 380
Kindred, Leslie, 15
Koopman, G. R., 81, 111, 265, 275
Koos, Leonard V., 27, 39, 287, 294
Krug, Edward A., 81, 111

Landis, Judson T., 51
Landis, Mary G., 51
Langfitt, R. E., 111, 321
Leggett, Stanton, 274
Leonard, J. Paul, 39, 40, 60, 341
Lewin, Kurt, 68, 81, 127
Limm, Henry, 275
Linn, Henry H., 260, 275
Logsdon, J. D., 321, 360
Lounsbury, John H., 138, 209
Loving, Alvin D., 61

MacConnell, Charles, 321
Manley, C. B., 310, 321
McCutchen, S. P., 32, 39, 58
McKown, Harry C., 138, 139, 159, 222, 224, 250
Meek, Lois H., 200
Meier, Arnold, 250
Melby, Ernest O., 131, 321
Menge, J. W., 16, 68, 81, 116, 131, 188, 328, 341, 347, 360
Midwest Administration Center, 126
Miel, Alice, 69, 81, 82, 111
Misner, P. J., 81, 111
Moehlman, Arthur B., 275, 295
Monroe, Walter S., 341
Mort, Paul, 131
Mudd, Dorothy, 322

National Society for the Study of Education, 131, 360
Newlon, Jesse, 16
Newsom, N. W., 295
Noar, Gertrude, 61, 322

Olson, E. G., 41, 61, 123, 131, 259, 275

Perkins, L. B., 275
Powdermaker, Hortense, 52
Prall, Charles E., 112
Progressive Education Association, 32–34, 39, 58, 380
Puner, Morton, 131

Quillen, James I., 123

Rasey, Marie I., 159, 164, 328, 329, 337, 338, 341
Reavis, W. C., 16, 275, 287, 294, 321, 360
Redl, Fritz, 152, 159
Reppen, Nels O., 93
Robinson, Francis P., 156
Roe, William S., 380
Roemer, Joseph, 88, 111, 294
Roethlisberger, Fritz J., 16
Russell, John D., 295

Saylor, J. Galen, 40, 60
Scott, C. Winfield, 131
Segel, David, 342
Sharp, George, 63, 82
Sheviakov, George, 159
Smith, E. R., 32, 39, 200, 342

Smith, Glenn E., 200
Smith, Joe, 251
Spaulding, Francis T., 34, 39, 342
Spears, Harold, 16, 61, 82, 86, 112, 200,
    345, 359, 360
Sternloff, Robert E., 366, 380
Stiles, Lindley J., 136, 160
Strang, Ruth, 160, 200, 222
Stratemeyer, Florence B., 131, 321

Thayer, V. T., 132
Thomas, Maurice J., 360
Travers, Robert N. W., 150
Traxler, Arthur E., 200
Trout, David, 342
Trytten, John M., 192, 289, 290, 295
Tyler, Ralph W., 112, 200, 342

Viles, N. E., 275
Vincent, William, 5, 131

Washburne, Carlton, 360
Webb, L. W., 207
Wilds, E. H., 18, 39
Wiles, Kimball, 69, 77, 82, 105, 112,
    380
Wilson, Russell E., 275
Wittenberg, Rudolph, 16, 82
Wrenn, C. Gilbert, 200
Wright, Grace, 55, 61
Wrinkle, William L., 182, 200

Yauch, W. A., 16, 82, 132, 360
Yeager, William A., 132, 342

Zechiel, A. N., 32, 39, 58

INDEX OF SUBJECTS

Academy, 21
Accounting methods, 287–291
Activities of school councils, 240–246
Activities program, 23
    credits and awards for, 213–215
    for economic experience, 291–293
    evaluation of, 215–219
    financing of, 210–213, 283–287
    organization of, 204–207
    purposes of, 202–204
    relation of to curriculum, 219–220
    relation of to guidance, 137–138
    relation of to student council, 235–236, 240–246
    scheduling of, 207–210
    school building plan for, 270–273
    student activities ticket, 211–212
    types of, 205–207
Administrative councils, 356–357
Anecdotal records, 163–167

Barriers to growth, 374–376
Board of education, earlier administrative role of, 344–345
    legal powers of, 343–344
    policy role of, 345–346
    relation of to citizens committees, 347–348
    relation of to superintendent, 348–350
Budgets, 276–283

Cardinal Principles, 28–29
Citizens commissions, 347–348
Classroom planning, 267–268
College, preparation for, 33–34
    College days, 48
    Michigan college-secondary school agreement, 36
Committee of Ten, 27
Community, 113–130
    advisory committees from, 119–120, 121–122
    attitude toward schools of, 113–114
    citizens commissions, 347–348

enriching instruction through, 123–124
    evaluation of, 129–130
    public relations, 114–116
    PTA, 120–121
    role of principal in, 124–130
    role of superintendent in, 116–117
    student representation in, 122–123
    surveys of, 118–120
    use of school plant for, 261–262
Community college, 26
Community school, 53–54
Core curriculum, 54–60
    background of, 56–57
    classroom appropriate to, 267–268
    extent of, 55–56
    fallacies regarding, 58–59
    purpose of, 54–55
Cost of high school, 282
Counselors, 24, 146–149
Critical incident technique, 364–366
Cumulative records, 167–181
Current scene and curriculum, 50–54
Curriculum, meaning of, 62–63
    role of teachers in, 63–65
    setting social climate for, 65–69
Custodian, duties of, 259–261

Delinquency, 9
Democracy and education, 18
Developmental tasks, 202–203
Drop-outs, 29–30
    relation to failure, 329
Duties of principals, 85–91, 351–355
    delegation of, 89–93

Early high schools, 22
Eight-Year Study, 32–33, 58
Elementary school, 30–31
Employment of youth, 20
Enrollments, effects on character of student body, 329–331
    increase in, 11, 17, 22–23
Evaluation, of principal's growth, 361–380; by critical incident-technique,

364–366; factors aiding growth, 376–378; factors blocking growth, 374–376; in relation to purpose, 362–364; by self-analysis, 369–373; by teacher judgments, 366–369
of pupil growth, 330–334
of student activities, 215–219
Evaluative criteria, 34, 216, 221, 378, 380
Experience curriculum, 31

Faculty meetings, 101, 106–107
Failure, 325–327
in elective courses, 331–333
remedial help, 333–334
in required courses, 331
results in drop-outs, 329
Flexibility, of schedules, 310–318
of school buildings, 263
Funds, administering, 276
accounting of, 287–291; forms for, 289–291
budget for, 276–283; criteria of, 279; divisions of, 279–280; staff planning of, 280–283
for school activities, 284–287
student participation in, 291–293

Grouping students, 335–341
ability grouping, 335–338
other kinds of sub-groups, 339–340
relation to core classes, 340
role of difference in groups, 337–338
social maturity as base for, 338–339
Group guidance, 152–153
Group planning, 69–73
criteria for, 75–77
efficiency of, 77–79
results of, 72–73
role of teachers in, 72–73
setting for, 71–72
Guidance, 24, 47–49
contributions of, 137
definition of, 133–134
relation of to student activities, 137–138
relation to instruction, 135–137
role of counselor in, 146–149
role of testing in, 149–150
through core classes, 140–145
through one-period classes, 140–143
through the home room, 138–140

History of secondary school, 21–38
Holtville, Story of, 54, 61
Home, decline of, 8–9
Home room, 24, 138–140

Illinois Study, 36
Individual enrichment, 42–46

Junior high school, 24–26

Kalamazoo decision, 22
Knowledge, increase of, 9–10

Latin Grammar School, 21
Leadership, training in, 12–14
Life Adjustment Program, 36–37
Loneliness of principal, 1–3

Marking, 181–186
failure, 325–329
Michigan Study, 35

PTA, 120–121
Parent-teacher conferences, 189–197
Principal, role of, 5–6, 11–12
as example, 67, 69
as supervisor, 85–110
cautions regarding, 357–358
See also Training of principals
in community relations, 113–130
in coördinating guidance, 157–158
in counseling students, 155–157
in group planning, 73–74
in helping teachers, 108–109
improvement of status, 354–355
in line of authority, 351–355; relation to superintendent, 351–353
need for, 358
in program change, 64
in relation to efficiency, 77–79
in setting climate, 65, 67
in student participation, 248–260
in treatment of staff, 69
Problem census, 65–66, 70–72
Problems facing principal, 4–6
Production, increase in, 20
Promoting, 323
arguments for failure, 325–327
attitudes of teachers, 323–325
in elective courses, 331–333
remedial help, 333–334
in required courses, 331
values of success, 327–329
Public relations, 114–116

Pupil adjustment, 183–185
  and grouping, 335–341
Pupil records, 161–199
  anecdotal, 163–167
  check lists, 186–187
  conferences, 189–197
  cumulative, 167–181
  data needed, 162–163
  faculty planning of, 198–199
  importance of, 161–162
  letters, 187–189
  marks, 181–186, 197–198

Reading, 45–46
Regents inquiry, 34
Remedial instruction, 333–334

Schedule, 296–321
  blocking for longer periods in, 310,
    315; plans for, 311–317
  criteria for, 308–310
  faults of, 298–301, 309–310
  grade level planning of, 318–320
  importance of, 296–297
  methods of developing, 302–308;
    interpreting to parents, 307–308;
    group plan, 305–306; reducing
    conflicts, 304–305; staff help in,
    306–307; tabulating choices, 303
  needed changes in, 318
  scheduling shorter periods in, 315–
    318
School plant, 252–274
  importance of, 252–253
  planning new buildings, 263–273
  relation to program, 263–270
  responsibility of teachers for, 253–
    254
  role of custodians, 259–261
  role of lay citizens, 261–262
  role of principal in maintaining,
    273–274
  students' role in care of, 254–259
Secondary school, changing role of, 6–
  11, 19
  role of standards in, 329–331
Self-analysis by principal, 369–373
Social climate of schools, 65–69
  importance of, 65–66
  reducing barriers in, 67–69
  relation to supervision, 97–99
Student councils, 224–250

Student participation, activities of, 240–
  246
  background of, 224–226
  commission, plan for, 235–237
  confusion regarding, 226–229
  do's and don'ts for, 247–248
  faculty support for, 232
  in handling funds, 291–293
  in planning buildings, 270–272
  in planning schedules, 320
  in school-community groups, 122–123
  in school government, 224–250
  recent trend toward, 229–231
  representative base for, 232–233
  role of principal in, 248–250
  status for, 237–240
  steps in development of, 231–234
  total participation in, 233–234
Study committees, 121–122
Supply inventory, 283
Superintendent of schools, 348–350
  cautions regarding, 357
  delegation of powers, 349–350
  relation of to administrative councils,
    356–357
Supervision, 83–110
  as meeting needs, 101–102, 108–109
  by buildings, 95–96
  by central staff, 92
  by department heads, 93–94
  by principals, 90–91
  by purpose-coördinators, 94–95
  early concept of, 83–84
  evaluation of, 103–110
  purposes of, 96–97
  through class visiting, 103–105
  through committees, 107–108
  through faculty meetings, 106–107
  through interviews, 105–106
  through recognition of merit, 109–
    110

Teachers' judgments of principal, 366–
  369
Teachers, role of, 63–65
  and creativity, 101–102
  in group planning, 72–73
  in planning schedule, 318–320
  in planning school plant, 253–254
  in proposing problems, 70–71
  and morale, 97–98
  and philosophy, 99–100
  and selection of, 108

Testing, 149–150
Training of principals, 3, 12–14, 377–378
Trends since 1930, 40–42
   list of, 266–267
   summary of, 59–60

Urbanization, 7–8

Vocational education, 48–50

Writing, 44–45